Reconceptualizing School-based
Curriculum Development

9300646
LEAA
£27.00

Reconceptualizing School-based Curriculum Development

Colin Marsh
Christopher Day
Lynne Hannay
Gail McCutcheon

The Falmer Press
(A Member of the Taylor & Francis Group)
London · New York · Philadelphia

UK   The Falmer Press, Rankine Road, Basingstoke, Hampshire, RG24 0PR

USA   The Falmer Press, Taylor & Francis Inc., 1900 Frost Road, Suite 101, Bristol, PA 19007

First published 1990

British Library Cataloguing in Publication Data
Reconceptualizing school-based curriculum development.
  1. Schools. Curriculum. Development
  I. Marsh, Colin
  375'.001
  ISBN 1-85000-500-1
  ISBN 1-85000-595-8 (pbk.)

Library of Congress Cataloging-in-Publication Data
is available on request

Jacket design by Caroline Archer

Typeset by Input Typesetting Ltd, London SW19 8DR

Printed in Great Britain by Burgess Science Press, Basingstoke on paper which has a specified pH value on final paper manufacture of not less than 7.5 and is therefore 'acid free'.

Contents

List of Tables and Figures

Preface

The term 'school-based curriculum development' (SBCD) is used in various ways in the literature but typically as a slogan for devolution of control, for 'grass-roots' decision-making, and as a representation of the polar opposite of centralized education. It is sometimes difficult to gauge the extent to which SBCD is increasing or declining because other synonyms for the term are also used, such as 'school-focussed', 'school improvement' and 'self-managing schools'. Added to this is the problem that studies of individual schools do not find a ready market in the publishing arena and so it is extremely difficult to read about actual examples of SBCD and thus to separate out the empirical evidence.

This book attempts to overcome some of these problems by focussing directly on SBCD. SBCD has occurred, and will continue to occur, in many countries and a special quality of this book is the attempt by the authors to bring together a collection of case studies from four countries, namely Australia, Canada, the United Kingdom and the United States of America. Although the contexts are very different, it is possible to discern patterns that cross these national boundaries, especially in terms of the motivations of SBCD participants and the processes that occur.

Several chapters are devoted to understanding *why* SBCD occurs in addition to *how* it occurs. An innovations metaphor is used, along with other factors to provide a theoretical basis for SBCD. The use of this metaphor implies that each staff member is motivated to initiate certain activities and not others, due to personal preferences and life cycle demands, peer pressures, and school or central office directives.

Individuals or groups of staff in schools (and in some instances school communities including staff, parents and students) may decide upon activities which they consider are innovatory and worth initiating; but they also might make decisions not to introduce other ones. In certain subject areas, there are strong pressures to continue with past practices while in other subjects there may be considerable incentives to try out new ideas. Some of the ideas advanced by staff within a school may never get beyond the discussion stage while others may be carefully planned and implemented.

Curriculum is largely driven by political considerations and the course of SBCD seems to veer widely and somewhat erratically as political leaders take up various priorities. Some of the political considerations are very evident in the case study chapters but also in the concluding chapter where future trends are considered.

The book is intended for a number of audiences. School principals and teachers will have a major interest in the book as considerable attention is given to their motives, strategies, activities and learning. In addition, parents, students and local community members will also find material of considerable interest, especially if they are concerned about local level, curriculum decision-making.

In section A of the book the emphasis is upon establishing the different contexts for SBCD in Australia, Canada, UK and USA and presenting a conceptual framework for SBCD. Section B provides four different case studies selected from the four countries. In section C the theoretical basis outlined earlier is re-examined in the light of the case studies. Finally, current and future issues are examined in some detail.

The practical examples, ideas and concepts incorporated in this book have been obtained from various sources in Australia, Canada, the UK and the USA. The authors have had wide and varied experiences in these countries and it is difficult to acknowledge individual sources, but special mention needs to be made of the contributions by John Olson and Bill Reid. Finally, sincere thanks are due to Lynne Schickert and Ann Sankey for their skilful typing of the manuscript.

Colin Marsh
Christopher Day
Lynne Hannay
Gail McCutcheon

Settings and Issues

Chapter 1

The Contexts: Australia, Canada, United Kingdom and United States of America

Introduction

School-based curriculum development is essentially a teacher-initiated grass roots phenomenon, and it is likely to survive in this pure form regardless of political and economic contexts. Over the years local and national governments in some countries have at different times provided support through funding initiatives, either indirectly through curriculum development agencies or directly through earmarked funding; whilst others have allowed SBCD to be largely self-nurturing. Inevitably, the quantity if not the quality of SBCD projects will vary as a result of the relative level of support received from outside the school itself.

There are, however, a number of constants across the countries represented in this book. For example, higher education seems to be involved in catalyst manifestation of the professionality of teachers who wish to improve learning opportunities for their pupils. Teachers demonstrate their commitment to this through individual and collective commitment to reflection, research, action and evaluation which occurs as much during out of school time as during in school time. As a result, thinking and practice is changed and curriculum materials are revised in ways which are relevant to particular needs identified in particular contexts.

This chapter provides a critical overview of the history of SBCD in Australia, Canada, UK and USA, its current educational and political contexts and consideration of forms which help and hinder its development.

Australia

In Australia, state governments have the major responsibility for education. By contrast, the Commonwealth government provides general finance to states and provides a national perspective by funding special projects (for examples, the Participation and Equity Project [PEP]), undertaking research, dissemination functions and consultancies (for example, via the Schools Commission and Curriculum Development Centre), and by specifying regulations and standards (for example, the Sex Discrimination Act).

Although the influence of the Commonwealth government in education matters has increased considerably over recent years (Tannock, 1983), it should also be recognized that each state (and the two territories, Australian Capital Territory and the Northern Territory), actively promote and protect their mandate to be the major provider of schooling within their geographical boundaries.

Each state education department is controlled by a minister of education who in turn is accountable to the state parliament. Each education department establishes schools for pre-school, elementary, secondary and post-secondary (technical) students and employs the teachers, and to varying degrees, determines the curricula. Pre-school is typically for 4–5-year-olds, elementary school is for 6–12-year-olds and secondary school is for 11–17-year-olds. All students going on to tertiary study complete twelve years of elementary and secondary school education. As noted by McKenzie (1986). 'until fairly recently, centralized control in most state systems was maintained through externally set student examinations and the regular (and vigorous) inspection of schools and teachers' (p. 6). Although there has been a decided shift toward devolution of control to individual schools, the structural changes to bring this about, and more important, the different attitudinal dispositions required, have been difficult to achieve in the short term.

Non-government schools in Australia have always been a sizeable group of schools outside direct government control. In each state they comprise about 25 per cent of primary and secondary students, with the majority of these being associated with the catholic church. Yet, although independent from state government control, they tend to follow curriculum and organizational policies similar to the government schools.

4

Canada

In Canada, legislative control over education remains firmly under the direction of the ten provincial governments and two territories. The jurisdiction over education was originally given to the provinces as one means of protecting the dual language and culture of the French minority in Canada. The federal government, perhaps because of the politically sensitive role of education, has not been involved in developing or suggesting the nature of curriculum for provincial schools. Occasionally, the federal government will provide extra grants for local school boards or provincial governments but it has not entered into the area of policy making.

The control over education is further divided between the provincial Ministry of Education and the different school systems. In over half of the ten provinces, more than one provincial school system exists within the same geographical area. There might be, for instance, a church school system, a minority language system and a public school system. In several provinces, there exists more than one church school system such as a Protestant and a Roman Catholic system. Each of these school systems is further broken down to local school districts or school boards. All three layers, Ministry of Education, school system and local school district, have specific areas over which they can make educational policy decisions. However, this varies from province to province.

Generally in most Canadian provinces, the Ministry of Education has jurisdiction over curriculum development. The Ministry typically forms a development committee comprised of teachers, teacher federation representatives, university faculty and, sometimes, members of the public or business representatives. This committee develops a general guideline which, once approved by the Ministry of Education, becomes the legal curriculum for the provincial schools. Most provincial Ministries of Education also provide a circular that lists the textbooks that may be used within their schools.

USA

In the USA, local school districts are the lynchpin of the education system. All states of continental USA (Hawaii has no local boards) have a number of school districts, totalling over 15,000. School districts can vary considerably in size, mode of operation and budget. Typically, each school district has a lay board, a superintendent and an assistant superintendent (with special responsibilities for curriculum) and central staff.

Of increasing importance over recent years have been the state boards. These are state departments of education, often with large professional staff, who have been exerting considerable influence (and in many cases, control) over local school districts in curriculum matters. The state's percentage of support for schools has steadily risen and specific legislative mandates have figured prominently.

The federal government does not have direct, national policies on education, and its financial commitment has been reduced over recent years. Notwithstanding it is still influential via various federal agencies dealing with civil rights, labour, humanpower needs.

There are many other agencies which influence curriculum development, directly or indirectly, and these include professional organizations who set guidelines and standards; educational publishers, who can have a major impact on what is taught, and in some subject areas, have given the country an unofficial national curriculum; testing organizations who can also influence the content selected by teachers.

UK: England and Wales

England and Wales offers a patchwork quilt of educational provision. There are 104 local education authorities which have responsibility for education within the framework of a national legislation which determines teachers pay and conditions of service and the governance and general curriculum of schools. Teachers salaries and the costs of running schools are shared between central and local government. In the 30,000 primary and secondary state schools and among the 400,000 teachers conditions vary. For example, the majority of children attend infant (5–7 years), junior (7–11 years), primary (5–11 years) or comprehensive (11–18 years) schools. However, some LEAs have developed systems of first schools (5–9-year-olds), middle schools (8 or 9 years to 12 or 13 years), junior high (14–14 years) and senior high schools (14–18 years). Within some LEAs there will be sixth-form colleges (16–19 years), tertiary colleges (16+ years); and about 10 per cent of children still sit an '11+' examination to determine whether they will attend Secondary or Grammar school. All students sit a national 16+ examination (the General Certificate of Secondary Education [GCSE]), and movement 'up' the school is in classes, by age, not by ability. Nursery schools (for 3–5-year-olds) are few in number, but an increasing number of infant schools have 'nursery units' and others admit children at the age of 4 years. Not all children in every school will have the same opportunities. Policies which affect curriculum and professional development, and schools' resources (for example, pupil–teacher ratio and per capita allowances) vary across LEAs. In secondary schools in some LEAs, the curriculum will include areas of study which reflect particular concerns of the ruling political party.

Each LEA has a Director of Education (sometimes called Chief or County Education Officer) who is accountable to the elected representatives through the Chairperson of the local authority Education Committee. The Director is him/herself advised by administrative and professional officers (local authority advisers/inspectors). Non-government schools (c. 5 per cent of all schools), are independent from state control, but are monitored by Her Majesty's Inspectorate (HMI). The national system is controlled by the Secretary of State for Education and Science, a member of the Cabinet. He/she is served by the Department of Education and Science (DES), within which HMI is responsible for monitoring standards and advising the Secretary. Until relatively recently there has been an unspoken agreement that LEAs and schools should be left in relative peace to educate their students. Since then national governments have expressed increasing disquiet with the nature and quality of local educational provision and have become much more interventionist. The Education Reform Act legislated for a National Curriculum for all schools and a national system of assessment for the core subjects in this (English, mathematics and science) at 7, 11, 14 and 16 years.

School-based curriculum development in England mirror these changes and represent both the relative autonomy of schools and teachers and, more recently, the increasing influences of central and local government.

Historical Roots of SBCD

In each country SBCD has grown within a different cultural tradition, and it is therefore difficult to point to a particular time period when it began. By its nature, much of SBCD has been and no doubt will remain a normal part of the professional lives of many individual teachers and schools as part of their continuing attempts to present the most effective learning opportunities for pupils.

Inevitably, much of SBCD work in the past will not have been documented, and that which was is likely to exist in mimeo from within teachers notebooks and schools in-house publications. However, during

7

the 1960s, there was a growing advocacy for this kind of work by educationalists and system managers operating in positions of influence outside schools. From this point public documentation increased, and it is here, therefore, that the story of the development of SBCD must begin. This account seeks to present a series of snapshots selected from the album of curriculum development which represent both the contexts and significant instances.

Australia

The high-points are relatively easy to establish such as the halcyon days of the incoming Federal Labor government in 1972 and its massive spending on education, or the upheavals at state level in the 1980s in Victoria and Western Australia when school-based decision-making became foisted upon communities, whether they wanted it or not. But more about these developments later in the chapter—an attempt must be made to trace the antecedents.

Education in Australia since the beginning years of the colonies has been a state concern. The very earliest schools in the eighteenth century were established to provide elementary education for children and to upgrade the moral fibre of many of the parents! The governors in charge of each colony administered the schools and tried to appease in-fighting and competition between different religious groups. Although these early church schools had their local decision-making councils they were dependent upon grants from the governor to remain in operation. After numerous attempts by governors to establish dual systems of national and denominational schools, a centralized system of elementary education in each state which was to be free, compulsory and secular, became established by a series of state Education Acts (Victoria was the first in 1872 and Western Australia the last in 1893). In effect this placed all decision-making with the central board in each state and which was in turn responsible to the respective Minister of Education. Each state raised its own taxes and a portion of this was allocated each year to the education portfolio.

Because there was no direct link between locally derived finances and school operations, it was not surprising that community-level decision-making rarely occurred. As settlers moved further and further inland and as the goldrushes encouraged even greater population mobility in the 1890s and beyond, more schools were needed in isolated, inland regions. The enormous areas of land (for example, one million square miles in Western Australia) dictated the need for centralized control of education in an attempt to provide a uniform and fair system for all children.

The only glimmer of community involvement occurred in some rural areas where declining numbers threatened to close a school. Small rural schools proliferated in farming areas but if an area proved uneconomic due to unreliable climate or poor soils, it was difficult to retain the necessary number of children. Rural lobbies of local members of parliament and various schemes to 'aggregate' school numbers were used by community members to ensure that their schools were not closed.

State level developments

It was not until well after World War II that various moves were made in education circles which might be construed as being related to SBCD. The Plowden Report, released in the UK in 1967 (Central Advisory Council for Education, 1967), advocated child-centred approaches and informal learning practices in primary schools. This approach became popularized as 'open education' and 'open learning' in many Western countries and especially in Australia. Because the emphasis was upon child-centred activities, it required teachers at the school level to make more of the curriculum decisions and to work cooperatively with other staff in planning units. The state education systems appeared to encourage this development by the building of new schools with open plan architecture from 1969 onwards. For example, two-teacher open units were built in South Australia in 1969 followed by multiple-area schools and 'flexipods' in other states such as Western Australia, Tasmania and Queensland (1970) and New South Wales and Victoria (1972). This is not to suggest that all teachers embarked upon more school-based decision-making simply because new flexible buildings were made available. However, there has been some evidence that a number of primary school teachers did get involved in SBCD activities as a result of these architectural changes (Angus, 1974).

Another interesting development occurred in the state of Victoria in the 1960s. Secondary education in that state was highly centralized with university-dominated syllabuses and external examinations in years 10, 11 and 12. When the year 10 examination was abolished in 1967 it enabled schools to have far more freedom over the first four years of secondary school. To encourage this move, the Chief Inspector of Secondary Schools (R. A. Reed), established a Curriculum Advisory Board (CAB) to advise on curriculum revision. He urged schools to devise their own local curricula and encouraged them to do so by allowing staff non-teaching 'curriculum days' for discussions and planning. The powerful teachers unions in Victoria also took up this challenge and their journal *Australian Teacher* became the mouthpiece for considerable educational debate (Dow, 1985). Curriculum reform in this context was definitely school-based, even though later political events caused a decline in its impact.

In another state education system, the Chief Education Officer (Director-General) in South Australia, A. W. Jones, produced his landmark document for teachers entitled *Freedom and Authority* memorandum (1970). This document also encouraged schools and especially school principals to plan for their own needs in curriculum development in consultation with teachers, parents and students. At the same time, organizational changes brought about a decline in the use of inspectors who had hitherto wielded considerable control in monitoring the dictates of a centralized education system. Tensions between school-based and central decisions did develop in this state to the extent that this newly found freedom for local schools was curtailed in subsequent official policy documents released in the early 1980s.

A state system which formally enshrined SBCD principles was in fact developed in the Australian Capital Territory (Canberra). It occurred in the smallest and newest of all government education systems and it specifically espoused devolution of decision-making powers to schools. The Currie Report in 1967 recommended this system and after subsequent public hearings, additional reports and considerable media debate, it came into operation in 1977. Under the regulations of the ACT Schools Authority, a school board is elected for each school and it decides broad curriculum policy. Teachers submit their curricula proposals to their respective school boards for approval and teams of principals and teachers visit schools to provide peer monitoring on the viability of these programs. The central office provides limited resources only for professional development, evaluation and research activities. Problems have occurred, however, with this system and these are described in a later section.

Up until this point, it would have been noted that only state government education systems have been used as examples to illustrate the growth of SBCD in Australia. Although non-government schools service approximately one-quarter of the Australian school-age children, there is less to report about their moves to SBCD because they have always been more decentralised. For example, catholic schools operate as community parish schools and there is consequently considerable local decision-making by religious leaders and lay persons. Notwithstanding, incentives to become more heavily involved in SBCD did emerge in the 1970s with the growth of Commonwealth government initiatives and subsequent earmarked funding grants.

Commonwealth developments

Increased involvement by the Commonwealth government in education had in fact already commenced in the 1960s. At first the Commonwealth government became involved in identifiable national problems, providing remedies that could be implemented quickly and which were highly visible and attracted considerable attention from the public. In 1964 Commonwealth Secondary Scholarships were introduced to encourage students to stay on to year 12 of secondary school and then proceed to tertiary study. Also in 1964 government and non-government schools were given capital grants to build science laboratories and to purchase the necessary equipment. In 1969 funds were provided to enable schools to build or to extend their school libraries.

A major development occurred in 1972 when a newly-elected Labor government took office. Within eleven days of taking office, the Prime Minister established a 'blue ribbon' committee of eleven, chaired by Peter Karmel to enquire into education in Australian schools. The Karmel Committee recommended seven major programs that were urgently needed to overcome gross inequalities in education and which were estimated to cost $467 million. The Schools Commission, later to be renamed the Commonwealth Schools Commission, was established by Act of Parliament in 1973 to implement these programs.

Of special interest here were the programs which encouraged community participation in curriculum decision-making and incentives for individuals to experiment with innovative programs.

A number of community-based projects were funded during the 1970s and 80s which focussed on parent and student skills needed for school-level decision-making. Persons from all states interested and involved in SBCD were brought together for a National Conference on SBCD held in Sydney in 1977.

The Innovations Program commenced in 1973 with the express purpose of supporting individuals (teachers, community groups, parents, students) who wanted to experiment with a 'good idea'. It created an exciting precedent by providing funds directly to individuals rather than via the state education hierarchies. During the period between 1973 and the demise of the program in 1981, several thousand projects were funded. Some of the projects used non-traditional settings

11

such as residential field centres; a great number of the projects used the funds to design and produce different learning materials; and some projects enabled students to initiate new and exciting activities.

Another major organization that was created by the Commonwealth government in the 1970s was the Curriculum Development Centre (CDC), established by Act of Parliament in 1975. This was created at a time when commonwealth-state relationships were at a high point, and previous cooperative ventures between states augured well for a centralized agency which could provide leadership in curriculum development activities and provide information services.

The inaugural director, Malcolm Skilbeck, a scholar of international reputation, was a driving force in SBCD-oriented projects at CDC. One project in particular, Teachers as Evaluators Project, under the directorship of Phillip Hughes, was initiated in 1977 to provide teachers with the necessary skills to undertake their own curriculum evaluation activities. Although the project was terminated in 1982, it was very successful and many teachers in all states benefited from attending workshops and receiving teachers' guides and information about school-level evaluation.

Two other national bodies have also had significant but less major roles in furthering SBCD in Australia. A research funding organization, the Education Research and Development Committee (ERDC) funded a number of school-focussed research studies in the 1970s. One major study, the Curriculum Action Project, directed by D. Cohen and M. Harrison (1982) undertook an analysis of SBCD in secondary schools across all state systems. They were quite pessimistic in their conclusions, noting that 'although SBCD is widely proclaimed as being in practice in Australia, the Curriculum Action Project study indicated that SBCD is not in fact being implemented in the vast majority of Australian secondary schools' (p. 263).

The Australian Council for Educational Research (ACER), apart from its testing role, provides funds from time to time for special curriculum projects. In the 1970s it produced some valuable materials on evaluation techniques and item banks for classroom teachers (for example, Piper 1976 and 1977). More recently it has initiated some major studies to highlight the problems of academically-oriented secondary school curricula and the need to develop programs which are more broadly-based and student-centred (for example, Batten, 1987).

Canada

School-based curriculum development has not been institutionalized into Canadian legislative reality. The provinces and the territories maintain exclusive jurisdiction over curriculum policy making although they might turn over some degree of responsibility to local school systems.

Historically, Ministries of Education have formed curriculum-writing committees that produce curriculum guidelines for provincial schools. Typically, the composition of the committee represents the various stakeholders such as teachers, subject-area groups, universities, teachers' federation and/or the general public. Teacher members form the majority on most committees.

The nature of the curriculum guideline produced by a provincial committee somewhat determines whether SBCD is encouraged. Some guidelines are prescriptive and teachers are allowed very little room to develop documents for either their classroom or the school. More recently, however, these documents have been general in nature and do require further development at the school or classroom level. When this happens, as currently in the province of Ontario, SBCD has the opportunity to flourish. This is not curriculum development in the sense of total creation of the document and policy, but does provide for some degree of local development and ownership.

The provincial curriculum guidelines created for elementary schools have typically been more general, thereby encouraging curriculum development at the local school district level. This has not always meant an increase in SBCD, as a district level committee might be responsible for developing a curriculum. The Ontario elementary document, for example, *Education in the Primary and Junior Divisions* (1975) is a very general statement of areas that should be included in the learning experiences of children. The teacher, or the school district, is responsible for developing a more detailed program. This has provided the opportunity for SBCD in instances where practitioners opt to develop programs. A similar degree of flexibility appears to be developing in British Columbia with proposed changes to the *School Act*. The changes include a upgraded primary structure where children progress at their own rate. In the proposed changes, 80 per cent of the Grade 4–10 curriculum would focus on provincially authorized programs, while the remaining 20 per cent would consist of other provincial programs or local programs at the local school district's discretion. While still emphasizing the centralized role of the Ministry of Education in developing curricula, the changes do seem to open the door for some SBCD. How this is operationalized will have to wait until the policy is implemented in the 1989–90 school year.

Secondary schools have usually had far less leeway in developing programs. As will be discussed later in this chapter, the Ontario government has mandated that courses of study, based on the provincial guideline, be developed for each course taught in each provincial high school. In some schools, this policy has led to active SBCD while in others it has been implemented in a cursory manner. The changes proposed for British Columbia seem to create the opportunities for some SBCD at the secondary level. The suggested graduation requirements mandate that a student must successfully complete thirteen courses. Eleven of these courses must be from the provincially approved list while up to two courses can be locally developed. The proposed regulations, therefore, provide some opportunity for locally developed courses. Whether they are developed by district level committees or schools will differ across the various school districts.

While SBCD has not been incorporated in a meaningful manner into Canadian educational practices, other agencies have been involved in supporting the concept of the teacher as a curriculum developer. Two national organizations have been particularly active: the Canada Studies Foundation and the Science Council of Canada. Both groups have funded teachers' involvement in development materials and unit curricula for classroom usage.

Teachers' Federations have been the other agency actively supporting SBCD. The British Columbia Teachers' Federation has had a strong department advocating and supporting SBCD for several decades. Their 'Lesson Aides' service provides a vehicle through which provincial teachers can share with colleagues the material they have developed. The Ontario Secondary School Teacher's Federation has been active in assisting its members during this current round of SBCD. For instance, they have published a booklet on developing curriculum, offer frequent curriculum workshops, and sponsor a major curriculum conference each year.

However, Canadian educational history has not documented a strong movement or an example of institutionalized SBCD. Canadian curriculum scholars, similar to those in other countries, are divided in their response to the lack of SBCD. Some have reacted by developing curriculum development models to be used at the provincial or local levels (i.e. Robinson, Ross and White, 1985; Pratt, 1980). A few Canadian academics have focused their attention on how curriculum development actually occurs (Hannay and Seller, 1987; Orpwood, 1985; Butt, 1981; Young, 1979). Others have turned to what happens after the provincial guideline has been developed by becoming interested in the implementation process (Fullan, 1982).

Perhaps the lack of SBCD in Canada has created the interest in another focus which suggests regardless of who develops the written curricula, the teacher is the ultimate developer as user (Oberg, 1980). Curriculum scholars interested in the teacher's role have been actively investigating the role of the teacher's personal practical knowledge in interpreting curriculum documents and in deciding on classroom practices. For example, Connelly and Clandinin (1988) suggest that:

> . . . it is possible that any one teacher will discover and create a variety of potentials in the text depending on his or her particular curriculum situation, the students, the community, and so forth. This matter of different readings is multiplied when we think of the consequences of this notion for different teachers reading the same text, each of whom may have multiple readings of the materials (p. 151).

Each teacher, then, becomes a curriculum interpreter and a developer. In this perspective, the emphasis shifts to the lived curriculum as opposed to the written document. Given the Canadian context of centralized control over curriculum development, this might well be the only way that some aspect of SBCD can survive.

USA

Local school districts since their inception in the nineteenth century have had a strong emphasis upon community participation in developing curricula. Over the decades various terms have been used to portray major emphases such as 'child-centred' approaches, 'progressive education', 'curriculum reform', 'school improvement' and 'school effectiveness'. Although a number of these terms are related to school-based curriculum development (SBCD) it is surprising that this latter term has not featured prominently in the educational literature in the USA.

Since the mid-1970s there has been a major effort at all levels to bring about school improvement/school effectiveness. School-level groups have been, and continue to be, involved in SBCD activities. The literature is replete with guidelines and case studies (for example: Loucks-Horsley and Hergert, 1985; Lieberman and Miller, 1984; McLaughlin and Pfeifer, 1988), of how teachers can initiate and implement SBCD projects. Yet, the ever-increasing pattern is one of state-level control via the alignment of textbooks (new guidelines on selection criteria and adoption procedures), scope and sequence subject guides (frameworks) and wide-ranging testing programs. Teachers, as the ultimate delivery agents, still have opportunities to adapt and change the curriculum, but the opportunities for them to have a major input into curriculum planning seems to have been reduced greatly.

UK: England and Wales

It is no accident that the growth of the curriculum development movement itself began in the 1960s, when school populations were increasing, and the notorious selection examinations at 11+ years were diminishing alongside the growth of neighbourhood comprehensive schools which all students in a given catchment area would attend. Now, 90 per cent of all children transfer from primary schools to comprehensive without examination. Clearly there was a need to develop curricula which would be relevant to all students. Alongside these structural changes in the provision of education, and the raising of the school-leaving age from 15 to 16, colleges of education were producing teachers imbued with the new progressive, child-centred approaches espoused by the Newsom Report on secondary and the Plowden Report on primary schools (Central Advisory Council, 1963 and 1967).

National developments

A major feature in the educational landscape of England and Wales in the 1960s and 70s was the growth of national curriculum development projects. Major participants in this growth were two national funding agencies. One privately-funded foundation (Nuffield) and one publicly-funded body (the Schools Council) together accounted for many developments. The Schools Council is of particular interest, since it represented a partnership between teachers' professional associations, LEAs, and central government. Subject associations (especially the National Association for the Teaching of English, the Association of Teachers of Mathematics, and the Association for Science Education) accounted for more; and teachers and LEAs played a crucial collaborative and supporting role in such projects as 'Geography for the Young School Leaver' and the Humanities Curriculum Project. Often, higher education played a leading role through the directing and/or evaluation of curriculum development work (for example, Keele Integrated Studies Project).

Exceptionally, projects were initiated by groups of teachers and gained major funding. The Schools Mathematics Project (SMP) is one example. The history of many of these projects has been summarized in a series of case studies and responses (Stenhouse, 1980), but there are four features which are characteristic of most:

1. teachers were rarely involved in their initiation or design;
2. most of the projects were not school-based;
3. few of the projects had evaluation as a built-in feature;
4. most of the projects failed to take full account of the problems of impact and take up by teachers in schools.

Stenhouse was one of the pioneers of the curriculum development movement, advocating the need for the teacher to be actively and centrally placed within any curriculum development work (Stenhouse, 1975). In curriculum development, 'the error is not one of location of initiative (i.e. central government versus grass roots development); the error is in adopting the conception of curriculum development as something distinct from curriculum research' (Stenhouse, 1981). In writing reflectively about a number of curriculum development projects he was critical of optimism expressed by some influential groups about curriculum change as a means of improving schooling:

> It is rather the fashion at the moment to suggest that those involved in the Nuffield and Schools Council projects were naively optimistic about curriculum change as a means of improving schooling. Some may have been. But on the whole it was those in the system who were absurdly optimistic: especially perhaps local education authorities and some HMIs. In 1969 when I predicted at a conference that projects would fail in terms of the expectations being held of them because of lack of investment in dissemination and in-service training, I was attacked as being absurdly pessimistic. (Stenhouse, 1980)

In the late 1970s, the Schools Council commissioned an evaluation of the impact and take up of its own curriculum development projects (Steadman *et al.*, 1978–81). This revealed — to no-one's surprise — that many of the projects had failed to have any effect upon schools, teachers or teaching. Indeed, a high proportion claimed to have no knowledge of project material which was directly relevant to their students. Those which had been adopted had built into their design schools participation through piloting from an early stage and network support after the project itself had ended. The research-development-diffusion or centre periphery model of innovation had clearly been ineffective, and the time was right for support for school-based curriculum development. The Schools Council in its last few years of existence, moved many of its resources toward support for school-centred curriculum development. When the Schools Council was terminated by the government in 1981 (Plaskow, 1985) and replaced by a Schools Examinations Council and a School Curriculum Development Committee consisting of government nominees, the latter continued in its support for SBCD work. In 1988, however, the SCDC too was dissolved, and the Secretary of State for Education and Science took direct responsibility.

During the 1960s and 1970s, then, a number of apparently contradictory developments had taken place. First, there was the well-publicized and painstakingly documented move towards more intervention into school life from the centre, leading to ever increasing calls for more public accountability and prescription. The so-called 'Great Debate' launched by Prime Minister Callaghan in 1976 effectively signalled the end of the consensus which had allowed LEAs and schools to operate with relative autonomy. It was a clear signal that they had 'failed to deliver the goods'. Since then there have been increasingly more assertive initiatives by central and local governments which have contributed to establishing limits to teachers' freedom in deciding on the curriculum. Less well documented, however, were the plethora of parallel and uncoordinated developments in school-based curriculum development of all kinds. These two trends illustrate a struggle for the control of the design, delivery and evaluation of schools' curriculum developments which continues today.

Government initiatives

Curriculum development projects were accompanied in the 1970s and 80s by more policy-oriented reports on the curriculum initiated by local and central government politicians which were becoming increasingly interventionist into all aspects of education. At a national level the trend was towards increased advice from the centre. The Bullock Committee reported on language and the Cockcroft Committee on mathematics (DES, 1975 and 1982). HMI reflected the emerging interest of government with further reports on primary and secondary schools (DES, 1978 and 1979). The DES itself (not to be confused with HMI who advise Government) began to assert itself as an instrument of government, and began to require information from LEAs on schools' curricula.

From these developments, *The National Curriculum 5–16* consultative document was produced (DES, 1987) and its contents enshrined in the Education Reform Act. This was the culmination of a public shift towards a view of education as a process which is predominantly a preparation for adult and working life.

Non-government initiatives

At the same time that one part of the government was producing prescriptions for curriculum development, another part was supporting SBCD, as were LEAs, higher education, and teachers themselves, through, for example, the Association for the Study of the Curriculum (ASC) and the Classroom Action Research Network (CARN).

In many LEAs schools were encouraged to 'bid' for financial support for their initiatives — as noted by Keast (1982), this action supported the belief that 'teachers are most likely to attach importance to interesting issues which they themselves have identified'. Other LEAs built up curriculum development support services through planned programmes of secondments of serving teachers who leave their own schools for periods of one to three years to work with colleagues in different schools in support of school (and sometimes LEA) identified curriculum and professional development needs.

In the late 1970s, the Schools Council took an initiative which was to have far reaching consequences. Through the introduction of Programmes 1 and 2 the Schools Council adopted a development strategy in which it provided 'seeding' money to support locally identified needs. 'Programme 2' was specifically intended to provide speedy small scale (£500) funding in support of school-based initiatives. The resulting grass-roots projects had an authenticity and practitioner appeal which were lacking in many more high-powered, 'centralized' project materials. Many of these whole school, department and individual teacher initiatives have been subsequently documented and exist now as a testament to the success of SBCD which is adequately resourced (Thomson and Thomson, 1984; Oldroyd, Smith and Lee, 1984; Day, 1984 and 1986).

Perhaps the most controversial examples of SBCD are those which are carried out largely by individuals or groups of teachers in schools, often with little or no system support, and which are labelled 'action research', a form of participatory research carried out by practitioners into their own practice (Corey, 1953). Essentially, it is a term used to describe a family of activities in professional and curriculum development. In England, this kind of work was given impetus and support by

19

Stenhouse, who argued forcibly that, 'curriculum research and development ought to belong to the teacher' and that there could, therefore, be no educational development without teacher development (Stenhouse, 1975). John Elliott, a co-worker on Stenhouse's Humanities Curriculum Project (1970) and a colleague of his at the University of East Anglia, developed the notion and practice of action research through such projects as 'Ford T' (Elliott and Adelman, 1973a and 1973b) and the Teacher–Pupil Interaction and the Question of Learning Project (Elliott, 1981), and a number of seminal papers (Elliott, 1980, 1983, 1984 and 1985). In the late seventies Elliott and others formed a national and international network of those who were committed to this form of curriculum and professional development. CARN (Classroom Action Research Network) continues to form a focus for this work, through its conferences and publications. Since the mid-seventies there has been a mushrooming of writings in the area of action research (Nixon, 1981; Hustler *et al.*, 1986; Armstrong, 1980; Rowland, 1984; Rudduck and Hopkins, 1985). It is interesting also to note the emergence of an active 'action research' section within the British Educational Research Association (BERA).

The Current Situation

Australia

The extent of SBCD activities as we approach the 1990s is far from clear. Perhaps a major hurdle mitigating against the growth of SBCD has been that moves for school-based activities have resulted mainly from the efforts of Commonwealth and state administrators who have initiated moves for devolution, rather than it being a groundswell of grassroot demands. Accounts by visiting overseas educators (for example, Murphy, 1980; Gatherer, 1984) commented favourably upon the moves toward regionalization and SBCD activities but saw little evidence of parental involvement or demand for increased responsibilities. It may be that the widely publicised devolution of curriculum decision-making in many state systems has been rather superficial and that, as a result, the traditional, centralist structures and processes remain intact.

At the Commonwealth level, agencies and programs can change with remarkable rapidity. Programs, although successful, can be terminated forthwith, due to changes in the political climate. The Commonwealth Schools Commission and its programs (for example, PEP) has recently been terminated (October 1987) with its functions being transferred to the Department of Education. CDC appeared to be set for termination as part of widespread financial cutbacks in 1981, but after several years of uncertainty, it now appears to be reasserting itself as a major national agency and with a significant role to play in encouraging SBCD activities.

However, it is at the state level where major developments have occurred but only in a few states. Again it might be argued that these developments have been politically inspired and therefore could also have short lives, but to date, the new structures put in place promise considerable potential for SBCD. The two examples singled out for special attention are Victoria and Western Australia, although some interesting developments have also been occurring in South Australia and Tasmania.

In 1982 in the state of Victoria, the incoming Labor government had the opportunity to capitalize on a groundswell of support for SBCD from large sections of the community and from teacher unionists. Using a series of Ministerial Papers (Fordham, 1983 and 1984) the Minister of Education announced that new structures would soon be established by his government.

A state Board of Education, which provides for parent and community representation, was established in 1983 to provide advice directly to the Minister of Education on policy issues. Legislation was also passed creating a school council for each school, with one half of the positions in elementary and secondary schools being allocated to parents, community members and students. School councils have the powers to select the school principal, the mix of teaching specializations and the priorities of the school curriculum. At each school, the council members are also directly involved in planning and implementing their school improvement plan (SIP) for which they receive funding from their local education region. The SIP plans enable school councils to plan new curriculum approaches and to evaluate existing practices.

Although problems have emerged within the Victorian system such as principals being concerned about the diminution of their responsibilities; a lack of professional development funds to foster decision-making skills for teachers, parents and students; and tensions between head office frameworks for curriculum areas and school-based initiatives — it does appear that major progress with SBCD ideals is occurring.

In Western Australia, a major enquiry into secondary education in 1984 (Beazley Report) has resulted in significant structural changes for government schools operating in this state system. Although a number of the recommendations applied to the restructuring of specific

21

subjects in lower and upper secondary school, there were also rec-ommendations which have facilitated the development of SBCD. For example, a school council structure has been recommended for each school and a pilot program is currently in progress to determine viable ways of establishing this. Individual schools have been allocated funds to give them independence in determining such areas of need as profes-sional development and the use of teacher relief days. After the initial period of transition to a new unit curriculum structure for secondary schools it is envisaged that individual schools will have far greater opportunities to plan and implement their own school-based units (Marsh, 1988).

These developments in Victoria and Western Australia have estab-lished new structures for SBCD which are likely to be maintained well into the 1990s. Although some modifications will undoubtedly occur to SBCD priorities as participants adjust to the new structures, it is most unlikely that major reversals to centralist forms will occur in the near future in these two education systems. Whether other Australian state education systems get involved to the same extent is problematical. If any major problems occurred in Victoria or Western Australia over the next few years this would harden the resolve of other states not to move in the same direction.

Canada

The political and geographical reality of Canada makes it difficult to describe one Canadian context related to school-based curriculum development. The geographical size of most provinces and some of the local school districts has necessitated legislative authority over edu-cation to be shared by several different layers pf government.

School-based curriculum development in Canada exists within this multiple-level context. While in some provinces SBCD is encouraged, in others it would be contrary to provincial legislation. In British Col-umbia, for example, there is some indication that there is a degree of school-based curriculum development occurring within clearly defined parameters. The British Columbia Ministry of Education requires that locally developed courses be approved and registered with the Ministry. There are approximately 900 such curricula currently registered. How-ever, these curricula are only for special courses not covered by Ministry documents as the Ministry does not permit provincially mandated courses to be locally developed. Any province-wide course must be developed by a provincial committee. The local school boards are neither encouraged nor responsible for adapting the provincial curriculum to their context.

The province of Ontario provides a different context for SBCD. The Ministry of Education actively encourages local school boards to adapt the provincial curriculum guidelines and to produce what is typically called a 'second-generation document'. Often the development of second-generation documents happens at the system rather than the school level. Sometimes, however, this activity takes place at the school level. Recently, the Ontario Ministry of Education has mandated that courses of study based on the general provincial guidelines be developed for each grade 7 to grade 13 course. This policy, *Ontario Schools: Intermediate and Senior Divisions (OSIS)* has resulted in a great deal of school-based or collaborative inter-school curriculum development. Whether this activity is developmental or a procedural 'cut-and-paste' effort, depends upon the individual practitioners involved. In some schools, according to a recent study by the Ontario Institute for Studies in Education field centre faculty (Leithwood, 1986) the development process results in a re-issuing of past practice to fulfil the legal requirements of the Ministry of Education. Other schools, such as the case study reported in chapter 4, have used this policy to foster curricular and instructional change. As the policy is only four years old, it remains to be seen whether it is a means of institutionalizing school-based curriculum development.

USA

It is not possible to provide an overall judgment about current levels of SBCD occurring in the USA because of the enormous diversity occurring at district and state levels. However, some states, such as California and Florida, do appear to be encouraging SBCD developments quite strongly. For example, the School Improvement Project (SIP) in California has provided individual schools with state funding for the creation of School Site Councils to plan and implement local changes over periods of two to three years (Marsh, 1987).

Professional associations are also active in promoting school-based school renewal. For example the National Education Association (NEA) has recently initiated a project with twenty-six schools whereby NEA specialist staff provide on-site assistance to school staffs on restructuring processes such as needs assessment, developing effective instructional strategies in harmony with students' learning styles and fostering a positive school climate (McClure, 1988).

Yet, these examples of SBCD may be the exception rather than the rule. The literature is replete with numerous efforts by states to legislate learning. These state-initiated efforts to control curriculum are diametrically opposed to SBCD endeavours. They include various laws and mandates and focus on such aspects as specifying time requirements for the school year and for the school day, mandating specific subjects, setting graduation requirements, mandating procedures for the adoption of textbooks, specifying the scope and sequence of topics to be covered in various subjects and grades, and mandating a testing programme at specific grades in certain critical areas (Glatthorn, 1987, p. 135).

UK: England and Wales

In the 1980s there have been:

- fundamental changes in the organization and funding of INSET;
- a new and imposed pay-structure and conditions of service for headteachers and teachers, including the five 'Baker' days, which are explicit and legally binding, and the ending of the Burnham Committee (in which employers and employees met to determine, through negotiation, teachers' pay and conditions of service);
- the introduction of a national appraisal scheme, probably including classroom observation, which the Secretary of State has the legal power to enforce;
- fundamental changes in the roles and tasks of headteachers and teachers (i.e. profiling, GCSE, open access to pupil records, national curriculum and testing, TRIST/GRIST, local financial management and the promotion of vocational education and the enterprise culture via the TVEI, the DTI and others);
- fundamental changes in the governance and management of schools and teachers (i.e. increased powers for governors, local financial management, grant-maintained schools, city techs, the break up of the ILEA, changed roles of advisers, officers and members. (Bolam, 1988)

All of these changes signal increased workloads and increased stress levels for the majority of teachers who are involved. From a management perspective, they also signal the need for more and better 'managed' professional and curriculum development opportunities.

The imposed growth of school-based curriculum development in

England and Wales through radical changes both in the organization and funding of INSET (DES, 1986) and in pay and conditions of service for teachers (DES, 1987) has made the management of SBCD a priority issue. In the Grant Related In-service Training (GRIST) scheme, LEAs were directed to take explicit responsibility for in-service and curriculum development in their own schools through an annual central grant system. In each of the LEAs in England and Wales, schools must now draw up annual development plans based upon identified need. These are submitted annually to the LEA which must then analyze and collate, and together with its identified priorities and those identified nationally, submit proposals to the DES within certain guidelines. Within this system, LEAs must monitor and evaluate their programmes. The system is not quite as egalitarian as it might be, for 'national priorities' which are identified by central government attract a 70 per cent grant, whereas local priorities attract 50 per cent. Furthermore, this innovation cannot be seen entirely separately from the curriculum initiatives which have been taken by the government. The national curriculum, national systems for its assessment and testing, and the local management of schools by governors all have implications for the way in which the new SBCD will be perceived by teachers, many of whom already feel that their autonomy is under threat through the introduction of appraisal systems, 'directed time' (A minimum number of hours per year which the teacher must work); and the imposition of five days per year which schools must use for professional and curriculum development.

Despite the increased financial and human resources now available for the promoting of SBCD, success will still depend upon the commitment of the individual teacher and school. This commitment may well depend to a significant degree upon the extent to which teachers believe themselves to have been actively consulted and whether they can observe that this consultation has resulted in action which will both involve and be of practical benefit to them and their students.

In one sense the initiatives taken by management in the 1980s provide more opportunities for teachers to engage in SBCD, and they appear to devolve more power to schools as providers of their own curriculum development. Yet at the same time they have decreased the opportunity for teachers to gain full-time one-year secondments to pursue, with LEA support, their interests unless they coincide with those of national or local government or their school. Teachers, it seems, may exercise control of the curriculum only within ever more detailed guidelines, defined by others. Furthermore, the scale of the reduction in full-time secondments — almost 70 per cent across all higher education institutions in 1987/88 — may result in a reduction in staffing levels in higher education and this may result in less external support for SBCD.

Key Factors Contributing to the Growth of SBCD

The historical accounts provided so far would seem to indicate that SBCD is likely to remain an essential feature of school life in the 1990s and the foreseeable future. A number of agencies and institutions operating at national and state levels will continue to influence the growth of SBCD. Further, there is no doubt that the nature of intervention by government in the business of managing the curriculum and professional development will continue to exert both positive and negative influences.

Australia

A major factor which now appears to be influencing education in general, and SBCD developments in particular, is that ministers of education now wield considerable power within their respective state systems. In previous periods, ministers of education provided little more than ceremonial leadership, leaving all the policy decisions to the public service head of each state education system, who had the designated title of Director-General. These traditional rules of conduct no longer seem to apply. Ministers of education have abolished the directors-general position in two states. These politicians are now showing great interest in all facets of education and they are producing changes with remarkable rapidity.

National bodies such as CDC and the now defunct Commonwealth Schools Commission have had a major impact upon SBCD developments. Many of the SBCD developments have emanated from projects initiated by individuals associated with these institutions such as M. Skilbeck, P. Hughes and G. Boomer.

Tertiary level academics through their research projects and consultant activities have been a considerable spur to SBCD. For example, academics associated with action research at Deakin University have initiated many school-based projects within the state of Victoria. Action research, which enables teams of people to engage in actions to solve commonly agreed upon school problems, can be extremely valuable in developing SBCD skills among teacher participants (Carr and Kemmis, 1986) but also with parents and senior students (McTaggart, 1984).

Academics have also been largely responsible for the publicizing of SBCD concepts and projects through their writings. An important early book on SBCD concepts applied to the Australian scene was produced by Walton and Morgan in 1978, although Skilbeck's articles on SBCD (1974 and 1975a) but published in the UK, pre-date this volume. A number of publications on SBCD and sponsored by the CDC were produced in the late 1970s such as those by Soliman *et al.* (1981) Rawlinson and Spring (1981), Rawlinson and Donnan (1982) and Walton, Hunt and Maxwell (1981). Since then, general curriculum books which have highlighted SBCD principles include those by Brady (1987) and Marsh and Stafford (1984 and 1988).

However, it should be noted that most of these publications on SBCD have been confined to explanations of the term and methods for achieving good results. These assertions may have been too heavily weighted to pronouncements and exhortations and too little on problems associated with SBCD. As indicated above, one of the few research studies on SBCD in Australia (Cohen and Harrison, 1982), was far from positive in its conclusions. In fact there has been a dearth of published accounts of SBCD in action, apart from the occasional higher degree theses.

Interested groups representing various community parent groups, ethnic and religious affiliations, have been active over recent years in seeking out more community participation in education. They have had their successes in states where they have been able to form active pressure groups, such as the religious groups in Queensland in the 1970s who were successful in forcing the government to ban the teaching of Man: A Course of Study in Queensland government schools (see Marsh and Stafford 1984 and 1988). Other successes with school-level decision-making have been largely due to the funding opportunities and community programs provided by the Commonwealth Schools Commission. For example, PEP funds have enabled various parent and student groups to undertake skills training workshops to equip them more appropriately for their role on school councils.

A small number of talented and enthusiastic school principals have demonstrated that SBCD practices can work in their respective schools and within their local regions they have had considerable influence upon other schools and local educators. However, because of the different contexts and circumstances, it is unlikely that the efforts of individual school principals have been circulated to a wide audience in Australia.

The establishing of a school council to become the major policy-making body for each school community has been an interesting development in a number of states during the 1980s. For example, legislation was introduced into Victoria in 1983 to require this for all government schools. ACT schools have had a similar structure since the creation of the ACT Schools Authority in 1976. Other states also have school councils except that their function tends to be mainly advisory.

It is difficult to gauge the impact of school councils upon SBCD in general. The few published accounts of school council activities point to many unresolved problems relating to lack of democratic representation, conflicts with teaching staff and especially the school principals, and lack of group decision-making skills by council members, especially parents and students (Alexander, 1985; Manning, 1982; and Andrews, 1985).

Teaching staff operating in the various education systems are of course a key factor in that any real growth in SBCD activities is dependent upon their enthusiasm, support and skills. As will be indicated in the following section, there are some major factors militating against teacher support such as promotional/transfer systems which prevent the occurrence of long-term appointments, and the debilitating legacy of centralized decision-making. Yet there are many teachers, including an increasing number in systems such as those operating in the ACT and Victoria, who are very keen to take on more school-level decision making. Their commitment to SBCD tends to encourage their peers and a cumulative effect can be created in particular schools. It can be argued that teachers are the lynchpin for SBCD to really take off as a major development in education.

Canada

Although the Canadian literature on SBCD is not extensive, two recent case studies of Ontario (Hannay and Seller, 1987) and Quebec (Butt, 1981) are illustrative of key factors involved. Both studies stress the importance of reflection in the development process, the dual role of document production and teacher in-service education, and the teacher as the decision-maker with real alternatives.

USA

A number of writers have been involved at first-hand in school improvement projects in the USA over recent years and many of their findings have relevance to SBCD. For example, some key factors include the school culture, teacher ownership and collegiality, local problem-solving and action research, networks, implementation strategies, review and evaluation processes (Lieberman and Miller, 1984; McLaughlin, 1986; Huberman and Miles, 1986; Anderson and Cox, 1988). These key factors are analyzed in some detail in subsequent chapters (chapters 2, 7 and 8).

UK: England and Wales

Primarily because of the increased intervention of central government into all aspects of schooling already, schools have been forced to undertake systematic SBCD as part of public accountability procedures — in particular, through formal demands for curriculum review, the introduction of a national curriculum and national testing, assessment and teacher appraisal schemes.

Additionally, the structures now places upon LEAs, schools and teachers through 'rate capping' (a means used by central government to limit its financial support through imposing financial 'penalities' where government guidelines are breached), the LEA Training Grants Scheme, local financial devolution, new powers of school governors, and imposed conditions of service have, paradoxically, ensured fewer opportunities for teachers to leave the school premises and take advantage of off-site in-service and curriculum development opportunities. These have either become too expensive, or too troublesome to arrange (teacher replacement cover is not always available or appropriate); or they require too much energy from teachers who are already engaged in working, in 'directed' time and on 'Baker' days (named after the Secretary of State for Education and Science of that name) on, for example, finding ways of implementing new curricula and examinations and testing procedures.

SBCD offers what seems to be an ideal way forward. It appears to be cost effective for, since most of the developments are 'on-site' it does not involve the same cost of buying in replacement time for teachers who, in the part, pursued off-site studies. In addition, it allows more teachers to participate in developments. LEAs and schools are, therefore, engaged more and more in promoting it. Whether it will provide better value for money in any other than the strict economic sense, remains to be seen. There is no doubt, then, that structural changes in funding control and the governance of schools have served to encourage the growth of SBCD through provision of resources which are more easily used in this enterprise.

A further negative factor has also contributed to the growth of SBCD. Much traditional curriculum development has been carried out by small groups of 'experts', who were not always practising school teachers. Curriculum materials were often developed, packaged and disseminated (through a range of strategies) to schools in what has been described as a 'centre-periphery' model of innovation (Schön, 1981) which took no account of principles of user ownership or the need to negotiate meanings. Even when new or modified curricula reached schools they were often left unread or partially implemented. The failure of much of this kind of curriculum development has been well documented (Steadman *et al.* 1981; Parsons *et al*, 1983). We have seen that even in the 1970s dissatisfaction with this model had led to the development of alternative models which involved potential users in the in-school development and piloting of new curricula. The Humanities Curriculum Project and Geography for the Young School Leaver (Stenhouse, 1980) are examples of the 'social interaction' model. Even so, these developments were usually led by people from outside the schools, and barriers to implementation remained.

In any discussion of factors which contribute to the growth of SBCD it is also important to note that the teaching profession in England and Wales has, since the mid-1970s, become all-graduate entry. (Before this, teachers could enter the profession either through university and subsequent one-year postgraduate training or after three years training at a college of education which resulted in the award of Certificate of Education; and some undertook a four-year course of training which culminated in a BEd (Bachelor of Education) degree.) Although no hard evidence exists, it is worth surmising that as the number of non-graduate teachers decline, so may the perceived needs to move outside the school for further development.

A further significant positive factor is that SBCD is at least in theory able to match perceived needs of teachers to their work contexts and to minimize problems of transfer and utilization of knowledge by giving them ownership of planning, action and evaluation of their own learning. In addition it may be much more grounded in classroom practice so that whether the curriculum being developed is in the form of materials, syllabi or teaching strategies, it is likely to be directly relevant to the teacher and his/her immediate needs, the needs of functional groups within a school, and the needs of the school as a whole.

Finally, it is important to note that SBCD enables networks to grow which already exist in schools. Within the LEATGS system, (LEA Training Grants Scheme previously referred to as GRIST), schools are required to produce annual development plans and to monitor these. Needs identification, target setting and review of the curriculum is, therefore, now a formal requirement for LEAs and schools. While this requirement enables either individuals or networks of teachers with schools to 'bid' for resources in any given year, it is worth noting that the extent to which implicit principles of collaboration and collegiality are implemented will depend upon the will and effectiveness of management.

Factors Limiting the Growth of SBCD

Australia

A major factor operating on the Australian scene relates to the disparity between rhetoric extolling SBCD and the actual support structures provided to participants (Prideaux, 1988). Most education systems in Australia have issued formal statements and bulletins during the 1970s and 80s couched in terms such as 'school-based', 'devolution of control' and 'decentralized decision-making'. However, to make SBCD a reality requires new levels of skills for participants and time to practise them. To a large extent, education systems have not provided the support structures needed. Little information has been disseminated about decision-making models, professional development workshops have been very few in number, and no major increases in non-teaching time have been allocated to teachers to enable them to undertake planning activities. In fairness to senior education officials the economic restraints of the 1980s have given them little opportunity to increase financial incentives for schools wanting to embark upon SBCD. Alternatively, it might be argued that senior education officials had other agendas in mind in that they had no intention of devolving major curriculum decision-making roles to school communities.

Another limiting factor is the suddenness with which SBCD changes have been thrust upon schools. Mention has already been made about the top-down edicts including legislative changes which were enacted in Victoria over recent years. Sudden policy changes have also occurred in some other states, such as in Western Australia and in South Australia. Teachers can become very stressed by the myriad of demands placed upon them. Creating order out of all the policy changes in addition to the stresses of daily teaching can become a major problem for teachers. Many might opt not to become involved in SBCD activities because they can not cope with all the additional demands and the lack of lead time to get adjusted to them. Prideaux (1985) refers to teachers' lack of interest in SBCD in South Australia because central office officials did not produce clearly enunciated policies and reasonable time schedules for implementing them.

Of course the suddenness of the SBCD changes in many state education systems have been at least partly due to political dictates. Ministers of education and their staff have endeavoured to bring about changes which could demonstrate to their respective electorates that they have implemented significant changes during their terms of office (three years) and therefore should be re-elected for a subsequent term.

Accountability questions about schools and teaching have been a major public issue since the mid-1970s in Australia. Fuelled by claims by some interest groups (for example Australian Council for Educational Standards) that standards are falling, especially in terms of numeracy and literacy, educators have been hard pressed to refute these claims. As a consequence, senior officials have tended to introduce more stringent guidelines for all schools relating to such aspects as literacy tests, and secondary school graduation requirements. There has been far less inclination to encourage school communities to develop their own approaches and solutions to raising levels of literacy and numeracy.

These centralizing trends may even be accelerated in the near future as state ministers of education explore ways of economizing with their respective education budgets. For example, at recent meetings of the Australian Education Council (participants are all state ministers of education and their chief education officers) moves have been made to examine the feasibility of using curriculum units and resources developed by other state systems. Thus, this sharing of units between states could lead to a form of common or national curriculum which would be available to students in all schools throughout Australia. Whether this degree of cooperation eventuates is far from certain, but there would be major cost savings for the various education systems and it would produce, of course, an escalation of the centralizing tendencies and a decrease in decentralizing moves such as SBCD.

The present system of staff appointments, transfers and promotions operating in most education systems in Australia is largely based on promotion by seniority. It is also due to education systems officials' insistence on uniformity of provisions to schools in all areas, whether they are remote, isolated farming or cattle station areas or located in metropolitan centres. As a result, teachers are typically required to do country teaching service several times during their teaching career and almost without exception as their first teaching appointment. Union pressures have produced a system of promotion lists and appeals to ensure that no teachers are given preferential locations. The actual allocation of appointments is done by head office personnel in each state using a combination of seniority, experience and qualifications as their major criteria. School principals are not involved in interviewing prospective staff (although this is now happening to a limited extent in Victoria).

Such a system is not very conducive to attempts to build up a stable and cohesive staff for a particular school community. Ideological differences can often occur between staff members. Some staff members may not develop any commitment to SBCD activities because of their short period of time at a school and because they are aware that they could be transferred in the very near future. Although efforts have been made recently in some states to enable some staff appointments to be based on merit rather than seniority and to require teachers to spend longer periods of time at a school before being eligible for transfer — current staffing procedures are still a major deterrent to the growth of SBCD.

Finally, mention should also be made of the decision-making and group process skills needed by participants in SBCD activities and the general lack of them by most teachers, parents and students in Australia. Many of the teachers would not have received training in these skills in their pre-service teacher education programs. Professional development programs for teachers were readily available through Commonwealth funding during the 1970s and 80s and a number of those programs did develop SBCD skills, but unfortunately the entire professional development program was terminated in 1986. State education systems are unlikely to have the funds to maintain anything other than a very minimal program of professional development, whether these are provided centrally or whether the relatively small amounts are devolved for individual schools to use.

A similar depressing picture applies to parents and students. For those parents and students involved in school community activities during the 1980s, the Commonwealth Schools Commission did provide some training programs, especially through the PEP program. A number of glowing accounts have been published about their successes, especially in Victoria (Andrews, 1985; Darling and Carrigan, 1986). However the termination of the Commonwealth Schools Commission in 1987 is likely to end, or greatly reduce, any future funding for these school community participants.

Canada

The Canadian literature on SBCD tends to focus on two limiting factors, namely the problem of centralization and the teachers' lack of skills, experience and motivation.

As noted earlier, jurisdiction over education remains firmly under the control of provincial governments. Each province further subdivides control over educational policy with the school systems within the province and the local school districts. Historically, provincial governments have waxed and waned between centralized and decentralized control over curriculum development. In times of centralization, the schools have received prescriptive documents outlining what they should be teaching, while in times of decentralization the guidelines have been general philosophical statements from which to base the school curriculum.

The educational history in Ontario over the last thirty years provides an interesting example of the ebb and flow of the centralization-decentralization continuum. Similar examples can be found in the other provinces.

In the 1950s elementary education in Ontario was governed by a curriculum commonly referred to as the 'Grey Book' (Podrebarac, 1981). The Grey Book was perceived as a highly prescriptive account of what teachers should be teaching and when they should be teaching it. The document prescribed the content, the page numbers in the textbook and the date the material should be taught. Inspectors evaluating a teacher would check to see if the teacher was in 'the right place for that specific date'. During the reign of the Grey Book, school-based curriculum government was not encouraged and might even result in negative evaluation.

The Grey Book was replaced by *The Formative Years* in 1974. This provincial document resulted from the recommendations of the Hall-Dennis Commission. The published recommendations of the Hall-Dennis commission, *Living and Learning* (Ontario Ministry of Education, 1968), located responsibility for curriculum decision-making at the school board and individual school level. Teachers were assigned the responsibility for curriculum programming. Consequently, in a very short time period, Ontario teachers were thrust from teaching from a prescriptive curriculum document to designing their own program based on the more philosophical document, *The Formative Years*. This latter document contained many significant changes for teachers: it emphasized a developmental approach to teaching and learning; advocated an enquiry or discovery approach; and perceived the teacher as a curriculum developer. According to *The Formative Years*:

> School staffs, both as individuals and as a collective body under the leadership of the principal, have the task of planning classroom programs specifically adapted to the children for whom they are responsible (Ontario Ministry of Education, 1975, p.4).

The intent behind this move towards decentralization was to shift the emphasis from control of policy/curriculum development by a few high-powered professionals to control by the wide cross-section of educators within the province (Podrebarac, 1981). However, the decentralization provided a great deal of difficulty for teachers used to a prescriptive document. A provincial review of *The Formative Years* and the accompanying document *Education in the Primary and Junior Division* conducted in the mid 1980s suggested that the philosophy underlying these documents had not been implemented in classroom practice. Consequently, the shift back towards centralization has begun again. In the last few years, the provincial Ministry of Education has been producing documents outlining the curriculum in more depth. A recent document *Science is Happening Here* is a typical example. While this document still reflects the philosophy of *The Formative Years*, it provides far more specifics on content and teaching methodologies. However, local school boards and schools are still expected to develop more detailed local curriculum documents based on the document *Science is Happening Here* so the pendulum has not yet swung totally back to a centralized position.

The pendulum swing in Ontario provides an example of the context in which school-based curriculum development exists. During a period of centralization, little school-based curriculum development officially occurs. Possibly due to the division of powers in the Canadian constitution, SBCD in Canada exists within this constant pendulum-swing between centralization and decentralization.

USA

A major factor limiting school-based curriculum development in the USA is the current preoccupation with state legislative controls. It has enabled much greater 'lay' input and less 'professional' input into educational policy-making. This downgrading of the role of professional educators has been accelerated still further in some states where certification and teacher tenure requirements are based on qualifying examinations and not professional education programmes.

The new legislative requirements are emphasizing performance indicators which are supposedly measuring 'quality education' but their uses are far from proven. It has brought about stifling effects of bureaucracy (Boyer, 1983). Boyer maintains that

> more emphasis needs to be placed on decision making at the building level. However, some still advocate top-down solutions such as increased graduation requirements for all students, increased length of instructional time, and the adoption of specific instructional strategies as standard practices. People who would solve the school's problems in this manner appear to be ignoring the changing professionalism of the teacher and to be failing to take advantage of the increased education level of the parents. They are also ignoring the findings of a number of scholars in other fields regarding the nature of effective modern organization. (pp. 189–90).

UK: England and Wales

The very kinds of intervention into the management of the curriculum of schools which contribute to the growth of SBCD may also limit its effectiveness; for where the new SBCD with its increased resource support is perceived to be a management tool or enshrined as part of local and national accountability system — in short, where motives are suspect — then teachers commitment to it may be limited, and the intended reality of SBCD may become buried beneath a rhetoric of documentation. Structural and political changes may, therefore, produce, for some, a negative effect.

A second potentially limiting factor in the 'new' system is that it relies for its success upon the will and the ability of management of leadership in schools to encourage participation in significant decision-making, collaboration among staff, and collegiality in its approach to need identification. There will be many school principals who neither have the wish nor the necessary management skills to achieve this.

Planning for staff development must be both reactive (in response to the articulated needs of individuals and groups from within and outside the school) and proactive (as a result of systematic identification of individual and institutional needs). Inevitably this kind of planning requires the time, energy, and skilled commitment of principal and senior management. It requires the development of systems of communication, consultation, support, review, monitoring and feedback which are credible and valid to all concerned, in which all concerned have an investment, and into which all concerned feel able to place their trust. The successful development of such systems will depend to some extent on the priority which is given and seen to be given to staff development by the headteacher.

Teachers themselves might also be limited in their ability to carry out SBCD for, as is demonstrated in the case study, new levels of research and human relating skills will often be required. Nor should it be assumed that all teachers would wish to bear the burden of responsibility for curriculum development. The need for support for acquiring such skills is not formally recognized, although evidence of the difficulties in, for example, need identification is well documented (Bolam, 1982).

Finally, there are dangers intrinsic to the exclusive use of any one system for development, for it runs the risk of being limited to either the confirmation of existing prejudices, the sharing of ignorance or discipleship of some charismatic, influential individual. If we rely only on our own perceptions of need, relevance and worth, without taking into account the limitations of our own perceptions and socialisation (what Skilbeck calls 'localism, parochialism and conservatism' (Skilbeck, 1984), then SBCD may become predictable, parochial (Henderson, 1979) and inbred. Without cross-fertilization with teachers in other schools, and without access to new ideas or 'critical friends' from outside as well as inside the school, there may be insufficient ideas of quality and impact.

Evaluative Evidence about SBCD

Australia

SBCD in Australia has been promulgated as a policy by senior officials from national education agencies, and more recently, by state education systems. The top-down enunciation of this policy may appear to be paradoxical for a concept which is typically associated with local initiatives and 'grass-roots' activities.

It is also surprising that the concept of SBCD has been subject to very little critical scrutiny. Since the term was advanced by senior officials in the Commonwealth Schools Commission and the CDC in the 1970s it has become a popular slogan for educators but few evaluative studies have been initiated to explore the viability of it to the

Australian scene. The evaluative studies that have been undertaken during the 1970s and 80s can be categorized as:

(a) Commonwealth Schools Commission case study reports;
(b) reports/articles published by school principals;
(c) research studies;
(d) school level evaluations.

As part of the requirements to receive a grant from the Innovations Program of the Commonwealth Schools Commission during 1973–81, recipients were required to provide evaluative data about their project, written up in the form of a case study. In many cases an external evaluation consultant was funded to assist them with this task. A number of these case studies have been published (for example in a summary document by Fraser and Nash (1981). The case study reports typically concentrate upon successful examples of SBCD but they also contain important caveats about school-level problems.

From time to time innovative principals have documented school-based programs that they initiated at their school. They vary in quality from brief exhortatory accounts to comprehensive case studies (which may have also been used for credit for graduate diplomas or degrees). Recent examples include those published by Peljo and Howell (1980), Williams (1980), Whelan (1982) and Adams (1984).

A number of postgraduate theses have been completed over the last decade and which have focussed on aspects of SBCD (see review by Marsh, 1986). The more recent ones have used case study approaches and ethnographic techniques as their major thrust for collecting data (for example, Prideaux, 1988). Only one major national study has been undertaken which included a number of survey questionnaires and case studies of individual schools (Cohen and Harrison, 1982). Although it would be difficult to generalize from some of the case studies included in these research studies, it is unfortunate that official policy documents on SBCD do not appear to have consulted this source of information.

Over recent years a number of comprehensive school-wide evaluations have been undertaken, especially by private schools, using the New England Association of Schools and Colleges Model (1972). This model relies upon a formalized system of procedures whereby staff collect data about teaching practices, and then an external panel visit the school and produce a final report. Very substantial reports on individual schools have been produced by using this approach and they can include valuable data on SBCD issues.

Although various discrete studies have been produced about SBCD there is a paucity of data about overall patterns within and between states. It would appear that some major evaluative studies of SBCD operating within educational districts, regions and states are urgently needed so that policy makers and more especially Treasury officials can be convinced that this mode of organization has financial advantages in addition to the often cited pedagogical advantages.

Canada

While Canadian curriculum literature contains many calls for increased involvement by classroom teachers in school-based curriculum development (Young, 1979; Common, 1986; Oberg, 1980), the literature also emphasizes why SBCD is not a prevalent manner of developing curriculum across the nation. A major problem often cited is the role of the teacher within the bureaucratic and legislative division of power.

Through her investigation of SBCD in the province of Alberta, Young (1979) suggests that teachers are generally willing to accept school districts and provincial governments' initiatives in establishing curriculum policy and that, consequently, teachers are willing to consider themselves as implementors rather than developers. She suggests that:

> . . . it may be said that a school district, due to its centralized nature, reinforces the natural inclination of teachers to enclose themselves within the four walls of their classrooms and thus inhibits participation in curriculum decision making.

Common (1986) makes a similar assertion, when she claims that while teachers have the potential of being curriculum reformers they tend to be defenders of the status quo. She suggests that teachers may have been granted de jure authority but they are unable to earn the de facto authority necessary to engage in curriculum reform. De facto authority presupposes teachers are experts on the knowledge to be taught and the methods of teaching that knowledge. However, Common suggests that in too many cases teachers have neither kind of expertise.

In the Canadian context, similar to the contexts mentioned in the literature from other countries, is the concern expressed by teachers that they do not have the jurisdiction to make the necessary decisions involved in SBCD. Smith (1983) suggests that a sense of decision-making space is an important consideration. If the teacher-developers are required to develop their curricular product within the narrow parameters of a provincial guideline, then they might feel they do not have sufficient decision making space from which to design a curriculum. Certainly, in times of centralization as described in the earlier section, this would be the case. The perception of a narrow decision making space, prescribed by Ministry of school district policy, might account for the teachers' lack of interest in being actively involved in SBCD.

In summary, SBCD is not the established means of developing curriculum in Canada although called for by the curriculum scholars within the country. Seemingly, the centralization of curriculum policy making either at the provincial or school board level, provides little opportunity for teachers to develop curricula for their school or their classroom. However, other scholars suggest that even if centralized policy making did not exist, teachers lack both the skills and the inclination to be involved in SBCD. Perhaps, this perspective should be tempered by Oberg's (1980) assertion that when teachers carry out their interpretation of an externally produced curriculum guide they act simultaneously as developer and implementor.

USA

Although the term SBCD has not figured prominently in the American literature some major evaluation studies have been undertaken over the last decade which relate to school-level curriculum development.

The Rand Study (Berman and McLaughlin, 1977) involved case studies of 293 curriculum projects across a number of states. McLaughlin (1979), one of the co-directors of the study, maintains that the most successful projects were those which required teachers at their local school to work out styles of teaching and classroom techniques which best suited them, within a broad philosophical framework. That is, 'implementation is a "mutually adaptive process" between the user and the institutional setting . . . the goals and methods are made concrete over time by the participants themselves' (*ibid.*, p.20).

The Dissemination Efforts supporting School Improvement (DESSI) (Crandall, 1983) was also a major study of 158 schools in ten states studied over a three-year period. Huberman and Miles (1982), in their case studies which comprised part of the DESSI study, concluded that teacher commitment at the school level comes with mastery of new practices and that this mastery heightens the sense of ownership. These authors considered that teacher ownership at the school site could be developed successfully even with strong advocacy and prescription from personnel having superordinate positions.

Similar findings were produced by Odden and Marsh (1987) and

Marsh (1988) in their studies of Californian schools. They concluded that local school curriculum reforms were successful when district leaders articulated and translated state policies into district visions and policies. They noted that staff teams 'were able to blend top-down initiation of the reform direction with bottom-up participation in developing and implementing the programs' (Marsh, 1988).

A number of studies have examined the leadership role of school principals and other senior teachers in bringing about curriculum change at the school level. Studies by Rutherford and Huling-Austin (1984) and Hall *et al.* (1982) have pointed to the multifaceted, highly fragmented and busy role of secondary school principals in school improvement programmes. Hall and Rutherford (1983) have isolated a small number of 'styles' which seem to be of special significance for school improvement in primary and secondary schools.

UK: England and Wales

The adoption of SBCD by national and local government as a means of both encouraging the development of teachers' professionality and ensuring the implementation of policy is potentially conflicting, since an increase in participation in need identification and curriculum development, even within a general framework of curriculum implementation, may well lead to a questioning of both curriculum content and management structures and subsequent demands for change. The new SBCD is, then, a strange mix between top-down initiatives and grass roots activities (though central government has reserved the right to turn off the resource tap through its system of monitoring and annual 'progress reports').

It is true also that the promotion of the new SBCD is as much rooted in perceptions of economic value for money as in educational ideology. There is some evaluative evidence to support the development of SBCD as an effective means of growth in schools, though much of it is rooted in individual case studies and in the 'action research' literature (Skilbeck, 1984; Nixon, 1981; Hustler, 1986; Oldroyd, Smith and Lee, 1984; Oldroyd and Hall, 1988; Thomson and Thomson, 1984). Examples of support for SBCD from LEAs and higher education are readily available, and some have been described earlier, but it is more difficult to find evaluations of these. In Project SITE (Baker, 1980 and 1982) the evaluation revealed that there were problems of

1 the ability of schools to carry out their own needs analysis,

2 the causal relationship between INSET and the edification of teacher behaviour,

3 the different perceptions and expectations of the extended consultant's and providing agency's role. (Bolam, 1982)

There is no tradition of curriculum evaluation in England, and such evaluations that do exist are formative (Schools Council, 1973; Shipman, 1974; Tawney, 1973 and 1976). However a tradition is rapidly beginning to be established through LEATGS, other externally funded work, and an Education Reform Act which ensures at least paper accountability.

Conclusions

It seems that school-based curriculum development is more deeply embedded in the fabric of educational practice in Australia and England and Wales than in Canada or the USA, although the need for it has been continually stressed by the academic community and the various teachers' organisations in each of these countries. Certainly SBCD is not anywhere institutionalized as a primary means of developing curriculum.

School-based curriculum development has been defined as, 'the planning, design, implementation and evaluation of a programme of students' learnings by the educational institution of which those students are members' (Skilbeck, 1984). The implication of this definition is that curriculum development and curriculum research are inseparable and that, since teachers are central agents, curriculum development is about teacher self-development (though it is worth noting that this self-development may be influenced by the (sometimes conflicting) interests of a number of interested parties with investments in the school — not least the students, but also colleagues, parents, governors and so on).

The case for SBCD has been established on the grounds of:

1 demands for the increased autonomy of the school in curriculum making;

2 'top-down' modes of control have created dissatisfaction;

3 schools need to be responsive to their environment and this requires the freedom, opportunity, responsibility and resources to determine and direct their affairs;

4 schools are best fitted to plan and design the curriculum, and to construct the teaching and learning of specific programmes;

5 teacher self-actualization, motivation and sense of achievement

are integrally bound up with curriculum decision-making which is the staple of teachers' professional lives;

6 the school is a more stable and enduring institution for curriculum development than regional and national bodies.

Involvement in SBCD requires a redefinition of the teacher's role to include a more active participation in determining educational directions. This causes potential problems as, in accepting a centralized educational policy, teachers have often performed a more conservative role in maintaining the status quo.

If teachers are to develop curriculum then we have to help them prepare for this change of direction. First, the curriculum development process must be reconceptualized to include teacher development. Teachers will need to gain the necessary skills to perform curriculum leadership roles so they are not dependent on external resource people. Second, the development process will have to be considered not merely in terms of document production but as a reflective process encompassing such issues as what children should learn and the past practices of the teachers involved. Third, the curriculum development process, similar to the current conceptualization of the change process, will have to be considered as an ongoing, time-consuming activity that must be grounded in classroom practice. As such, curriculum development will have to be viewed as a more circular and problematic process, with those assigned the responsibility for facilitating curriculum development no longer employing linear, ends-means curriculum models. Fourth, the process of developing curriculum will need to be considered as a skill-based activity which includes such areas as problem formation, generation of alternatives, and leadership. Lastly, teachers will have to accept the role of curriculum developer as part of their professional responsibility, not as another 'add-on'.

A reconceptualization of the development process as school-based with skill-based teacher expertise poses several considerations for teacher education programs and school organizations. Teacher education programs, whether pre-service or in-service, will have to assist teachers in gaining the necessary reflective ability to make curricular decisions and in acquiring the facilitative skills necessary to develop curriculum. Teachers will need to learn to make curriculum decisions and justify them on educational grounds.

If schools are to increase their involvement in SBCD then several organizational changes must be considered. First, the frequent pendulum swing towards centralization will have to cease. If teachers are to design curriculum for their own schools and classrooms, then they must not fear a policy shift that could negate their efforts. Perhaps centrally designed documents will have to become more general philosophical statements which serve as a guide to document production at the local level. Second, more teachers must be provided with in-school time to work on SBCD. It is important that teachers have time to reflect with their colleagues and to develop curriculum as a group rather than in isolation.

A move towards SBCD would help teachers define and shape the challenges facing their schools and their classrooms. Such involvement would empower teachers to reflect on their own practice and become curriculum reformers, rather than defenders of the status quo or implementors of curriculum developed by others. Through this process, then, teachers would assume professional control over their working environment.

If, in the future, SBCD is really to 'become a movement which engages the energies of teachers but, even more dramatically, of pupils, parents and a large variety of social groups' (Skilbeck, 1975), then those who take management responsibilities for its development must ensure that teachers who are expected to participate in their own and their school's developments are enabled to do so through training which helps them to adopt new roles, to understand better the deliberations which underpin curriculum issues, and equips them with appropriate research and problem solving skills. Managers themselves will need to face the consequences of this kind of 'enabling' for their own structures which must place emphasis upon collegial rather than hierarchical sub-cultures in schools and local education authorities. As yet there is no evidence that this issue has been addressed with any seriousness of purpose and planning by the managers themselves. SBCD remains essentially an act of faith.

Chapter 2

Toward a Reconceptualization of SBCD

Over recent years a number of educators have contributed to the literature on school-based curriculum development (SBCD) providing conceptual frameworks for studying the myriad of actions and decisions that occur daily in school classrooms.

In this chapter, the concept and practices of SBCD are systematically analyzed. After categorizing various types, SBCD is reconceptualized in terms of several key variables and a set of developmental stages. To pinpoint issues for those undertaking SBCD activities, attention is given to ideal conditions and to recurring problems. Finally, special consideration is given to ways of evaluating SBCD projects, partly because of its valuable feedback to participants, but also because it is a means of demonstrating the viability of SBCD to policy-makers concerned about matters of accountability.

Introduction

In many Western countries during the last two decades the term School-Based Curriculum Development (SBCD) has been used as a rallying cry for various innovatory educational practices. There have been variations in terms such as 'school-focussed' rather than 'school-based' and 'curriculum decision-making' rather than 'curriculum development'. Further, some would argue that SBCD is a slogan, while others prefer to conceptualize it as a method or technique. These variations need to be considered before proceeding any further with an analysis of SBCD.

Some would argue that SBCD highlights the vexatious matter of centralized control of education versus decentralized control. As can be noted by recent developments in the United Kingdom, there is no guarantee that a well-established decentralized system can withstand a concerted onslaught by political rulers intent on superimposing a centralized system.

After many decades of highly centralized control by state systems in Australia, there have been general flirtations with SBCD, and more recently, some serious relationships involving the mandating of local community control. The Canadian scene, with its checks and balances, appears to be accommodating considerable school-level autonomy within systems of provincial and federal control. In the USA, increasing state controls have been very evident over recent years.

A literal definition of 'school-based' might imply that all educational decisions are made at the school level. Apart from independent and 'alternative' schools operating as separate entities, it is highly unlikely that this situation pertains to systemic schools (for example, government schools, schools in a school district). The term 'school-focussed' is a weaker interpretation in that it suggests that decision-making, at whatever level it occurs and by whom, is undertaken in terms of the interests and needs of school communities. This latter term could apply to a whole range of highly centralized decision-making activities. Expressed along a continuum, 'school-based' is closer to the extreme of individual schools being responsible for all curriculum decisions, whereas 'school-focussed' could be represented as a middle position between the centralized and decentralized extremes.

The term '*curriculum development*' has wide connotations and is used to describe the various curriculum processes of planning, designing and producing, associated with the completion of a particular set of materials. It can also include teaching activities associated with the implementation and evaluation of a set of materials. One might ascribe such elaborate activities to a well-funded curriculum project team, but the scale and range of these activities could well be beyond the scope of individual school communities. As a result, the term 'curriculum-making' is preferred because it signifies a less grandiose range of activities for school personnel. Walton (1978) makes a further distinction when he suggests that SBCD may typically involve *creating* new products or processes but that it can also involve *selecting* from available commercial materials and making various *adaptions*. The latter two processes, of course, require less time and funds and a lower level of commitment from participants. Yet, it can be argued, that SBCD tasks should be embarked upon only if they are manageable and can be achieved within a relatively short space of time. Certainly adaptions and selections are more manageable activities than creating new materials but they raise in turn, problems of ownership and internalization.

There is yet another interpretation of curriculum development which is far less materials-oriented than those mentioned above. It can be argued that teachers should not merely be involved in activities which enable them to implement curriculum materials more effectively, but that they should engage in wide-ranging inquiries of concern to them. Connelly and Ben-Peretz (1980) argue that teachers' engaging in educational enquiry will grow professionally from these activities even though, as a result of these experiences, they may be less inclined to implement curricula designed by others.

Without doubt, education systems and agencies have used the term SBCD as a *slogan*. It conjures up action at the local level, it connotes participation, grass-roots control, and many other attributes which are held to be near and dear to the general public. In a more cynical vein, it could also be stated that SBCD has been used by senior officers in some educational systems to deflect the blame for educational crises or is used as a means of cost-cutting from head-office budgets (Hunt, 1981; Fitzgerald, 1973).

Other writers argue that SBCD is an amalgam of ideas which can be construed as an *educational philosophy*. Skilbeck (1974 and 1984) puts together such terms as 'teacher and learner working together to produce the curriculum'; 'freedom for both teacher and pupil' and the 'school's responsiveness to its environment' to produce a theoretical position about SBCD. He argues at length for structures and policies to be developed at the school-level and for there to be shared decision-making by all participants, especially teachers and students. Fullan (1982) supports teacher involvement in change at the school level and he has produced various factors and strategies which could be viewed as a model for SBCD.

The literature is also replete with various accounts of SBCD as a *technique*. Case study accounts in particular have focussed upon particular techniques which seem to work. Some writers have produced particular procedures such as the person-centred approaches by Loucks-Horsley (1985) or the management-centred approaches by Caldwell and Spinks (1986) and Day, Johnston and Whitaker (1985). Others have concentrated upon ways of making SBCD work more effectively by the training of special in-house consultants (Sabar, 1983); and leadership skills and qualities for school principals (Leithwood *et al.*, 1984; Rutherford, 1984).

What is SBCD?

Definitions of SBCD, reflect to a large degree, the predispositions of the respective authors. For example, Skilbeck (1984) defines SBCD as: 'the planning, design, implementation and evaluation of a programme of students' learnings by the educational institution of which those students are members' (p.2). This definition in itself may seem quite acceptable but in accompanying descriptions, Skilbeck is emphasizing particular aspects such as shared decision-making between teachers and students; that SBCD is internal and organic to the institution; and that it involves a network of relationships with various groups and is characterized by a definite pattern of values, norms, procedures and roles.

Harrison (1981) perceives SBCD as a combination of participants' intended curriculum (a progressively-modifiable plan); their operational curriculum (what actually happens to the person/s) and their perceived curriculum (their perceived situation and outcomes). She maintains that these 'three phases of curriculum interact, as an interlocking set, bringing about continuous evaluation and decision-making, for progressive modification of the curriculum' (p.52).

Other writers try to map the infinite varieties of SBCD in their attempts to explain what it is. For example, Brady (1987) postulates twelve different variations of SBCD using a classification system based upon *type of activity* (creation, adaptation, selection of curriculum materials) on one axis and *people involved* (individual teachers, pairs of teachers, groups, whole staff) on the other axis.

There are certainly many variations of SBCD and a single definition cannot do justice to the many different permutations. In addition to the variations of *type of activity* and *people involved* there is also a time commitment dimension. As a result, it is possible to construct a three-dimensional model as illustrated in Figure 1. The time commitment dimension can be a crucial element because one-off activities, no matter how successful, will have little enduring effects on the school community unless they are part of a well-developed, on-going plan. Of course, activities which continue beyond a teaching term of two–three months can falter due to lack of time, and competing priorities. Changes in staff at the end of each teaching year can cause further problems for the development of long-term SBCD activities.

Taking an example from the matrix in Figure 1 a typical SBCD activity might be the *adaption* of a primary science workbook by a *small group of teachers* as part of a *short-term plan* to upgrade their teaching of science in the upper primary grades. A more ambitious undertaking based upon the matrix cells in Figure 1 could be the *creation of new*

Figure 1: A matrix of SBCD variations

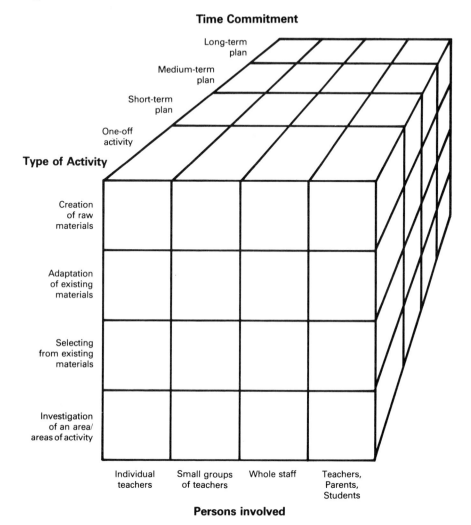

materials for a local community unit by a *team of teachers, parents and students* as a *long-term plan* to be completed over a period of one calendar year.

Knight (1985), in a recent meta-analysis of fifty empirical case study accounts of SBCD in the United Kingdom, also noted the diversity of scope and emphasis in these studies. Some of the variations he discovered were:

		Number of cases (N = 50)
levels	whole school changes	13
	multi-departmental changes	13
	departmental changes	9
	single teacher changes	15
type of activity	wide range from minor changes of existing content to a complete review and renewal of the curriculum.	
leadership roles		
primary schools	– 8 out of 9 projects were initiated by the principal	
	– most assistance from advisory specialists	
secondary schools	– mainly heads of department	
	– organisational constraints were often cited	
	– projects were mainly for lower ability and non-academic students	
planning	– motives were mainly overcoming perceived deficiencies of provision and pupil needs	
	– direction of activities were planned mainly by teachers, some assistance from external specialists	
implementation and evaluation		
	– few implementation difficulties were reported	
	– 41 of the cases had successful outcomes	
	– specific evaluative data was only collected in 17 cases.	

In later chapters of this book a number of case study accounts of SBCD are described and analyzed. Although some authors include individual teacher projects in their examples of SBCD (for example, Knight, 1985, as cited above) that practice will not be followed in this book. All examples included in subsequent chapters are based upon groups of persons from a school community working on particular SBCD projects.

Why Become Involved in SBCD?

There are very many reasons why individuals become involved in SBCD. Although SBCD applies to parents and students as well as teachers, it is the latter group who typically get directly involved. To simplify the analyses, the initial discussion focusses upon teachers.

Teachers have a major interest in their craft. Maximum satisfactions are achieved if they are able to teach in ways which suit the majority of their students. The occasional successes they have with extremely difficult students makes their endeavours well worth the effort. They guard very jealously those particular strategies or 'recipes' which seem to work (Lortie, 1975; Huberman, 1980).

Sometimes the problems are beyond the resources of an individual teacher and he/she needs to exchange ideas with others and perhaps even work collaboratively with a colleague on a particular problem. These experiments in cooperative ventures will only occur if the conditions are amenable and psychologically safe for the individual teachers.

Stated another way, teachers may embark upon SBCD activities if they have particular *needs* but these will be tempered by the *limits* of their particular teaching environment. Miles and Ekholm (1985) refer to a balancing out of these two factors. Teachers will be highly motivated to participate if there are important needs to be satisfied but only if these can be accommodated within the value system of the school community. Day *et al.* (1985) point to four factors which can affect the directions that teachers might take and that some compromise between them is always needed. These four factors include *predilections* of what teachers would like to do, *situations* that have to be taken into account and wider external factors of *expectations* and *prescriptions* (such as by legislation).

In figure 2 the motives for teachers to become involved in SBCD are conceptualized around two major factors, namely *current level of job satisfaction* and *educational innovations*. It is argued that job satisfaction is a key variable. If teachers are satisfied with what their students are achieving, especially as this often requires some very careful attention to the use of particular resources and methods, then they will be reticent about changing this state of affairs. The frenetic activities which can typically occur in a days teaching, make many teachers long for periods of stability and even homeostasis. Teachers, as a result of their socialization into the profession, do not tend to opt for avante-garde initiatives. Few want to be labelled as radicals or mavericks. The majority want the security of regular and predictable patterns of classroom activity.

Figure 2: Major factors affecting participation in SBCD

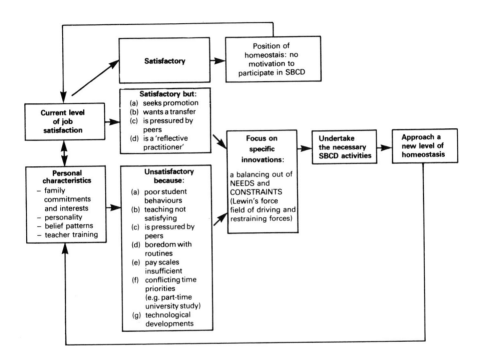

However, as indicated in figure 2, there will be some teachers who want to participate in SBCD activities even though they are relatively satisfied with their current teaching position. For example, those teachers seeking promotion realize that they need to do something extra to give themselves a chance of earning promotion. They might consider that their active participation in an SBCD activity could be a useful way of highlighting their particular strengths and details of this activity could be included in their curriculum vitae. Then again there might be teachers who are prepared to reflect upon their current practices — they have the ability and the desire to problem-solve about their teaching (Schön, 1983) even though they are relatively satisfied with their current position.

In addition to those teachers who might be in the category of being satisfied but mobile, there is the much bigger group of teachers who would be dissatisfied with their present teaching position. A major reason for their dissatisfaction might be poor student attainments in their particular subjects or individual students performing poorly across a range of subjects. Another reason could be their dissatisfaction with inadequate resources, timetabling constraints or insufficient preparation time. A related reason might be sheer boredom with the system of rules and regulations and teaching practices.

This leads us to the second major concept included in figure 2, namely *educational innovations*. There is always likely to be considerable debate and lack of agreement about what are effective *means* and *ends* of schooling. Despite the considerable impetus given to studies of effective schools over recent years, there is still no unequivocal evidence about the superiority of specific methods of teaching. There is also considerable disagreement about the purposes of schooling as witnessed by opposing views in the literature about vocational and academic goals.

It can be argued, therefore, that educators in general, and teachers in particular, are very susceptible to educational innovations. There are various pressures from the media, educational suppliers, professional associations and head office personnel for teachers to try new teaching practices. A new item of instructional hardware or a recently produced curriculum package may be perceived to be the solution to a pressing classroom problem. The nature of teaching is such that narrowly formulated procedures cannot be used in *all* learning situations. Experimentation, adaptation, modification is often what is needed and teachers are frequently encouraged (and sometimes coerced) into trying out particular innovations.

For some teachers it may be quite exhilarating and fashionable to try out an innovatory practice. This is related to the 'faddish' aspects of education. As noted by Kirst and Meister (1985), many changes in education occur in cycles and appear to be related to economic and social events. Particular emphases about schooling which are dominant in one decade might become dormant for some years only to reappear years later amid considerable media attention. As a case in point, the attention given to the production of national science projects in the 1950s in the USA has reappeared again in the 1980s in that country.

However, teachers have to balance out competing forces when making decisions about whether to use an innovation or not. As indicated in figure 3, as a result of considering needs and constraints, teachers may decide to try out some innovations and not others. The process they undertake may be akin to the force field of 'driving' and 'restraining' forces as noted by Lewin (1948) many decades ago. As indicated in figure 3 some of the driving forces can be very influential but so too are the restraining forces. Clearly, only those innovations which are perceived to have a majority of dominant driving forces will in fact be adopted. The majority, in all likelihood, will be rejected. Fullan (1982) makes this point succinctly when he states that:

> It should be clearly understood that I am not saying that teachers are 'intrinsically' uninterested in serious education change. The truth of the matter is that the culture of the school, the demands of the classroom, and the usual way in which change is introduced do not permit, point to, or facilitate teacher involvement in exploring or developing more significant changes in educational practice. (p. 120)

Every teacher develops his/her own unique configuration of driving and restraining forces as outlined in figure 3. Two or more teachers will only be willing to interact on SBCD activities if they perceive mutually supportive results from sharing their ideas and preferences (a mutual linking of configurations).

The final phase of model, as indicated in figure 2, is for pairs or groups of teachers to undertake their chosen innovatory SBCD activities on the assumption that improved teaching and learning situations for themselves and their students will be the result. They are likely to be seeking a new position of stability, a different set of relationships and procedures which will provide them in turn with a reasonable degree of homeostasis.

As indicated at the beginning of this section, SBCD can involve parents and students as well as teachers. It is argued that the conceptual model (figures 2 and 3) applies also to parents and students. For example, parents through their formal contacts (for example, school councils) and informal meetings can lobby for changes and the adoption of certain innovations if they perceive that there are problem areas and issues to be resolved. On the other hand, they may be the restraining forces who feel strongly that certain innovations proposed by the teaching staff should not be adopted.

Students, especially through their student councils, can also provide opinions and advice which can be influential in determining final decisions about certain innovatory programs. However, it has to be conceded that students' level of influence is likely to be minimal in many school communities.

Figure 3: Force field for using an educational innovation

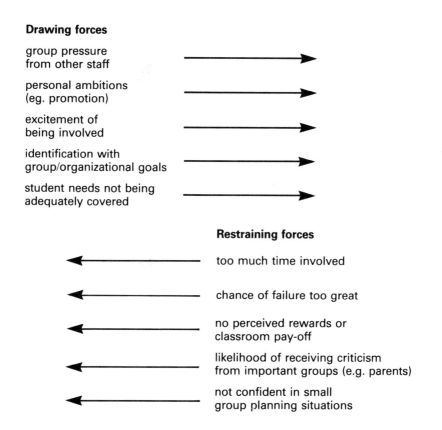

Drawing forces

group pressure
from other staff

personal ambitions
(eg. promotion)

excitement of
being involved

identification with
group/organizational goals

student needs not being
adequately covered

Restraining forces

too much time involved

chance of failure too great

no perceived rewards or
classroom pay-off

likelihood of receiving criticism
from important groups (e.g. parents)

not confident in small
group planning situations

SBCD — As an Ideal

Notwithstanding the caveats made earlier about the great diversity of approaches to SBCD it can be instructive to examine patterns and behaviours which might be expected of SBCD in *ideal* school community situations. In particular, it is useful to examine the following aspects:

(a) *mission — school goals*
(b) *readiness of participants — teachers, parents, students*
(c) *leaders/change agents*
(d) *group dynamics and school climate*
(e) *time — provisions, allowances*
(f) *resources — financial, organisational*
(g) *professional development*
(h) *processes*

Mission — School Goals

In an *ideal* situation members of a school community are able to be directly involved in decision-making. This democratization of decision-making is crucial if it is of concern that all participants, and especially parents and students, are to be active participants.

Although systemic schools will always have some connections with their respective head offices, it is desirable for each school to have maximum freedom in determining and directing its schooling activities. Each school should have the opportunity to devise goals which are of special benefit and significance to its students.

Goodlad (1984) maintains that a useful strategy for school communities is to commence with major categories of educational goals and then consider specific emphases required to optimize their application to particular school settings. Four categories of goals are commonly mentioned in the literature, namely academic, vocational, personal and social. Academic goals tend to be rated highly by teachers and parents. Students at high school levels tend to rate vocational goals ahead of other goals. Special interest groups will be able to muster strong arguments why some of these goals should be given a high priority.

Readiness of Participants

Although there will be the occasional teacher who has well defined and clearly formulated goals for SBCD, many will not have thought about them. As noted by Lieberman and Miller (1984) teachers are chiefly concerned about daily rhythms, rules, teacher–student interactions and feelings. Ideally, there needs to be a core of teachers who have developed beyond these immediate concerns and have strong beliefs and a vision for what their individual school community can achieve. Further they must be willing to share these beliefs and engage in discussions and working parties to achieve their goals.

A considerable amount of research has been undertaken over recent years by Hall and associates (1975 and 1977) on the developmental stages teachers seem to undergo as they are introduced to and proceed to implement a curriculum innovation. Applying this developmental concept to SBCD it can be argued that the same principle applies, as indicated in table 1.

Some teachers might never get beyond stage I. That is, they are quite content to work entirely within the confines of their own classroom

	Stage	Major Priorities
Stage I	Individual experimentation	(a) Not confident in working with others (b) Not willing to share ideas
Stage II	Exchanges ideas	(a) Willing to 'swap recipes' informally (b) Willing to try out other teachers ideas
Stage III	Seeks out information	(a) Finds out informally about tasks and expectations (b) Does some independent searching out (eg. Resource Centres)
Stage IV	Participates with minimal responsibilities	(a) Takes on roles which require limited leadership skills (b) Prefers to adopt a 'low profile' in terms of participation
Stage V	Active participant	(a) Is a major participant in the activity (b) Is willing to organize and lead various activities
Stage VI	Undertakes major leadership roles	(a) Is prepared to initiate and plan activities (b) Monitors achievements and takes steps where needed to maintain group productivity and direction

Table 1: Developmental stages of participation in SBCD

and have next to no contact with other staff members. Almost as 'safe' in maintaining the privacy of one's own classroom is to share ideas informally over lunch breaks but never to divulge specific details about what is happening with one's students (stage II). Huberman's (1980) term of swapping recipes is a very appropriate one to describe stage II teachers. The details that teachers reveal about 'ingredients' may be deliberately very vague but they share a common bond — their anecdotes are based on real-life events which have happened and which are significant to them.

Although it is feasible that some teachers might miss out stage II, it is likely that a number will not as they tend to be cautious and want to find out about ongoing and proposed SBCD activities before committing themselves. Because of their already busy schedules, few teachers will agree to additional workloads, especially if this means that this will reduce the time they have with their classes and for which they get their intrinsic rewards. Thus stage III teachers tend to seek out information and advice from experienced SBCD participants, either at their own school or at neighbouring schools.

Teachers at Stage IV are those who have agreed to be participants in SBCD ventures but they typically opt for low-profile, low visibility roles. They may not be entirely convinced about the viability of the project or perhaps it may be a lack of confidence on their part.

By contrast, Stage V teachers are very active participants and will spend a major portion of their non-teaching contacting other teachers, planning activities and generally undertaking tasks related to SBCD projects. This may entail making announcements to staff at lunch-times and other 'high profile' activities. It often entails a considerable amount of after-school activities for them such as contacting educational suppliers and school personnel at other venues.

Stage VI teachers are those who have had considerable experience with SBCD activities. They have built up a reputation within their school and they are looked upon to initiate and manage new activities. They may have a formal status position in the school such as that of Principal, Deputy Principal, or Head of Department, or they may be recognized as an informal leader.

The object of detailing the stages of SBCD (table 1) has been of course to indicate levels of readiness ideally needed in a school for SBCD to flourish. Of course, if the majority of staff of a school are operating at stage IV and above then it is highly likely that major SBCD projects will be achieved. However, because of transfers and the appointment of newly-graduated teachers it is quite possible that a school staff could have a number of staff members at stages I and II. In this case it would be far more difficult to initiate and maintain an SBCD project.

However, it should be noted that the stages are not necessarily related to age or experience or maturity levels. For example it is quite possible for a relatively inexperienced teacher to be operating at stage V, or for a very mature teacher to be only operating at stage I.

The stages of SBCD (table 1) can also be applied to other school community participants, namely parents and students. Many parents may consider that they have little to offer their local school community, due to language difficulties, work and home commitments, or lack of education. For parents to be involved in SBCD activities requires time to build up the trust and rapport with the local school staff. Parents with highly developed interpersonal, communication and organizational skills are needed to encourage a wider representation from parents. Some of the more articulate parents might be operating at stage V (table 1) in a very active and committed school community, but it is more likely that the most interested parents are only at stage IV. In an ideal SBCD situation, potential parent leaders have the opportunity to experience training programs on interpersonal skills, procedures for running meetings and other related activities to ensure that a growing number of them develop the skills and the confidence to become active participants in SBCD projects.

Similar strategies and resources are needed to obtain student participation in SBCD activities. In those school communities where students are active members of SBCD projects (operating at stages IV and V in table 1), considerable funds have often been needed to spend on student training (for example small group skills, meeting procedures, council member responsibilities). Additional student resources have also been needed (for example, time allowances for students to attend meetings and for payments, access to telephone and xeroxing facilities). Ideally, students can make a valuable contribution to SBCD activities but in a number of school communities problems can arise between the stake-holders due to misunderstandings, patronising actions by teachers and parents, and conflicting interests.

Leaders/Change Agents

Over the last decade a lot of attention has been directed toward the role of school principals as change agents (for example, Bolam, 1982; Hall and Hord, 1987; Leithwood *et al.*, 1984). In addition, other school personnel, such as deputy principals, heads of department and senior teachers have also been singled out for special attention. Each school will have its unique combination of teachers some of whom may have had experience as change agents or have the potential to do so.

Change agents tend to be very special people. Lieberman *et al.* (1987) suggest that they have well developed 'entry characteristics' as well as 'on the job skills'. For example, some of their 'entry characteristics' built up over a number of years of teaching and professional development activities might include:

(a) expertise in curriculum development practices;
(b) sound academic background in a number of subject areas;
(c) finely tuned administrative and organizational skills.

But, in addition to these characteristics they have the flexibility and sensitivity to tackle each SBCD venture as a new task, to seek out ways of establishing rapport among stake holders; to build trust, support and direction; and to assist teachers bring about their own empowerment.

Sabar (1983) advocates that change agents need to be given substantial periods of training to ensure that they can lead SBCD activities successfully. To support her claim she describes a training program in Israel where selected coordinator/change agents were given release time for one full day per week for two years and additional intensive workshops totalling 400 hours. During this program participants concentrated especially on the roles of group leader and curriculum specialist.

Ideally, it would be invaluable to have at least one teacher on a school staff who had received special training as a change agent, along the lines suggested by Sabar (*ibid*).

In addition, charismatic leaders do emerge from time to time on school staffs but with movements of staff due to promotional prospects, it is unlikely that they stay at the same school for many years. Ideally, a relatively stable staff is needed for SBCD activities to become a significant element of an ongoing school improvement program.

Group Dynamics and School Climate

The building up of collegiality between participants is a fundamental process in any SBCD endeavour. Leaders of SBCD activities are obliged to work hard to break down individualism and to establish new organizational structures to allow group activities to develop and prosper.

The literature is replete with numerous techniques for building group cohesion and developing a positive school climate. For example, Organization Development (OD) is a technique used over the last several decades to promote reflexive, self-analysis between staff members. Teachers involved in OD are encouraged to improve the effectiveness of their working groups — to change the functioning of these groups through improved communication skills and by adopting new roles. This technique typically requires the services of an external consultant to initiate the process.

Action research is another problem solving process which relies upon teachers selecting problems and then exploring, negotiating and assessing solutions. The process is often initiated by external consultants but once commenced, their role is typically that of resource person. Teacher participation in Action Research activities can often lead to heightened awareness of group needs and can help to build group cohesion, regardless of the specific outcomes of the project.

Action research has the potential for enabling teachers (and parents and students) to pursue basic educational issues and dilemmas. For example, McTaggart (1984) has documented how action research was used in selected Australian schools to engage parents and teachers in solving school-level problems. Olson (1982) argues that a dialectical approach enables participants to deal with contrary points of view, and this is an integral part of action research cycles.

These techniques and other problem-solving approaches can be used in ideal school situations to create and maintain high levels of staff support and collegiability. Unfortunately, high levels of collegiality can easily be lost due to unforeseen incidents involving personal conflicts or the loss of key participants through staff transfers or promotion.

Time

Because teachers are contracted to teach specific subjects to certain classes over a specified number of hours, this is a fixed commitment which can rarely be modified. In some education systems in the USA the number of hours are included in teachers' contracts. In the U.K. the Secretary of State for Education and Science has recently negotiated new pay scales which require all teachers to work for 1265 hours over 195 days a year.

Few teachers would want their contact time with students reduced as they gain considerable satisfactions and intrinsic rewards from face-to-face teaching situations. Herein lies the problem. If teachers are committed to irreducible periods of time with their classes how can time be found to plan and organize SBCD activities? In ideal school situations efforts are made to provide the time needed by the use of such devices as:

1 extended morning tea and lunch breaks;
2 early closing of the school once per week, fortnight, or months;
3 before school and after school meetings;
4 workshop and planning activities at the beginning or end of a vacation period;
5 use of salary reserves to appoint relief teachers to enable regular staff members to engage in SBCD planning activities;
6 obtain project funds from external agencies to buy time for SBCD projects for regular staff members and for parents.

A number of these solutions of course, depend upon the goodwill of the staff and there is a limit to the extent and the frequency with which they can be used. Those solutions involving finance might be viewed more positively by many staff but in times of financial restraint they are only available if special needs can be demonstrated.

Because SBCD requires far more interaction with other teachers (and ideally with parents and students) the matter of effective use of time also requires a fundamental reanalysis by individual teachers. It is possible to find time for SBCD activities if a high priority is given to them. Day *et al.*'s (1985) approach for school principals has application to classroom teachers. A simple exercise to record the use of time in a typical school day can be most enlightening for teachers. In addition, Day *et al.* include some of the following suggestions:

1 keep long-term goals (of SBCD) in mind even while doing the smallest task;
2 do your thinking on paper;
3 set deadlines. (p.89)

It is up to leaders in a school to be aware of and to encourage individual participants' effective use of time as well as making time available via timetabling rearrangements and other strategies as outlined above. In an ideal school community these strategies would be highly developed.

Resources

Although 'time' is undoubtedly the major resource in a school, other important resources are those which can be classified as *financial* and *organizational*.

There is little data available about the costs involved in school-level curriculum decision-making. Criticisms are made from time to time about the financial excesses of highly centralized education systems especially in terms of an over-abundance of head office officials, and the production of extensive curriculum materials which are inadequately disseminated and sporadically used by teachers. Yet, the devolution of decision-making to schools does not necessarily mean that costs will be less or that more efficient financial practices will result. In fact, the costs could be considerably more, dependent upon the types of SBCD activities embarked upon.

In table 2 a checklist of resources for SBCD is included, based upon an organizational framework developed by Caldwell and Spinks (1988). The list is quite extensive and formidable. Caldwell and Spinks argue that the salaries of teaching and general staff need to be calculated and included in all SBCD activities so as to reflect the true cost of each undertaking. In addition, a number of relief days may need to be provided for selected teachers to enable them uninterrupted time to plan a specific program or to make visits to other schools. Consultants may also need to be hired to provide expert advice on specific aspects.

Apart from these financial costs for personnel, there are many other costs. Professional development programs may be needed to acquaint

SBCD Project _____ _____	3. Resources required
1. Purpose _____	A. Personnel _____
	Teachers _____
	General staff _____
	Parents _____
	Consultant _____
2. Plan for Implementation _____	B. Relief days for teachers _____
	C. Professional development _____
3. Plan for monitoring/evaluation _____	D. Materials and equipment _____
	E. Minor materials _____
	F. Services _____
4. Plan for providing feedback into the system	G. Travel _____
	H. Reserve _____

(*Source*: After Caldwell and Spinks, 1988)

Table 2: A checklist of resources needed to undertake SBCD

SBCD participants with a specific set of skills or techniques, such as those associated with 'evaluation' or 'needs assessment'. There may also be a need to purchase new equipment and materials if these are an integral part of a particular SBCD project. Services such as printing can also be a significant cost. If meetings with personnel in other schools and institutions is a necessary feature of the SBCD activity, then travel costs must also be included in the budget.

In an ideal situation, the financial resources available for SBCD are considerable and well managed. Finance committees, consisting of administrators, teachers and parents would be an ideal group to take on the responsibility of planning and monitoring the financial aspects of SBCD activities. As indicated in table 2 it is crucial that SBCD undertakings have resource costs linked to all planning decisions.

Professional Development

Although many school communities welcome the opportunity to be given responsibility for curriculum decision-making, a number of the participants (teachers, parents, students) may be lacking in certain skills. For example, teachers might have well honed skills of instruction but might have little experience or confidence in working cooperatively with others in small groups. A number of parents might be unaware of meeting procedures and techniques for delegating tasks to work groups. Senior students could be overflowing with enthusiasm but overawed by the group situations, and as a result, very reticent about giving opinions on specific matters.

Ideally, professional development programs should address the needs of teachers, parents and students. Activities which are scheduled (for example, a workshop on the role of values teaching) should include participants from each of these categories. There are considerable benefits for teachers, parents and students to explore issues cooperatively and to acquire a better understanding of each other's priorities and backgrounds.

Because of limited budgets it is unlikely that school communities are able to mount a number of professional development programs in a given year, but an indication of the potential range is given in table 3. For convenience, the professional development needs in table 3 are categorised as Task-Oriented, Interpersonal and Subject Area Focus. The first two apply to teachers, parents and students whereas the last applies only to teachers.

Major Areas of Need	Ways of Servicing Needs
Task oriented	Within-school activities
(a) Problem solving approaches	Seminars
(b) Needs assessment	Workshops
(c) Selecting and evaluating commercial materials	Co-teaching assignments
(d) Evaluation process	
	Lesson demonstrations
Interpersonal	Video-tape presentations
	Small group meetings
(a) Working in teams	
(b) Resolving conflicts	
(c) Achieving group goals	
(d) Evaluating team projects	Out-of-school activities
(e) Leadership skills	
	Visits to 'lighthouse' schools
	Extended workshops
Subject Area Focus	Weekend camps and seminars
	Field trips
(a) Concept building	Residential conferences
(b) Achieving higher-order skills	
(c) Specialised teaching styles	
(d) Testing	

Table 3: Professional Development: Major areas of need and ways of servicing them

Although some experienced teachers and parents might have well developed interpersonal and leadership skills, it is likely that many key participants in school communities do not. Workshops on topics such as 'problem solving approaches', 'resolving conflicts', and 'achieving group goals' could be invaluable for developing commitment to the SBCD activities in train.

The logical venue for a majority of professional development activities is the school campus. As indicated in table 3 a number of within-school variations are possible such as seminars, class demonstrations and videotape presentations. However, there might also be sound reasons for having other venues associated with a weekend retreat or field trip.

There are, of course, other opportunities for professional development via formal courses leading to diplomas and degrees available from universities and colleges, and summer-school workshops and adult education courses. Many teachers and parents might make use of these individual forms of study to acquire specific skills and understandings. Other ways of acquiring information include brochures, manuals and books mailed to schools or available from resource centres, libraries and commercial firms.

The range of potential professional development activities is considerable. Ideally, school community members would have access to a number of them, dependent upon their particular priorities and times and financial constraints.

Processes

Dependent upon the scale of each SBCD activity, it is crucial that particular procedures or processes are considered and agreed upon by school community participants.

A particular school community might rely upon one or two key persons, such as the Principal and a Deputy-Principal to do most of the planning and to communicate their planning details to others. This rather authoritarian approach might be deemed appropriate in certain communities.

Alternatively, another school community might have a non-directive approach to planning, allowing greater opportunities for participants to talk out issues, engage in debates and dialogue and to generally explore matters in considerable depth before reaching a decision. Olson (1982) argues for this dialectical approach and the need for participants to reconcile contraries when looking at various solutions to particular SBCD concerns.

A middle-ground set of procedures is suggested by Caldwell and Spinks (1986) who maintain that specific activities such as planning, budgeting, management and evaluation need to be carried out but by teams representing the various interest groups within a school community. They recommend that a *policy team* (which could include parents and students as well as teachers) make decisions about such matters as school goals and needs, and the direction and range of activities to be undertaken in the short and long term. The *project teams*, comprised mainly of teachers, are established to undertake specific SBCD tasks. Each project plan and budget has to be approved by the policy team. The number of projects are limited to one or two each term and there is a rotation between different subject areas so that over a period of several years, most school subject areas have been examined, and where necessary, revised. This particular approach, entitled the Collaborative School Management approach (Caldwell and Spinks, 1988) is an eminently practical way of organizing SBCD activities with its emphasis upon brief reports (maximum of one page reports), checks and balances between the policy and project teams, and strategies for reducing conflict.

Ideally an elaborate set of processes is needed for SBCD activities to be successful and for the gains to be maintained over longer periods of time.

Problems that Participants can Experience with SBCD

At a superficial level it is possible to list a number of problems that teachers and principals experience in undertaking SBCD activities. Commonly listed ones include:

(a) lack of time — to plan, to reflect, to develop curricula;
(b) lack of expertise — knowledge, understandings, skills;
(c) lack of finance — for materials, for teacher relief days;
(d) externally imposed restrictions — by employers, parents;
(e) a threatening school climate — numerous resisters, lack of effective leadership.

These problems should not be underrated as they are very real and are often given as the reasons why particular SBCD activities have been abandoned. However, it can be argued that there are more deeply-rooted problems about SBCD which need to be considered.

One major problem revolves around the dichotomy of 'policy' and 'action'. Many educators argue that teachers are concerned predominantly with 'action' relating to how to teach specific topics and how to develop particular curriculum materials. They are not concerned about policy issues and theoretical curriculum questions. This may be due to several factors such as their relative isolationism in the classroom, or their perceived low status in the education hierarchy and lack of empowerment or their lack of academic training in policy studies.

The effect of this dichotomy is that if head offices devolve both policy *and* action decisions to individual schools it is likely that they will be unable to cope with both tasks. Either head offices will need to give more guidance and information about policy matters or provide considerably more funds for professional development to enable school staffs to develop these skills. The rhetoric of devolving policy decisions to schools rings hollow if little assistance is given to schools to achieve these ends. As noted by Hunt (1981) and Prideaux (1985 and 1988) with reference to two Australian state education systems, senior officials may have used SBCD slogans in the 1970s because it was fashionable to do so, and then retreated from this position in the 1980s because of purported teacher opposition to it, when in reality the problem may have been due to inadequate attention being given to policy issues and processes.

Another major problem relates to teacher attitudes, and values and levels of motivation (Skilbeck, 1984). There will be some members of a teaching staff who for various reasons have negative reactions to any form of SBCD. It may be that they have had unsuccessful experiences with SBCD in the past at another school. Alternatively, it could be that their type of teacher training and the consequent style of teaching that they have adopted and developed is perfectly satisfactory to them and they are therefore opposed to any change. They may perceive that they have insufficient time to become involved in SBCD. Whatever the reasons there can be sizeable numbers of teachers on a school staff who act as a resister group.

So long as strong leadership is available the presence of a resister group is not necessarily a deterrent. They can be useful for creating spirited discussions and arguments so that more teachers are challenged to reflect upon particular issues. The school level leaders need to be reconciled to the fact that commitment to SBCD is a slow process and that they won't automatically achieve positive levels of acceptance in their early forays.

A third problem revolves around hierarchical structures typically found in schools which are antithetical to the establishing of democratic, cooperative forms of SBCD. In many education systems teachers are perceived to be at the bottom of the hierarchy — decisions are filtered down to them (Young, 1985). Somehow the conflict between this hierarchical subordination and professional status of teachers has to be resolved. Teachers do respond to the opportunity to being involved in particular forms of local decision-making especially if they can see that this might enable them to 'transcend their traditional low position in the educational hierarchy' (*ibid*, p. 407). How to achieve these break-throughs is dependent on the ingenuity and perseverance of the change agents/leaders. Rewards may need to be offered, especially intrinsic rewards for work done. Recognition of their participation by giving them some relief from classroom teaching, or by the provision of small honorariums, may be the kinds of reward which will, over time, encourage teachers to want to develop professionally and to increase their levels of self-esteem.

A fourth problem relates to aspects of localism, parochialism and conservatism which can often dominate SBCD practices (Skilbeck, 1984). Too often, superficial 'tinkering' by a few active individuals can occur and, because of their limited vision and/or experience, the resultant changes can be less than desirable. Worse still, on some occasions powerful lobby groups can bring about changes at the local level which produce curricula that are lacking in breadth, or are biased and outdated. It is a vexing problem. On the one hand it is desirable for school community members to concentrate upon their unique needs and to attempt to accommodate them in any curricula they produce. By so doing however, they may omit or minimize wider issues about a topic or subject area that might be deemed to be essential by subject specialists.

Evaluating SBCD Efforts

To provide useful feedback and to ensure enhanced credibility for SBCD, it would seem that evaluation activities need to be included in any SBCD project. Unfortunately, this is rarely the case. Because most SBCD endeavours involve a small group of participants with limited resources, it is not surprising that few of them make any effort to evaluate their impact in any systematic way. There are a number of interesting case study accounts in the literature, often written by one or more participants, but they tend to be glowing accounts complete with exhortations and positive conclusions. Few of these accounts provide details on inputs (in terms of time, finance, materials) or any indicators of outcomes (student achievements or attitude changes).

Just as SBCD is all about participants' making their own decisions about curriculum, the same logic must also apply to evaluation efforts. That is, participants should plan and carry out their own evaluative efforts and only use external evaluators in exceptional circumstances.

Harlen *et al.* (1977) suggest that participants in an SBCD project can draw up a very worthwhile evaluation plan by reflecting upon the following:

(a) the aim of our work and our priorities;
(b) the nature and range of learning experiences provided for our students;
(c) the progress of individual students;
(d) the organization and use of space and facilities in our classrooms;
(e) teaching methods;
(f) teaching materials;
(g) continuity in a child's experience from grade to grade;
(h) the work load, pressures, responsibilities and morale of the staff. (p. 1)

Ideally one or two members of an SBCD project should take responsibility for organizing the evaluation activities. Other participants in the project need to be reminded about the type and range of data which each is expected to collect. Time lines and schedules for the collection and analysis of data need to be carefully planned and implemented.

To overcome criticisms that evaluations of SBCD projects are typically effusive accounts by committed stalwarts, it is necessary to consider some possible performance indicators. These need not be time consuming and highly sophisticated statistical measures. Rather, they can include commonsense indicators such as:

Students: basic statistics on any changes in attendance levels/truancy rates;
changes in library borrowings;
numbers involved in borrowing special equipment for projects;
attitude scales to measure changes in attitude about specific topics;
rating scales;
changes in achievement in end-of-term tests.

Parents: attitudes toward a new curriculum or subject;
opinions about changes in their children's work habits/attitudes.

Teachers: self-report inventories;
diary entries;
observation schedules completed by a colleague;
interviews undertaken by a colleague.

Specific data collected from these sources can enable participants in a SBCD project to make certain assertions about the level of success of their activity. Hopefully some of the data collected will provide indicators of some definite improvement in such areas as student attitudes, or skills. It is also important to collect sufficient descriptive information about each SBCD project so that comprehensive portrayals can be made for wider audiences. Although it might be anticipated that SBCD teams will develop their own unique approaches to evaluation, various models have been produced which do appear to be quite successful. For example, the GRIDS scheme developed by McMahon *et al.* (1984) provides detailed advice to principals and senior staff for undertaking evaluations of school-based projects. Action research processes as outlined by Elliott (1981) and Kemmis and McTaggart (1984) build in evaluative elements into their spiral of activities. Day (1981) has produced strategies for teachers to use to evaluate their own classroom practices. A procedure which enables teachers to produce details of cost-effectiveness measures as part of their project plans has been developed by Caldwell and Spinks (1986 and 1988).

Which ever methods of evaluation are finally developed and used, it is crucial that the SBCD participants make the important initial decisions. It is also important for them to remember that evaluative data, systematically collected and analyzed, is an important element of any SBCD project with which they become involved.

Concluding Comment

Although school-based activities have been practised by teachers over the decades, it is only over recent times that SBCD accounts have figured prominently. In particular, educators are beginning to examine more closely the concept of SBCD and the factors which facilitate and inhibit it.

In this chapter an effort is made to analyze the meaning of SBCD and to prepare a reconceptualization of the term. A model which attempts to explain why persons get involved in SBCD activities is developed, along with explanations about ideal conditions and impediments.

Each country has its own unique contextual factors which can facilitate or impede the development of SBCD activities. In section B of this book case study accounts are provided of SBCD ventures in four western countries, namely Australia, Canada, United Kingdom and the United States of America.

Section B

Case Studies

Chapter 3

Australia: Establishing a Unit Curriculum for Years 8–10 at River Valley Senior High School

This chapter documents how two innovative administrators in a local high school began to experiment with new structures in their school. Their concerns about the need for a more flexible curriculum with subjects that catered for the needs of the high and low achievers led them to experiment with a vertical timetable and daily sessions of pastoral care with vertical age groups.

It was most fortuitous that these two administrators took these initiatives when they did. Within two years a major state education system initiative entitled the Unit Curriculum *for all lower secondary school students (Years 8–10) was created and senior officials were seeking out a small number of schools to pilot the new curriculum structure. Not unexpectedly, River Valley Senior High School was invited to become a pilot school and it was given additional staffing and resources to undertake the new role. This chapter explores how staff at River Valley Senior High School became involved in a small scale SBCD activity initially and prior to the state education system initiative which led to a major SBCD activity being undertaken.*

Background Details

School Initiatives

River Valley Senior High School commenced in 1978 as a very different high school, with senior staff being specially selected and the school architecture being based upon open area concepts. The inaugural Principal was meticulous in his creation of school structures during his five years at the school. This enabled the next Principal, who arrived in 1983, to be more adventurous knowing that a solid administrative structure had already been established.

The new Principal had a special vision for his school. He wanted to offer students a wider range of subjects, and in particular, he wanted to cater for the many students from working-class backgrounds who seemed to be disinterested in attending school and were largely disruptive when they did attend.

The Principal and his Deputy Principals began exploring the possibilities of several innovations, namely a pastoral care system using mixed-age Teacher Advisory Groups (TAG) and the use of vertical timetabling for year 11 students and options in lower school. In July 1984, the Principal and the male Deputy Principal visited two innovative secondary schools in South Australia practising vertical timetabling (Seaton and Burra High Schools) en route to an education conference in Sydney, with the conference theme of 'Revitalizing Secondary School Structures'. They gained a lot of insights about vertical timetabling in particular, and upon their return began to experiment with possible variations. It would appear that they were 'developing a mission', as conceptualized in figure 2 in chapter 2.

System Initiatives

As a result of widespread disapproval of the curriculum for lower secondary schools (years 8–10) which had been in place in all government schools in Western Australia since 1970, an enquiry into secondary education was initiated by the state government in 1983. The resulting study, the Beazley Report (1984), was wide-ranging in its list of recommendations including:

(a) all subjects should be offered as units of study for twenty-four or thirty hours;

(b) each unit should be clearly defined in terms of prerequisites, course objectives and assessment procedures;

(c) all school subjects should be grouped into seven curriculum components;

(d) in years 8–10 each student should study at least one unit from each of the curriculum components;

(e) students and parents should have the right to be involved in unit selection.

Due to pressures and incentives provided by the then Minister of Education, the state education took immediate steps to make changes at the secondary school level. An implementation team of senior education officials was appointed in 1985 to operationalize the various recommendations of the Beazley Report. They resolved that all secondary students should:

(a) study units of forty hours duration;

(b) be assessed on each unit and awarded an A, B, C, D or F grade;

(c) complete twenty-six units per year;

(d) redo a unit or take another unit at the same stage level if they failed a unit.

Early in 1986 the Beazley Implementation team discussed a timetable for full-scale implementation of the Unit Curriculum with the Minister of Education. Preliminary plans were made for a small group of high schools to 'pilot' the Unit Curriculum scheme in 1987, prior to all high schools being involved with it in 1988. The term 'pilot school' was somewhat of a misnomer in that the schedule of implementation had already been decided upon and no amount of feedback, positive or negative was going to change that. Nevertheless there were advantages in having a small number of schools involved in trialling it, to find out about particular problems and to experiment with ways of solving them.

The Principal and staff at River Valley Senior High School wanted to be involved very badly as a 'pilot' school and with considerable justification. They had already gained considerable experience in related areas such as pastoral care and vertical timetabling. They had been willing to take chances and to be innovative. The Principal put forward a detailed proposal to the Education Department seeking their approval and informing them of their willingness to be a pilot school.

The authoritarian response from the Education Department criticized their proposals on the grounds that their base units were inappropriate and that their submission was premature. Although smarting from this refusal, senior staff still continued to explore ways of improving their lower school curriculum. They were not shaken by the departmental response. If anything it strengthened their resolve.

Toward the middle of 1986, decisions were finally made up by the Education Department about the number of pilot schools to be involved in the pilot scheme in 1987. For various reasons, possibly expense and control, it was decided that the number of pilot schools should be very small. They had to represent different metropolitan regions, small district high schools as well as senior high schools and private schools as well as government schools. In searching for a suitable senior high school in the south-west region, senior officers considered River Valley Senior High School but there was not a lot of support for it. Some officers had long memories of previous altercations with the Principal. Fortunately, River Valley Senior High School also had its supporters among senior departmental staff. One superintendent in particular championed the cause for River Valley Senior High School and gave his personal assurance to monitor its progress if it was nominated as a pilot school.

Chronology of Events and Persons Involved

Events Prior to the Pilot Year of 1987

Once the formalities of staff acceptance to become a pilot school had been achieved, the Principal and senior staff had only seven months to do all the preparations needed prior to implementing the Unit Curriculum in February 1987.

The following week in May 1986 after the Principal had obtained staff acceptance, the male Deputy Principal organized a three-hour afternoon workshop for all staff. At this workshop the Deputy Principal invited staff to use butcher's paper in small groups to sort out how they might translate their existing subjects into units. These staff meetings were to be the first of many cooperative group activities by staff during the remaining months of 1986.

An interesting feature of activities in 1986 was that existing structures were used to channel staff efforts (see figure 4). The only additional committee was a Vertical Timetabling Management Committee. The Principal, Deputy Principals and Senior Master Science were heavily involved in this Committee ensuring that unit details could be computerized, that appropriate timetabling choices and grid lines could be accommodated. To assist with these tasks, Tom and Barry Jones, Senior Masters of Science and Mathematics respectively at two metropolitan high schools, were contacted. Over a period of several months they put in many hours of work to produce computer programs for clerical record keeping (for example student hand-out slips and class slips); a report printing system; and most important, a computer program to enable a new timetable to be constructed each term.

Subject Faculty Meetings were also extremely important as each subject team had to ensure that their existing subjects were translated into units. In many cases this meant rewriting objectives, reallocating and revising content and teaching activities and redesigning forms of assessment. Some funds were available to give release time for subject teachers to work uninterrupted on these tasks for blocks of one to two days.

The Features of the Unit Curriculum During the Pilot Year (1987)

The following is an account of some of the major features of the Unit Curriculum as it evolved during 1987.

School timetable

A vertical timetable operates for years 8–10. The school works on a six-day cycle with six periods each day of fifty minutes duration. There is also a twenty minute TAG period each day. The timetable is based on six grid lines of subject choices.

A new timetable is prepared for each term based upon student choices. The units prepared by subject departments all operate on a forty hour, one term basis. The one exception is physical education, health education and vocational education which are timetabled over two terms, or a semester.

Teachers are required to teach eighteen units for the year. The usual pattern over the year is a five-unit term followed by a four-unit term. Senior teachers have a reduced load usually fourteen units for the year. Teachers in charge of subject areas have a reduced load, varying from fourteen to seventeen units per year.

Students are allocated a unit of study on each grid line of the timetable, based upon choices they have made previously. Typically, students take six units each term. At the end of each term students are awarded a grade for each unit taken (A,B,C,D,F) and are then allocated another set of six units, again based upon their choices.

In year 8, twenty-one of the twenty-four units are required units.

Figure 4: Implementation of the Unit Curriculum River Valley

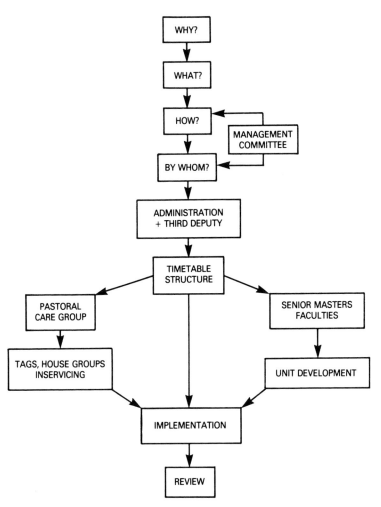

In years 9 and 10 requirements are established per component area. Year 9 students are required to do eighteen units from seven component areas out of a total of twenty-four units. Year 10 students are also required to do eighteen units out of twenty-four units.

The units for each component are organized into unit maps. Units are arranged across six stages of difficulty. Details about each unit and prerequisites associated with it are made available in a specially compiled student handbook. This information provides the basic information from which students will select their choice of units for each term.

At the beginning of each term students are given their new timetable. Students who failed units in the previous term are not permitted to take further units in that component at a higher stage until they have repeated and passed the unit or passed a unit of a comparable standard. This is a necessary requirement but it does cause complications for the Deputy Principals who have to make unit choice adjustments on the spot for a number of students.

Teachers' role and responsibilities

A major task for teachers is to ensure that the units produced for their subject department are effectively communicated to students and parents, so that they are aware of them and will want to choose them.

Teachers tend to schedule a number of assessment points during each unit, consisting of objective tests, essays, assignments and laboratory exercises. If a student does not perform very well in any of the early assessments a note is sent home to the parents during week 6 or 7 indicating that a failure may be imminent and that specific actions need to be considered (for example, the need to consider transferring to a different pathway in a future term). Assessments for each unit have to all be completed by week 9 so that reports can be compiled (using computerized subject comments) and distributed to students and parents before the end of term.

Passing grades consist of levels A, B, C or D and are given according to the extent to which students achieve the objectives. A failing grade (F) is given if a student does not achieve the minimum objectives of the unit. Most staff maintain that it is essential for students to be present for at least six weeks of a ten week unit to be considered for a passing grade, otherwise a 'no grade', or 'has completed insufficient work to give a grade', or a 'fail' grade is recorded on the particular student's report card.

In some subject areas, especially English, mathematics and science, new units were developed to cater for the needs of the low achiever. For example an English Bridging unit (1.1) was developed and used in 1987. Although this appeared to be successful with some students, others did require additional help. The Academic Extension teacher has been used partly as a remedial teacher during this year.

Students' roles and responsibilities

Under the Unit Curriculum students have far greater responsibility for choosing the units they want to study and when they want to study them. The ten-week, forty hour units enable them to experience a number of different units each year and to make changes to their unit map if they find that they have developed new interests and skills. The vertical timetabling enables them to accelerate through the unit stages far faster than under the traditional timetabling structures.

By providing students with a relatively wide range of choices it is not surprising that some subject departments have attracted more students than others. For example, the choices made by students at the end of 1986 resulted in an increased demand for units in physical and health education and home economics. If changes are substantial this can of course have staffing implications and some additions and reductions in specific subject areas did occur at River Valley Senior High School at the beginning of 1987. Some of these unit preferences appear to have flowed on to year 11 in that student choices for year 11 subjects in 1988 revealed an increase in physical science, furniture and woodwork, business studies and physical education and a decrease in human biology, geography, maths II and III and physics.

Formal management of the unit curriculum

There are a number of groups responsible for the management of the Unit Curriculum together with the upper school programme and other responsibilities which comprises the total operation of activities at River Valley Senior High School. The *Management* group, comprising the Principal and two Deputy Principals, has formal responsibility for most of the organised activities. The group is heavily involved in policy decisions as well as day-to-day decisions relating to individual students and classes.

The *School Council* consists of six parents, six teachers, six students and the Principal. Committees of the council include Finance, Canteen, Grounds and Buildings and Education. An analysis of the minutes of their monthly meetings for 1987 revealed that the major agenda items related to fund-raising, the school bus, amenities in the school and canteen matters. Although matters relating to the Unit Curriculum might have been discussed at these monthly meetings they were not given prominence in the minutes. The *finances* of the school are the responsibility of the school Principal but day-to-day matters are controlled by the Bursar. There is also a Finance Committee comprising three staff members which makes decisions about the fees to be charged per subject area unit.

A number of changes have had to be initiated since the Unit Curriculum structure was introduced in 1987. Apart from levies for the School Council ($7), for General Amenities ($12) and for Library ($12), other charges are now calculated on the basis of units actually chosen. The costs per unit for maths, English, science and social studies were all $3.50 per unit in 1987. Higher costs were imposed for physical and health education, languages, business education, manual arts, horticulture and computing ($6) while art/craft was $8 and home economics $10. Thus for any term parents could be paying out $25–$40 a term or $80–160 a year, plus the standard levies of $31 per single student. If students change units then of course a new set of charges may have to be calculated. These complications are likely to have increased the workload of the Bursar.

Each term the clerical staff are required to put in overtime hours over a weekend to ensure that the reports are completed and available for distribution during the last week of term. It would appear that costs for extra clerical time will continue to be an additional expenditure each year.

Photocopying costs by staff have certainly increased since the introduction of the Unit Curriculum, although there are considerable variations per department. Some departments such as English, mathematics and home economics have experienced escalating photocopying costs between 1986 and 1987. Other departments have used other methods to reduce their costs such as the purchasing of their own photocopier (science) and the use of photocopied masters with spirit duplicators and Gestetners (mathematics).

The creation of ten-week units does cause problems in finding cheap, relevant textbooks. Existing textbooks tend to cover the content of a number of units (perhaps three to four) but students might not opt to study all these units, or even if they did, they might be studied in different years. Not surprisingly, staff have largely ignored texts and produced a lot of their own materials. This has necessitated widespread use of photocopying. The problem is unlikely to disappear in the immediate future. If student choices become stabilized into identifiable pathways then textbook publishers may become more active in producing textbooks directed at the lower secondary school market.

Another considerable cost under the Unit Curriculum is for paper. Large quantities of computer paper are used by the twenty-seven computers used at the school. Every student is given a new log card after each six day cycle. Handouts are used extensively by staff, again because of the unavailability of cheap, relevant textbooks. The organization of the timetable requires numerous memoranda from the administration to individual staff members. A major cost each year is the student handbook which for 1987 was 176 pages and cost $4000 to produce.

Informal management of the unit curriculum

Staff at River Valley Senior High School work very cooperatively together. There is a high degree of friendliness and conviviality.

Another appointment in 1987 was that of Curriculum Coordinator. This staff member, with considerable experience in social interactive roles in other institutions, undertook a number of duties during 1987. He produced a monthly *Curriculum Bulletin* which contained newsworthy items about how the Unit Curriculum was developing at River Valley Senior High School. He also provided assistance to staff in developing new units; he gave workshops on study skills to students; and initiated a mentor scheme to link up academically talented students with individual teachers willing to share their knowledge in specialised areas.

Linkages with feeder primary schools

For a number of years senior staff at River Valley Senior High School, and especially the Deputy Principal (female), have developed strong links with their primary feeder schools. Since 1986 a systematic series of activities entitled the *Continuity Program* occurs during the second half of the year.

Linkages with employers and local community

Efforts have been made in 1986 and 1987 to communicate information about the Unit Curriculum to local employers. It is not an easy task as employers are still not fully conversant with the bewildering number of changes which have been made to exit certificates over recent years.

During 1987 a number of staff have been involved in communicating with employer groups. The Youth Education Officer has been in contact with a number of employers as part of her duties to organize work experience for students. She has indicated that a number of employers do not understand the titles of many of the units and are also concerned about the significance of the different stages (levels).

The School Council is aware of the problem and has arranged invitational evenings for employers to find out more about the Unit Curriculum. More recently a seminar was held for employers to acquaint them with how the results of current year 10 students are recorded on certificates.

Emerging Patterns and Issues

In figure 1 in chapter 2, a matrix diagram was used to illustrate the three major dimensions of SBCD, namely *type of activity, people involved* and *time commitment*. It is quite revealing to apply these dimensions to the situation at River Valley Senior High School.

As depicted in figure 5, the processes took four years of active commitment by the school Principal and Deputy Principal to bring to a satisfactory conclusion. The SBCD process commenced with these two persons. In terms of personality they complemented each other very well. The Principal is very out-going, tenacious and convincing. The Deputy Principal (male) is very conscientious and quiet but also tenacious and persuasive in his own way. They were a very effective team.

Figure 5: Analysis of persons involved and type of activity

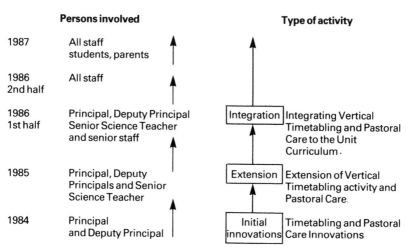

Over the years they gradually convinced other staff that their ideas about timetabling and pastoral care should be adopted.

The Principal and Deputy Principal seemed to attract like-minded persons. The senior science teacher was attracted to the challenge. He could see how computers could be used as the vehicle to bring about change in teacher planning and teaching. He was also fascinated by the process of change and the strategies that one could use to enlist staff support. He wanted to be part of the action and worked very hard as the unofficial third Deputy Principal. It is quite remarkable how successful he was. Staff treated him with considerable respect and did consider him to have special status in the school.

The Deputy Principal (female) was not an active participant initially. She preferred the traditional role of Deputy Principals of implementing system policy. It is possible that she felt overawed by the drive and charisma of the Principal. Nevertheless, she felt a need to be a member of the innovatory team and searched for a special contribution that she would make. She soon found this in the special links she forged with principals of neighbouring feeder primary schools. She was able to assert her authority in this relationship and at the same time to make a special contribution to the success of the innovation by preparing incoming students from primary schools (and their parents) for the new practices they would experience in their first year at River Valley Senior High School.

It took the Principal and Deputy-Principal two years (1984–85) to build up an effective team of participants. From then onwards they were the catalyst for others to join. Some heads of subject departments were the next to become involved, together with a few teachers who became excited about the potential of the innovations and were swept up in the euphoria of the change action.

The nature of the SBCD innovation, as indicated in figure 5, changed considerably over the years. It started off as an experiment with timetabling and a desire to do something about the pastoral care of students who were not responding to the traditional high school curriculum. Both these foci were extended in 1985 and 1986 as the chief architects of the innovation refined their ideas. This involved them in visiting 'lighthouse' schools in other states of Australia and being guest speakers at professional meetings and conferences. Their ideas on vertical timetabling and pastoral care were honed and refined by these experiences and interactions.

A major fortuitous event was the policy decision made by the state education system to adopt a *Unit Curriculum* approach for lower secondary schools and for this to be implemented, in the first instance, by a group of pilot schools. This decision provided the perfect opportunity for River Valley Senior High School. Their experiences with vertical timetabling and pastoral care were important elements of a Unit Curriculum approach. The senior staff at River Valley Senior High School had been experimenting with these elements for over two years while other high schools had minimal experience in these matters.

By being granted *pilot school* status, the senior administrative team were able to galvanize all staff into action and this occurred in 1986. They were able to integrate their ideas about vertical timetabling and pastoral care into a comprehensive plan for change. In due course, students and parents were notified of the changes although they had minimal inputs into the direction or scope of the changes. In 1987 the school was fully geared for action as the experiment was tried out in its entirety.

A more elaborate analysis of the motivations of the chief participants of the SBCD activity is provided in figure 6, using the conceptual structure developed in figure 2 in chapter 2. Although the majority of staff were satisfied with their teaching role at River Valley Senior High School in 1984 and had reached a state of homeostasis, the Principal was clearly not satisfied. Whether it was an aspect of his personality to want to be constantly striking out with new ideas because he perceived this to be the role of a good Principal, is not clear, but there may be some truth in this observation. He obviously enjoyed being visible among his fellow school Principals and took numerous opportunities at meetings and through the media to push his point of view and to publicize the innovatory happenings at River Valley Senior High School.

The Principal was responsible for challenging staff at River Valley Senior High School and causing them to reconsider their planning and teaching activities. He was clearly successful in goading them into action and which led ultimately to the school being accepted as a pilot school (lighthouse school) to experiment with the Unit Curriculum. As indicated elsewhere in this chapter the Principal may have overdone his efforts with system officials to enlist their support. A number of these officials were not enamoured by his abrasive style and very nearly overlooked River Valley Senior High School as a pilot school. They were wanting school principals who were more traditional and perhaps less threatening.

It is interesting to note, as depicted in figure 6, that the Principal's driving interest in the innovation had waned considerably by 1987. Although he could have made other arrangements he opted to take long service leave during the second half of 1987, at a time when strong

Figure 6: Analysis of motivations of key participants in the SBCD activity

PERSONNEL	Time Periods 1983-84	1985	1986	1987
School Principal Personal characteristics (a) flamboyant personality (b) likes to be 'first' with innovations (c) is willing to take risks (d) takes every opportunity through face to face contacts and the media to express his point of view.	**Satisfied with progress of school but . . .** (a) wants to establish River Valley SHS as a very different school (b) wants to establish a caring relationship for students.	(a) initiates a number of experiments within the school (b) takes every opportunity to 'advertise' his efforts within the education community.	(a) puts considerable energies into getting the school accepted as a pilot school. (b) is willing to leave the detailed plans of action to others.	Becomes interested in other matters and would like a transfer.
Deputy Principal (male) Personal characteristics (a) quiet person but friendly and with a well developed sense of humour. (b) strong commitment to the school – a foundation appointee. (c) is willing to move on an innovation when he has thoroughly explored it. (d) believes that you can only convince staff by being an active, well-organised 'doer'.	**Satisfied with progress of school but . . .** (a) is unhappy about levels of absenteeism and truancy and sees the TAG pastoral care system as a solution. (b) is convinced that a vertical timetabling system could work.	(a) produces a number of detailed schemes. (b) works hard with senior staff to get their support.	(a) extends procedures and methods. (b) wants to follow through meticulously to ensure success.	Wants to consolidate and get the innovations fully accepted.
Deputy Principal (female) Personal characteristics (a) quiet, confident. (b) authoritarian manner with students. (c) likes to develop her own areas of responsibility.	**Satisfied with progress of school but . . .** (a) is loyal to the Principal and willing to support his initiatives (b) is aware of the need to foster the support of catchment primary schools and develops this area as her special interest.	Takes steps to develop her interest in feeder schools.	Extends support and networks with primary feeder schools.	Wants to consolidate and get the innovations fully accepted.
Senior Science Teacher Personal characteristics (a) quiet, persuasive, task oriented (b) has experience in computing. (c) has had graduate training in change strategies. (d) perceives himself as the third deputy.	**Satisfied with progress of school but . . .** (a) wants to jolt staff into experiment-ing with innovations. (b) realizes must give them supportive help (eg. in computing) to get their cooperation. (c) wants to help P and DP (male).	Develops strategies for staff to use computers in their preparation and teaching	Develops strategies and time lines to ensure staff will be prepared for the Pilot Year experiment.	Accepts a transfer to a new position in the system where he is a process consultant to a number of schools.

leadership was crucial. During this leave period he began to explore other career prospects including careers outside of teaching. He had not reached a new level of homeostasis with the Unit Curriculum. Other directions and interests were now attracting his attention.

By contrast, the two Deputy Principals revealed during 1987 that they were consolidating their position and looking forward to arriving at a new state of homeostasis.

The Deputy Principal (male) concentrated his attentions upon fine-tuning the vertical timetable. His endeavours to get subject department heads to make decisions about staff workloads was beginning to get results in 1987. He also developed effective procedures for students to notify the administration of intended unit changes and to ensure that these changes were effected expeditiously. A new set of routines were now being established and the Deputy Principal was becoming more comfortable with the situation.

A major problem he was experiencing in 1987 and which had not been fully resolved in 1988 was teachers' union pressures to exert external demands on the internal workings of the school. The Deputy-Principal was very aware of the problem that some class sizes were far too high but he had developed a consensus system with staff whereby they received their share of large and small classes over the four terms of the school year. The teachers union issued an ultimatum in October 1987 that all classes in 1988 should not be greater than thirty-two students. If this happened, teachers were instructed by their union officials to use a system of dismissing the additional students from their respective classes. This externally derived decision was most upsetting to the Deputy-Principal and he had still not resolved the problem by the end of the 1987 school year. To a certain extent this decision had wiped out much of the staff commitment and flexibility he had carefully nurtured and promoted over the preceding three years. The teachers union had destroyed, if only temporarily, his goals of establishing a new level of stability among staff at River Valley Senior High School by the end of 1987.

The Deputy Principal (female) had consolidated her position by the end of 1987. She had established a new set of relationships with principals and staff of feeder primary schools. They perceived her to be the major figure responsible for liaison between their schools and River Valley Senior High School. She was respected as a concerned person and one who was able to ease the transition of their students into the high school situation. For her part, she had found her new homeostasis level. The liaison role enabled her to make frequent visits to other schools and to absent herself from the day-to-day timetabling concerns which she perceived to be the responsibility of the Deputy Principal (male). Further, her role as chief liaison officer gave her a new-found recognition and status which she clearly enjoyed.

The senior science teacher was a foundation staff member at the school in 1978 but had transferred elsewhere to receive promotion as a senior science teacher in 1980. He made a decision to transfer back to River Valley Senior High School in 1985 because he became aware of the exciting innovations being developed by the Principal and Deputy Principal (male). It appears that the Principal may have sought him out and taken steps to encourage him to transfer back to his school. Once back at the school he started immediately to develop strategies and plans for extending and refining the vertical timetabling system and for the provision of pastoral care. He had taken graduate courses in education, especially curriculum change and innovation, and had a strong interest in developing appropriate strategies and tactics which he and the administrators could use to bring about desired change.

Without doubt he had some extraordinary talents in simplifying problems and seeking out solutions. For example, he realised very quickly that the only way that staff would accept short-term teaching modules of ten weeks with the attendant, frequent turnaround of assessments and report writing, was by relieving them of some of the routine tasks. He envisaged that computers could be used much more extensively in planning courses (use of word processing to develop item banks of course objectives), for the recording and analysis of results, and for the production of reports (computerized bank of report card comments). His expertise in computing gave him a major advantage over the Principal and Deputy Principals and perhaps was a major reason why he was accorded special status in the school.

As indicated in figure 6, the senior science teacher seems to have been driven by some of the same motivations as the Principal. Once a new challenge had been resolved (or even partly resolved) he was ready to move on to the next. At the end of 1986, the senior science teacher was requested by head office to take up a senior position as change consultant to a number of schools in a nearby region. He accepted this challenge even though he made frequent return visits to River Valley Senior High School during the following year to assist them with various problems they had experienced in implementing the Unit Curriculum.

Although details of only four key actors at River Valley Senior High School are depicted in figure 6, there were other teachers who also became involved in the change process. Some of the subject department heads became interested early in the process and took part in some of the meetings. A few of the class teachers also learnt of developments and volunteered to assist in various ways. The camaraderie that developed, especially from 1985 onwards, provided a new atmosphere of excitement and challenge that staff found hard to resist.

Some of these developments are illustrated in table 4, using the developmental stages outlined in table 1 in chapter 2. The Principal had well-developed stage VI (undertakes major leadership roles) skills which he used to advantage to initiate and plan the various school-based initiatives. He was aided and abetted by the Deputy Principal (male) who took on more limited roles initially (stages IV–V Participates with minimal responsibilities/active participant) but soon acquired the skills and confidence to progress to Stage VI. The senior science teacher also had well honed skills and experience in leadership roles and operated at a stage VI level from the time he transferred back to the school in 1985. The Deputy Principal (female) operated at a Stage III (seeks out information) initially in that she was cautious about the proposed innovations and sought merely to find out further information. Once she developed her interest in the feeder primary schools she became a more active leader and organised and led various activities associated with this (stage V).

Other staff represented various stages from I–IV: The type of decision-making, especially relating to vertical time tabling required heads of department to make more decisions at the department level over such matters as department budgets and workloads of individual staff members. New leadership demands were thrust upon them and many enjoyed these experiences.

	1983–84 Stage	1985 Stage	1986 Stage	1987 Stage
Principal	VI	VI	VI	VI
Deputy Principal (male)	IV–V	V	V	VI
Deputy Principal (female)	III–IV	IV	IV	IV–V
Senior Science Teacher	–	VI	VI	–
Other senior staff	III	IV	IV–V	IV–V
Teaching staff	I–11	I–II	II–III	III–IV

Table 4: Development stages of staff at River Valley Senior High School

In addition, several class teachers without head of department status, were given special status in the school to undertake special liaison/change agent responsibilities. A *curriculum coordinator* was appointed to keep staff informed about developments in each subject area. This person produced a newsletter which appeared monthly. He also assisted some staff with their assessment procedures and he was generally a catalyst to assist with the change process. A *social coordinator* was also appointed to organize social events for staff and students. These ranged from weekly raffles to social athletic events to theatre and restaurant evenings. This person had a very pleasant, outgoing personality and he was very successful in developing and maintaining a positive school spirit among staff members.

These two positions had been planned by the school Principal as he appreciated the need to maintain strong staff support for the innovations. They were very sound strategies. In the process, the incumbents in these positions developed very valuable leadership skills and influenced the growth of leadership skills in a number of other staff at River Valley Senior High School.

Evaluation of the SBCD Activity

The author was contracted during the last six months of 1987 to undertake an evaluation of the Unit Curriculum as it had been developed by staff at River Valley Senior High School. To provide an overall focus for the study it was agreed that the following questions would be the central ones, namely:

(a) Has there been an increased range of student choices and pathways?
(b) Have the facilities for student counselling been adequate?
(c) Has the vertical timetabling system facilitated the introduction of the Unit Curriculum?
(d) Has the resource base been both comprehensive and adequate in enabling the Unit Curriculum structure to be developed?
(d) How effective is the Unit Curriculum, in terms of academic and social aspects, as perceived by students, teachers and parents?

The intention of the study was to collect a variety of information so as to portray as vividly as possible, the complexities and nuances of the Unit Curriculum as it had been developed and implemented at River Valley Senior High School. To that end a two-stage design was developed in which data were collected both informally and formally:

Stage One: The evaluator interacted with major users to collect information about what they perceived as being the major issues, problems and directions of the evaluation study.

Stage Two: The evaluator prepared and distributed appropriate questionnaires and checklist instruments to survey teachers, students, parents and other interest groups.

In Stage One, the evaluator spent a considerable amount of time collecting background information about the Unit Curriculum model in general and specific contextual details about how the Unit Curriculum had been conceptualized, planned and implemented at River Valley Senior High School.

Data obtained from document analysis and from interviews with teachers, students and parents provided the basis for the items included in the questionnaires and checklists for Stage Two of the study.

Teacher's Perspectives

There is clearly a large proportion of very young staff at River Valley Senior High School with 50 per cent being 30 years of age and under and 84 per cent being 40 years of age and under. The length of time that staff have been teaching at River Valley Senior High School is also significant. Those that were appointed in 1986 or earlier (59 per cent) would have experienced the early planning aspects (including the successes and failures) and in all probability, have a sense of ownership and commitment because of this. The staff appointed in 1987 (41 per cent) must have found the new Curriculum structure very confusing. Some may have been unconvinced about its viability or even opposed to it.

A majority of teachers consider that 'the previous "option" subjects now have a higher status as perceived by the students. Under the Unit Curriculum structure all units have equal time and similar assessment procedures. Consequently the status/stigma differentials between the traditional 'core' and 'elective' subjects have been removed although it may take a little time for attitudes to change on this matter.

One of the unintended outcomes of the Unit Curriculum in operation this year has been that students' choices of units have not been evenly distributed. Some units have proved to be much more popular than others and because of timetabling constraints this has necessitated some large classes, and in some cases, up to forty students per class.

The majority of teachers consider parents do not understand the Unit Curriculum and how and why units are selected. Perhaps teachers are indicating their frustration after various deliberate efforts to involve parents and to communicate new arrangements to them.

A very positive aspect of the Unit Curriculum was revealed by teachers in that they agreed that 'students are motivated to work hard because the ten-week units provide them with short-term goals'. This was also corroborated in the student checklist and parent questionnaire data.

Also, a very positive response was recorded by teachers that 'students are given plenty of opportunities to discuss pathways and to make sound decisions about unit selection'. The 74 per cent of the teachers who supported this statement is very reassuring for the successful implementation of Unit Curriculum at River Valley Senior High School.

Almost 40 per cent of the teachers have misgivings about their ability to counsel or their amount of involvement in pastoral care activities. This would seem to indicate that a substantial number of students are not getting adequate support from teachers through the TAG system. These results seem to indicate that the TAG system needs to be very carefully analyzed. As a matter of urgency, staff need to be acquainted with units and unit maps for all subject areas so that they can provide adequate information to their TAG group. Perhaps greater attention needs to be given to staff training in pastoral care approaches and processes.

It is also very reassuring to note that 73 per cent of teachers consider that the Unit Curriculum system has now made their lesson planning much easier. Eighty-six per cent of teachers indicate that 'the specifying of objectives for each unit makes my teaching more effective'. It would seem therefore that the practice of specifying objectives for each unit has been a very positive aspect of the Unit Curriculum, and, in the process, has made the planning of lessons much easier for teachers.

Developing appropriate assessment procedures which can be directly related to unit objectives is an integral element of the Unit Curriculum. Many teachers are very uncertain about this area of their teaching. It is not surprising therefore that 57 per cent of teachers agreed that they used a lot of assessments because they want to assess each objective properly. Many teachers may in fact be overassessing in their efforts to fulfil what they consider are the minimum requirements.

A considerable amount of effort was expended by staff in 1986 and 1987 to produce examination report comments which could be computer-read and printed. A considerable number of teachers (60 per cent) consider that they now provide adequate information to convey to students and parents but 40 per cent are obviously not convinced. Because of the short ten-week units it is imperative that a rapid system of reporting is devised and one which does not take away valuable lesson-time from teachers. If the computerized system is to be retained then it will be important to refine it further so that a much higher percentage of teachers are convinced about its effectiveness.

A very high percentage of the teachers (96 per cent) enjoy teaching the Unit Curriculum and 80 per cent of the teachers 'have as much enthusiasm about the Unit Curriculum now as they had last year'. It would seem that if River Valley Senior High School staff maintain this positive attitude toward the Unit Curriculum, it must succeed.

Items dealing with workload provide a more sobering picture. Eighty-one per cent of the teachers support the statement that 'the Unit Curriculum has increased their workload'. This is a very high figure and clearly teachers would not want this situation to continue year after year, or worse still, to escalate still further. Nevertheless, the workload problem seems to have been kept in bounds at present. For example, only 6 per cent of teachers indicated that their 'incidence of sickness and absenteeism had increased since their involvement in teaching the Unit Curriculum'. A stronger warning about the potential problem was revealed in another item where 42 per cent of teachers indicated that their 'workload commitment to the Unit Curriculum is causing problems to their personal and social life outside school'.

Students' Perspectives

It is very evident that future job aspirations is a major factor affecting the units students choose. Students agreed that they would 'get a better job having worked under the Unite Curriculum system'. These results are possibly symptomatic of the restricted economic conditions prevailing and the very real threat that many of these students may have a future of unemployment ahead of them unless they do something positive about it. There is, of course, no guarantee that the Unit Curriculum will assist students to get jobs and this may be an unrealistic expectation.

A worrisome set of responses is that 60 per cent of the students consider that they don't always get the units they choose. A number of questions might be raised about this result. Does it indicate that some units are proving to be much more popular than others and that these will need to be offered more frequently each year or the less popular units will need to be revised to enhance their level of popularity? Alternatively does it reveal that students are being inadequately counselled about the units they should be choosing, commensurate with their abilities and job aspirations? Are the students' expectations unrealistic and that they should not expect to get all their first choices in every term of the year?

Sixty-eight per cent of students 'would like to have two or three revision lessons at the end of each unit'. This might be interpreted as students desiring a last chance to review the main content of a unit before the final tests because they are pressured too much during the normal lessons. Yet most units would have a number of assessment points during the ten weeks and so revision lessons at the end might not be all that appropriate. Whatever the reasons, this item does indicate that students are concerned about passing and therefore are supportive of revision procedures which might improve their chances of success.

A similar feeling of unease about passing units is revealed by the 34 per cent of students who indicated that they are 'told that they are not doing well in a unit too late to stop them from failing it'. All kinds of questions could be raised about this item. Does it mean for one-third of the students that they don't receive sufficient feedback from their teachers? Which students comprise the one third — are they the students who are most at risk academically? Does it mean that poor results in early assessments in a unit are irreversible during the life-cycle of a unit? If this is the case it would seem to be at odds with the assumptions of criterion-referenced and mastery learning which are integral to the Unit Curriculum structure.

It is evident that students are very concerned about failing units (91 per cent) and that they 'try harder in class now because they can't stand failing' (81 per cent). Eighty-five per cent of students were worried about failing units, and that their fears were not allayed by the prospect of being able to take other units at the same stage. It might be argued that this fear of failing is a desirable motivational power to be operating in high schools. If it became overstressed by teachers then it could lead to an excessive degree of student anxiety with all the attendant behavioural side-effects.

On a more positive note, many students are coping with, and perhaps even enjoying, the heavy workloads imposed by the Unit Curriculum. For example, 82 per cent of students are trying 'harder in class now because they understand exactly what they have to do to pass a unit'. This supports one of the major principles of the Unit Curriculum structure and it is most commendable to note that such a high proportion of students consider that they are working harder and are willing to do so. It also suggests that teachers have communicated this aspect of the Unit Curriculum very effectively to their students.

For a considerable number of students (61 per cent) the workload is very heavy under the Unit Curriculum, but only 34 per cent indicated that they found it difficult to cope with all the work. The important question to be asked here of course is which students find it is difficult for them to cope? Are they students who made poor choices in the units they selected? Does it mean that the 34 per cent are mainly students with poor academic skills and/or attitudes to work?

Parents' Perspectives

A considerable number of parents (73 per cent) consider that they have a greater say under the Unit Curriculum about what subjects their children will study. However, parents were equally divided about whether their children had made satisfactory choices or not this year. There appears to be some contradictory evidence here but, notwithstanding, parents seem to be very supportive of their increased involvement under the Unit Curriculum.

Parents were very supportive about the advice teachers offered their children about unit selection (79 per cent). If anything, it seems that parents would like teachers to be more directive in 'telling students which unit selections are best for them'. This information has important implications for how TAG teachers should advise their students. It raises questions such as is it ethical for TAG teachers to recommend directly and prescriptively about units to be studied by certain students? Would it lead to accusations of 'empire building' if TAG teachers tried to direct students into particular subject areas? Should it be the students only who have the major and ultimate responsibility for choosing units they will study? If so, are there special skills that students need to develop to be able to undertake these tasks successfully?

It is very pleasing to note that a large number of parents (72 per cent) consider that 'there is a strong caring relationship between teachers and students at River Valley Senior High School'. A similar high level of support (72 per cent) was given by parents, that 'my child (children) can always get help from teachers at River Valley Senior High School'.

It appears that employers in the local area don't understand the Unit Curriculum (77 per cent) and that only a moderate number (43 per cent) are in favour of it. This must be a disappointing finding for River Valley Senior High School staff as they have taken a number of steps during the year to acquaint local employers with the Unit Curriculum. It could be that publicity about the Unit Curriculum to employers is a central responsibility for the Minister of Education who may need to have concerted campaigns using all the media, including television, radio and newspapers.

It is very evident that many parents know very little about the

Unit Curriculum (73 per cent). Although all kinds of literature have been sent home to parents during the year and parents nights have been held, it appears that parents are still very confused about Unit Curriculum and further strategies will have to be developed to overcome this lack of understanding.

A sizeable number of parents (62 per cent) consider that their children are 'happier at school now under the unit Curriculum scheme'. This also means of course that 38 per cent are less happy or are unchanged compared with the previous Achievement Certificate system. This figure might be construed by some as a disappointing result because one of the tenets of the Unit Curriculum is that students will be more self-motivated and happier.

Parents are clearly very concerned about their children passing sufficient units each term and they perceive the threat of failure to be a major motivation (78 per cent). A considerable number of parents (76 per cent) considered their children do 'get worried about failing units'. To a certain extent it might be desirable to have the threat of failure as a motivator (and which is commensurate with many life situations) but there is always the danger that the fear of failure could become obsessive for students and that this in time could adversely affect their mental, social and emotional development.

Parents were also concerned about assessment procedures which they perceive as not being fair to all students. For example, 82 per cent of the parents considered that 'children who miss work because of illness should not have "failed" recorded in their results'.

Concluding Comment

This SBCD example commenced as a small-scale activity over a two year period by the school principal and several of his senior administrative staff. Their drive and persistence attracted the support of a small number of teaching staff. Together they planned and implemented a pastoral care system using mixed-age Teacher Advisory Groups (TAG) and a vertical timetabling system for year 11 students and for options in lower school (years 8–10). Although it might be argued that these two innovations were implemented successfully and that most staff were involved in running TAG groups, it was not a total SBCD activity. The staff as a whole did not 'own' the innovations even though they followed the routines required.

The breakthrough which enabled a relatively minor SBCD activity to blossom into a major school-wide project came in 1986 when the state education system invited River Valley Senior High School to become a pilot school to initiate a new curriculum structure for lower secondary school students, the Unit Curriculum. It was coincidental but certainly advantageous for River Valley school staff that they had been involved previously in the small-scale SBCD activity described above. Now they were being asked to plan and implement a major innovation which had a myriad of implications for counselling, timetabling, teaching loads and student commitment.

Although some aspects of the new Unit Curriculum structure were prescribed by officials of the state education system, a number of planning decisions still had to be made by staff at River Valley Senior High School. As they were one of seven schools especially selected to trial a Unit Curriculum approach there were no models or precedents for the staff to follow. They had to plan their own version of the Unit Curriculum, make a number of critical decisions about priorities and schedules, and then follow these through to the implementation stage.

All staff were heavily involved and committed to developing their particular version of the Unit Curriculum. During the latter months of 1986 and during the pilot study period (1987) the staff worked intensively and cooperatively on planning new module units, orchestrating the different difficulty levels (stages), assessment points, and information documents and unit planners for students and parents.

The evaluation study conducted on River Valley Senior High School during July–December 1987 revealed that this major SBCD activity was a resounding success. Stake holders were generally very positive about their participation in the planning activities and about the perceived outcomes. There were minor criticisms of some elements of implementing the Unit Curriculum, but the overriding conclusion was a sense of achievement, a well developed spirit of congeniality and respect among stake holders, and a desire to move forward to further successes with the Unit Curriculum.

Chapter 4

Canada: School-Based Curriculum Deliberation[1]

The curriculum field is replete with models of how curriculum should be developed and, yet, there are very few case studies that describe the actual process. This chapter employs the experiences of two committees to illuminate the process of school-based curriculum development. The school involved was fairly typical of most high schools in the province of Ontario, Canada. Staff turnover was low and, as in most Ontario schools, the average age of the teaching force was steadily rising. The participants of both committees, therefore, were older and experienced teachers but were involved in a formal process of curriculum development for the first time. They began the project because their Principal had mandated participation in the development process as a means of addressing newly-legislated policy and of fostering school improvement. This chapter will explore their experiences and will analyze the factors affecting that process.

Background Details

Provincial Initiatives

In 1984 the Ontario Ministry of Education initiated major reforms of the secondary school curriculum stated in the policy document, *Ontario Schools: Intermediate and Senior Divisions (OSIS)*. The policy required major shifts in school organization, school-based curriculum development of courses of study, and student streaming procedures. The policy document clearly emphasized the role of the school staff in developing school-based curricula: 'Primary responsibility for the planning of curriculum lies with the principal and teachers of the school working in conjunction with supervisory officers and other educators employed by their school board' (*OSIS*, p. 12). The school Principal was legally responsible for ensuring that a course of study for each course in the school was on file in the office and available for public inspection. The school course of study was to be derived from a general provincial guideline produced by the Ministry of Education for each subject area. Another major change contained within *OSIS* required that a course of study be developed at three distinct levels of student ability: basic, general, and advanced.

A flurry of provincial guideline preparation occurred simultaneously with the implementation of *OSIS*. The philosophical direction of these new guidelines, which have been developed for almost every school subject area, has also constituted a major change for secondary schools in Ontario. Every document produced reflects an image of the learner as a 'self-motivated, self-directed problem solver'. Consequently, the new documents have emphasized a thinking skills, problem-solving approach to curriculum and instruction rather than a focus on factual content.

With the evident policy changes, secondary school principals were faced with a dual implementation problem: establishing a curriculum development process in their schools and modifying existing teaching methodologies to correspond with the new provincial curriculum directions.

School Initiative

The Principal at Timberline Secondary School[2] opted to view the new provincial curriculum initiatives as an opportunity for school improvement rather than as yet another administrative responsibility. The school administration viewed the curriculum development process as serving two different purposes. The first purpose was to develop the courses of study legally required by the Ministry of Education. Second, the Principal and Vice Principal also perceived that a reflective curriculum development process would provide an opportunity for teacher growth and school improvement. Consequently, they employed the development process as a means of fostering classroom curricular and instructional change.

In the 1984/85 school year the Principal initiated a five-year program of school-based curriculum development. He mandated that subject area departments develop a curriculum for each of their courses. They were to develop the grade 9 courses in 1984, the grade 10 in 1985, etc. The school administration reviewed each document produced and suggested modifications for refinement.

The school administration supported the development process in several different ways. First, they budgeted for release time so that most of the development work could be completed during regular school hours. Second, they financially supported the attendance of several Department Heads and teachers at out of district professional in-service sessions on curriculum development. Third, the administration provided consistent morale and practical support throughout the process. Lastly, they sought the support of the faculty from the Northwestern Centre, Ontario Institute for Studies in Education (OISE).

The author, an OISE Faculty member, first became involved in 1985 when she responded to the administration's request to review the curriculum documents (grade 9) created in the first round of the school's curriculum development process. She made specific recommendations pertaining to the individual subject areas' courses of study and more general recommendations concerning the process employed. During the 1985/86 school year, assisted by a research grant from the Social Science Humanities Research Council of Canada, the author worked with three committees to develop curricula and to concurrently study how the participants made curricular decisions. A verbatim transcript was produced from the audio-taped committee meetings and the participants were interviewed concerning their perceptions. The technical report (Hannay and Seller, 1987) describes the findings in depth.

This chapter examines the development process experienced by a History Committee and a Geography Committee in Timberline Secondary School. The History Committee only had one meeting and was unable to develop a common course of study for their department. The Geography Committee completed their task of developing a departmental curriculum. The following table lists the committee membership:

History Committee	**Geography Committee**
Rick	Archie
Ted	Mark
Herb	Jack
George	Ralph
	Peter
	Lynne (researcher)

The following sections of this chapter will outline the process followed by both committees and will provide a description of the participants. The emerging patterns and issues will then be discussed and the final section will analyze the successes and failures experienced by both committees. An examination of both the positive and the negative examples, provides insight into the process of school-based curriculum development.

The Participants and the Process: A Chronology of Events

The History and Geography Committees shared some common parameters. First, history and geography were housed in the same department with the same Department Head. Second, both committees were dealing with new provincial guidelines from the Ministry of Education that emphasized the same problem-solving philosophy. Third, both committees were operating under the same administrative mandate to produce curricula that reflected the changes in pedagogy and philosophy outlined in the Ministry documents. Fourth, the participants of both committees began the process because of the administrative mandate, not out of a personal need to develop a curriculum.

Members of both committees had taught at least fifteen years in Timberline Secondary School, though several individuals had been at the school closer to twenty-five years. They all had academic degrees at the Bachelors' level in their respective subject areas and had teacher training through the now disbanded teacher's colleges. Only one member of the History Committee had a Master's degree. This degree was in history and not in education. The same participant was the only individual to cite a continual effort at personally searching for additional professional development. He sought out professional reading, in-service sessions, and experiences that he felt would assist him in enhancing his teaching. The other members attended required in-service sessions provided by the school system but they could not cite any personally initiated professional development.

The process experienced by both committees is outlined separately below. An analysis follows in the latter sections of the chapter.

History Committee

The History Committee only had one two-hour meeting and then disbanded as a working committee. As mentioned earlier, the Department had a new draft guideline from the Ministry of Education that contained radical changes for the teaching of history. The guideline strongly emphasized the process of learning and focussed on problem-solving or thinking skills as opposed to content. The one meeting of this Committee, however, failed to address the major philosophical changes in the new guideline and focussed on the content shifts. They were far more concerned with examining, for example, whether World War One had been shifted from grade 9 to grade 11 than in discussing the underlying philosophical and pedagogical changes.

The personal beliefs of the participants definitely influenced their concern with content. Of the four person Committee, three members (including the Department Head) exhibited a strong content orientation. Generally, they saw their students as passively accepting the content and repeating the factual knowledge on a test. As Rick reported, 'Kids that can listen in class will absorb the material and they will have very little studying to do.' The fourth Committee member, however, evidenced a strong process orientation to teaching. He was more concerned with students gaining learning skills than in acquiring specific content knowledge. He defined learning as 'a holistic process . . . the transformation of experience . . . The most important thing is to provide a milieu in which you can invite people to learn'.

The Committee chair, the Department Head, rather than encouraging a discussion of the evident differences in the light of the new curriculum guideline, steered the Committee towards investigating the changes in content. He claimed 'I'm not real big on sitting down and spending a day talking about the philosophy of teaching'. Consequently, the History Committee did not explore any changes in pedagogy or philosophy that might be necessary for developing a new course of study based on the provincial guidelines.

The situation was further compounded by the Committee's attitude about the curriculum development process itself. Developing the courses of study had been mandated by the Ministry of Education policy and further reinforced through the mandate of their Principal. To a person, the Committee evidenced a great deal of hostility towards the development process. The Department Head blamed the Ministry of Education, 'The Ministry says you've got to get this done, we've got to get it done.' Herb, a teacher member of the Committee, displayed his resistance to the process during an interview:

> What we had to do is for everyone of these God damn things [courses of study], they wanted us to put 'what do we want to achieve?' And then 'what are the methods we use?' Well, the whole thing resolved into absurdity.

Another teacher, Ted, claimed, 'I see the courses of study that comes down from Toronto as an authoritarian thing. I see it as really maladaptive to teaching.' The Committee members perceived they needed a product to satisfy the school administration but considered the created product to be of little practical use to themselves. One member explained, 'I don't really have much use for a course of study or a curriculum. I seldom refer to it.'

Perhaps because the Committee avoided discussing the pedagogical and philosophical changes apparent in the new guideline, they failed to perceive a problem with their past practice of teaching history. Consequently, curriculum development was viewed as a task to be procedurally handled through reissuing past practices without reflection on these practices. The absence of such a discussion, in conjunction with their resistance to the development process itself, resulted in the decision to cease joint development of the course of study. Department members retreated to their individual cubbyholes within the department office and designed individual courses of study which reflected their individual orientations. The group curriculum development process ceased and the department failed to produce a common course of study.

Geography Committee

The members of the Geography Committee began the curriculum development process with very similar views to the members of the History Committee. They viewed the curriculum development process as necessary to meet the demands of the school administration and the Ministry of Education. They did not, initially, perceive that the process or the product would be useful to their teaching. Individual Committee members shared similar views regarding the importance of geography content over an emphasis on the problem-solving process. However, unlike their history colleagues, the Geography Committee created a joint curriculum and through the development process modified their perceptions of curriculum development and their ideas or methods of teaching geography.

The Geography Committee met for eight days throughout the school year and by their last meeting had produced a document of which they were very proud. The following section describes the gist of these meetings. The latter sections of the chapter examines the differences between the failed History and the successful Geography Committees.

While the Geography Committee entered into the curriculum development process because of an administrative mandate, through their involvement they began to view their existing curriculum and pedagogy as problematic. They did not start with a problem to be addressed but, through their deliberations, gradually added components to their criteria for making curricular decisions. This process of problem formation encompassed five out of the eight meetings. Throughout these five meetings they also made design decisions and worked on their product.

Meeting 1

Members of the Geography Committee entered into the development process with the intention of quickly designing a curriculum to meet the external needs imposed by the school administration and the Ministry of Education. They shared the same perception as the History Committee regarding the purpose of the development process. One Committee member, Archie, explained this during the first meeting:

> I mean [the Department Head] is just pushing the pressure down the ladder. He's getting pressure from the [Assistant Principal], and he'll [Assistant Principal] claim he's getting pressure from whomever . . . I believe it's the Ministry [of Education] that says you have to have all these nice concise little documents in your office when we [Ministry of Education] come around.

The Committee members did not envision the process being a long or involved one. In fact, during this first meeting they announced that they would 'wrap this up in two days'. Their original plan was to divide up the development task between Committee members and reorganize existing practice into two separate courses of study, physical and human geography:

> I think the best bet is you gentlemen prepare your physical geography [course], I'll prepare the human [geography] for the general [grade] elevens and Archie can prepare his for the advaanced . . . You can have copies of ours. We'd like a copy of your physical [geography course] . . .
>
> [meeting 1, p.3]

Very quickly, Committee members expressed concern with this proposed practice; not because they were dissatisfied with dividing up the curriculum task or with existing pedagogy but because they were experiencing declining enrolment in geography courses. A decrease in student enrollment in their subject area might result in a cancellation of geography courses and their reassignment to other teaching areas. Consequently, they decided to create a course of study that would combine physical and human geography as they perceived this approach might attract more students.

This was a difficult decision for the Committee. A comment from the teacher committee chair illustrates the concern with geography content:

How can you ever understand the world if you don't understand physical geography? Where the mountains come from? Why they're there? It is maybe not very necessary for the average person to know. There's going to be a problem there because teachers of geography obviously think that is essential to know.

By the end of the first meeting, the Committee had decided to work together to develop one curriculum that would integrate physical and human geography. They were still mainly concerned with the organization and selection of content, and generally ignored the thinking skills component of the draft Ministry of Education guideline. The process orientation was only raised by the author as she tried to encourage the Committee members to reflect on pedagogy.

Meeting 2

The second meeting of the Geography Committee focussed on reconceptualizing the content organization. Committee members began the session by reviewing the table of content from various geography textbooks with the intention of using these to organize the content of the course of study. However, given their previous decision to integrate physical and human geography, they quickly became dissatisfied with this approach. They questioned whether the textbook's approach was valid: 'What we have to do is sit down and say is this author of this textbook on line with human geography?' Eventually, after a lengthy discussion, the Committee selected five major themes that would be integrated throughout all units. This decision would remain the major organizational framework throughout their curriculum development work.

During this meeting, the Committee also developed a list of concepts that would be the major focus of the themes selected. Rather than focussing on individual facts, as in past practice, Committee members sought out concepts and generalizations that could be taught through different content choices. They also started to develop a growth scheme for geography skills that would encompass the 9–13 grade level continuum.

Throughout this meeting, the teacher members struggled with

whether a common curriculum would impinge on their personal teaching styles and instructional decisions. Archie stated his concerns, 'Jack does his [teaching] style one way, I do mine another. I think we have to come up with a document that's going to cover both.' The teachers also displayed a concern with the curriculum document being prescriptive and restrictive, as evidenced in a comment from Jack: 'I hope the office doesn't come and say, "Now God darn it, I thought you should be in Africa today and you are in China".'

The process leadership displayed by the author became crucial in addressing these concerns. Throughout the process she emphasized that a curriculum built around concepts and skills can empower rather than restrict the teachers. Several comments from the second meeting indicate this role:

> *Lynne:* But if you come back again to your content as skills and concepts, then it doesn't matter whether you're doing five or ten [units]. And that's the crucial thing, that somewhere along the line you are, either in an overview or in depth, you are having a progression of skills.
>
> *Lynne:* But if you're building on these themes then the content is irrelevant because you're teaching concepts.

During this session, then, the Committee had somewhat reconceptualized content organization and had begun to incorporate skills and concepts into their curricular planning. They still accepted that certain content was valid because of their past practice and had not yet questioned why that content should be included in the course of study.

Meeting 3

Meeting 3 was notable for several reasons. First, Committee members began to question what should be included in the curriculum. Second, with the author absent, some Committee members assumed a process leadership role for the first time. Third, they evidenced an acceptance of their role as curriculum developers.

For the first time in the process, Committee members perceived a need to rationalize their curricular choices by asking themselves why certain content should be included in the curriculum. For example, Mark asked:

> *Mark:* We should be able to come up with sort of an agreement as to why you're teaching [this]. Shouldn't we?

106

In this meeting, the Committee members started to view their past practice in more problematic terms. Rather than just accept past practice as given and acceptable, they questioned whether it should be included in the new curriculum. The development process became more of a reasoned discussion rather than a procedural task to be completed.

Meeting 4

Meeting 4 represented a crucial juncture for the Geography Committee. During this meeting they raised questions regarding alternative teaching strategies. The following extract from the Committee meeting provides some insight into the many facets considered by the teachers while contemplating a new teaching methodology:

Mark: Do you ever do role playing in geography or anywhere?

Archie: I have maybe once.

Mark: I never have. I've sort of toyed with the idea . . . How do you do it?

Lynne: [provides several examples]

Mark: I'd like to see that [examples] because I don't really know that much about role playing. I mean I know the general drift of it but I stop and think to myself 'mmhm, I can't'. Maybe I don't give enough thought to it.

Archie: I think role playing and most of those types of strategies demand a heck of a pile of preparation because the better they're prepared, the more successful they will be in the classroom. I find I just don't have that kind of time most times. I've never seen an example in my teaching career. You know, say in teachers' college or something like that . . . I think that is why I tend to stay away from it.

Mark: I always wondered how do you motivate them [students]? How do you get them to care that much [about role playing]. I mean you do it, I do it for the fun but some of the kids they don't want to spend the effort.

Archie: I think it's one of my greatest reasons for not doing this kind of stuff in the past was I never felt comfortable when it came to an evaluation. How do you evaluate?

Archie: I'll give it a great deal of thought because I really do think that in my teaching right now I'm looking for variety because I can see where I get into a rut.

[Meeting 4, pp. 48–53]

During this discussion, Committee members openly questioned their past teaching practice which had been primarily a lecture format. They noted the various factors influencing their lack of experimentation in alternative teaching methodologies. A major barrier was that these teachers lacked an image of how to incorporate interactive teaching strategies into their classroom practice as they had not experienced such teaching strategies while students in teacher's college or in their teaching careers. Committee members also raised the issues of additional preparation time, motivating students, and student evaluation.

However, even with the evident concern over incorporating new teaching strategies into their personal repertoire, in all subsequent curriculum decisions the Committee searched for alternative teaching methodologies. They now sought out strategies more consistent with the problem solving orientation evident in the new Ministry of Education geography guideline and with the concept/skill focus they were developing in their course of study. For example, later in the fourth meeting, Mark asked, 'Are there any simulations, games or anything like that about mining?'

Meeting 5

In the first four meetings, the Committee struggled with the content versus process continuum. As trained geographers, the teachers had a strong loyalty to geography subject matter which was frequently interpreted as geographical factual knowledge. However, the combination of the new geography guideline which emphasized a problem solving approach to geography and their deliberative discussions throughout the curriculum development process, forced the Geography Committee members to reflect on what should be the emphasis in a geography curriculum. Although this dilemma had been present throughout all of the group sessions, during the fifth meeting the group formally discussed the apparent changes. Ralph summarized the situation:

I think because we're subject matter specialists, by and large, that we have a tendency in the secondary level to be more content oriented than in the elementary level. Maybe what Mark is saying, that we are so content conscious that if we develop this format and force ourselves to go with skill objectives and that sort of thing, that hopefully, we come out with a happy medium.

The strong sense of group identity and the trust within the group that had developed during the year permitted Committee members to share their concerns and perceptions. During this meeting they freely investigated the differences in curriculum orientations between their past image of geography teaching and their developing image. Committee members became reflective of the differences and evidenced some degree of self-criticism.

By the end of the fifth meeting, the Geography Committee had succeeded in making their practice problematic in a positive sense. They had now developed criteria from which they could make curriculum decisions. Their criteria included: a thematic approach to subject matter organization; a focus on problem solving skills; interactive teaching strategies; the need to justify their content decisions; and their right to make curriculum decisions.

Meetings 6 to 8

While the Geography Committee had made design decisions and developed some of the components of their curriculum during the first five meetings, the real product work of the Committee took place during the last three meetings. They now applied the developed criteria to the curriculum as a whole and became very critical of their work completed earlier in the year and current suggestions. Because the Committee had invested a great deal of time establishing their criteria, they were now able to construct the written product relatively easily.

By the last Committee meeting, when the group reviewed their product prior to final printing, there was a sense of euphoria among the Committee members. Not only were the Committee members proud of the document they had developed, but they expressed a new appreciation for the curriculum development process itself:

Jack: We learned a lot from [the development process] so I think that's the important thing.

Archie: By doing it yourself, Lynne, you're going to write a document that you can use. By doing it collectively, you're going to use the document. All of us can use it.

Ralph: You have sources of interest that we all have. Like I have my little stash of goodies, okay? And then all of a sudden

it comes out, 'Geez, I never thought of using that.' You
get a whole different perspective [collective curriculum
development] than you get doing it [development] on an
individual basis. And you get a pride of ownership, too.

[Meeting 8, p. 114]

The curriculum development process presented a great deal of
difficulty for the Geography Committee. Table 5 summarizes the process
experienced by the Geography Committee.

One	Two	Three	Four	Five	Six–Eight
Concern with student enrollment	Select themes as curriculum organizers	Question emphasis on factual content	Search out interactive teaching strategies	Reflect on content vs process	Apply criteria of deliberations to curricular decisions
Select integrated curriculum	Start to develop concepts and general-izations	Develop growth scheme for geography skills	Develop interactive teaching strategies	Past practice made problematic	

Table 5: Motivations influencing the curricular decisions of the Geography Committee

As noted, the Geography Committee had begun the required project with the intention of modifying their existing courses to fit the paper
requirements of the school administration. Although this Committee
had not intended for the process to be either long or involved, it did
evolve into a major endeavour. Gradually, as they worked through the
process they developed an increasingly deeper understanding of both
their curriculum and the curriculum development process.

Emerging Patterns and Issues

The experiences of the History Committee and the Geography Committee provide insight into the process of school-based curriculum development. The emerging issues can be grouped into two major categories:
contextual factors and the curriculum development process itself. The
evidence suggests that four contextual factors affected the development
process: curriculum orientations, initiation source, leadership and availability of resources. The following section examines how the contextual
factors influenced the success or failure of the curriculum development
process.

Contextual Factors

Contextual factors refer to conditions already in existence when the school-based development project was initiated. These factors might be modified through the involvement of teachers in the development project. The contextual factors are applicable to other school-based curriculum development projects, however, their influence would vary according to the personalities involved, organizational climate, and legislated policies. The factors, which emerged during the data analysis, helped to explain the failure of the History Committee and the success of the Geography Committee. Although the four contextual factors intertwine throughout the process, each factor will be addressed individually.

Curriculum orientations

The curriculum development process, by its very nature, requires a consideration of what should be included in the curriculum. This includes reflecting upon individual and school philosophies. As noted in chapter 2, the literature suggests that teachers are often not interested, for various reasons, in addressing theoretical or philosophical issues.

However, in school-based curriculum development it is difficult to exclude philosophical or theoretical issues for several reasons. Obviously, the individuals involved bring their own personal educational philosophies to the group process and this can create conflict within the group. If the curriculum development process emanates from an innovation then there might be a conflict between the philosophy underlying the innovation and that of the development committee.

Miller and Seller (1985) developed a means of conceptualizing curriculum orientations that provides a useful lens to interpret the influence of philosophy on the two cases included in this chapter. They outline three meta-curriculum orientations: transmission, transaction and transformation. A *transmission orientation* emphasizes the subject matter disciplines, factual knowledge, and existing societal norms. The role of the teacher is directive and instruction is often didactic with students responding to the teachers' initiatives.

A *transactional orientation* assumes the student is rational and capable of problem-solving. The aim of transaction based teaching is to foster democratic citizenship skills through the development of intelligence in general and problem-solving skills in particular. The teacher becomes a facilitator who assists students in developing thinking skills, finding resources, and stimulating inquiry in the classroom.

A *transformational orientation* focusses on personal and social change. The goals are self-actualization, self-transcendence and social involvement. The role of the teacher is to help students develop skills that promote personal and social transformation through experiences that link the cognitive skills with aesthetic, emotional and spiritual dimensions of life.

The three meta-orientations provide a means of understanding the curriculum development process experienced by the History Committee and the Geography Committee. A common factor evident with both committees was the new directions for teaching history and geography contained in their new provincial guidelines. The history and geography guidelines contained a strong emphasis on problem-solving and interactive teaching strategies (transactional orientation) while both guidelines de-emphasized teaching content for content sake. The willingness to explore the assumptions of the different orientations was one factor influencing the school-based curriculum development process.

The members of the History Committee, as explained earlier in the chapter, failed to have such a dialogue. Three members of the Committee evidenced a very strong transmissional orientation and were primarily concerned with the shifts in content. They ignored the changes of philosophy contained in the new guideline. These three committee members also ignored the beliefs of the fourth Committee member who evidenced a transformational orientation. The inability or the unwillingness to enter into a dialogue on what students should learn through history was the major contributing factor to the failure of this Committee to develop a departmental curriculum.

Members of the Geography Committee initially evidenced a transmission orientation but gradually through their involvement in the process, began to shift their perspectives. The Committee did not have philosophical discussions *per se* but as they struggled with curriculum decisions they constantly referred back to the new guideline, their past practices and the curriculum they were developing. It was through making the design decisions that a discussion on alternative curriculum orientations was pursued. Their involvement in school-based curriculum development, then, became a professional development process that allowed the participants to reflect on past and future teaching practices.

Leadership

The different leadership styles between the History Committee and the Geography Committee was the prime reason why one Committee was able to explore alternative orientations and the other committee ignored the apparent differences. The History Department Head stated he had little interest in examining philosophical issues and wanted to produce the document to satisfy the administration. He saw little value in the development process per se. He also considered discussing curricular concerns or teaching methodology as an infringement on the privacy of the individual teacher. Consequently, the Department Head was unwilling to tackle his staff on their personal orientations or help them discuss their obvious differences.

The external researcher, in her role as a field developer, assumed the process leadership of the Geography Committee with the agreement of the Committee members. She perceived the curriculum development process very differently than did the History Department Head. Curriculum development was not only to produce a document but could provide a growth opportunity for the participants as they reflected on past practice and future practice in terms of the curriculum they were developing. She also believed that curriculum development was a circular not a linear process with a major emphasis on a reasoned approach. This leader helped the committee establish a trusting climate that supported an exploration of, and a respect for, alternative ideas. Through asking questions of the participants, this leader encouraged a reflective dialogue that resulted in a departmental curriculum of which the members were proud and that contained a major shift in curriculum orientations. The curriculum development process became a growth experience for the participants.

Initiation source

The initiation source relates to how the participants defined the locus of the problem. When a committee did not perceive there was a problem with their existing curriculum, the curriculum development process was not viewed as problem solving but as a task to be completed. Consequently, the locus of the problem was external and the task was defined in terms of the product requirement. The research on change suggests that external pressure is acceptable only at the initiation stage. However, if the participants do not accept ownership during the implementation phase then it is unlikely the project will be successful.

The History Committee and the Geography Committee entered into the school-based development project because of administrative pressure. Both committees initially exhibited a great deal of resistance towards the task which they perceived as a bureaucratic exercise. The History Committee maintained this perception while the Geography Committee adapted their attitude.

The History Committee resisted the curriculum development process and the assigned members evidenced a great deal of hostility towards the project. Their defined problem was not what should be taught in history but, rather, how to satisfy the administration with the least amount of effort. During their own brief meeting, the Committee did not express any concern with their existing programs or investigate alternative means of teaching history. The group composition perpetuated this attitude. All participants could be classified on Hall's (1975 and 1977) scale as being at stage 1 as outlined in chapter 2. Consistent with the characteristics of stage 1, departmental teachers were quite content to work in isolation from each other and resisted sharing their curriculum in use with others. This attitude might have been overcome by a leader who believed in the curriculum development process. In this instance, however, the Department Head agreed with his department that the curriculum development process served no useful purpose other than to satisfy the school administration. He also lacked knowledge about, and experience in, the curriculum development process. Because of these factors, the need for curriculum development remained externally motivated and was not related to the job satisfaction needs of the teachers involved. The lack of intrinsic motivation was a contributing factor to the failure of the History Committee to produce a departmental document.

The members of the Geography Committee entered into the school-based development project with very similar attitudes to that of the History Committee. However, this attitude changed through their involvement in the project itself. The external pressure was gradually replaced with an internal desire to create a curriculum and to reflect on existing practice.

When the geography teachers began the process they could have been classified as Hall's stage 1. By the end of the project, however, three teachers had moved to a stage 4 and one teacher evidenced behaviour reflecting a stage 5 level. The three teachers at the stage 4 level were participating in the project but lacked a willingness to accept an active leadership role. One teacher, who demonstrated stage 5 characteristics by the end of the process, had accepted this responsibility and was very involved in the process. A key factor in influencing this shift was the leadership of the Committee. The leader was used to assuming a change agent role and had expertise in curriculum development. She used a process of 'gentling' to help the teachers gain the confidence to take risks and share their professional expertise. Rather than challenge the teachers with an abrupt change in practice, she initially introduced issues that reflected the current beliefs of the members as to curriculum development and the teaching of geography. Gradually, as the process unfolded, the leader raised more complex concepts that encouraged the teachers involved to question their past curriculum development and teaching practice. The leader's understanding of the group members and constant encouragement allowed the participants to take the risks necessary to question their practice. Assisted by the facilitative leadership, the Committee gradually perceived an internal need for their involvement in the curriculum development process. Halfway through the process, one Committee member explained his revised view of curriculum:

> What does curriculum mean to me? It means getting down on paper the things that you're supposed to be doing within a course throughout the year, analyzing it and seeing whether you're doing the right thing and thinking about it. Thinking about what you're doing in the classroom. I think that is the real value to it anyway.

Resources

The fourth contextual factor impeding or enhancing the school-based curriculum development process is that of the resources available to support the curriculum development activity. Resources refers to materials applicable to the teaching process and assets that facilitated the curriculum development process. It is important to consider not only what resources are available to support the project but also whether the committees chose to take advantage of those resources.

As mentioned earlier in the chapter, the school administration had made various resources available to support the curriculum development process. Notably, they provided the resources necessary to release teachers from the classroom for curricular work and had arranged to have the support of the OISE Northwestern Centre. A member of the Geography Committee acknowledged this support:

> There doesn't seem to be any shortage of money. If we have something curriculum planned, there's no question about supply teachers or being out of the classroom for one day. They realize

that we're contributing something to the system so they're very supportive, all the way through.

The History Committee failed to take advantage of the resources being provided by the school administration. The Committee did not use all of the offered release time as they only met for one afternoon. Also, the Committee chose not to employ the curriculum expertise of the Northwestern Centre Faculty member although she had an academic degree in history and experience in teaching high school history.

The members of the History Committee did not search out new resources to support their curriculum nor did they share their individual expertise and resources with each other. The teachers appeared to consider these resources as private property and were unwilling to share or make them available for public discussion. By opting not to seek new resources or use existing resources for both the curriculum document and the development process, the History Committee failed to take advantage of an opportunity to broaden the curriculum process.

Conversely, the Geography Committee took full advantage of any resources available. The Committee far exceeded the allotted release time using a full eight days for the development process. They willingly accepted the assistance of the Northwestern Centre Faculty member not only for facilitating the curriculum development process but as an information source on substantive issues such as alternative teaching methodologies.

Committee members also used each other as resources. They acknowledged that individuals had special expertise in certain areas of geography and the Committee relied on these individuals to share their knowledge. Committee members exchanged their own experiences both to clarify alternatives under consideration and to offer further alternatives. As the process unfolded, individual members shared the resources they had collected during their teaching careers. In addition, various Committee members sought out community resources supportive of their new document. Gradually, they accumulated a collective resource file to support their curriculum.

The contextual factors provided a strong influence affecting the success or failure of the school-based curriculum development projects reported in this chapter. Initially, three of the factors were very similar for both committees. One committee, however, managed to overcome the initially negative influence to successfully complete their project. The fourth contextual factor, leadership, seemed to explain the different experiences of the two committees.

Curriculum Development Process

The preceding section described four contextual factors that impeded or enhanced the curriculum development process. The following section examines how these factors influenced the development process through specific reference to the Geography Committee. As the History Committee did not enter into a process, this committee is only addressed superficially.

Schwab (1969) maintains that curriculum problems arise out of practical concerns when something is perceived as unsatisfactory. Without the presence of a practical problem, curriculum development can become a theoretical activity that might not be attractive to practising teachers.

Initially, both committees did not have a practical problem and had difficulty in making their past practice problematic. In the case of the History Committee, they saw the development process itself as the problem and did not evidence any concern over the status quo. Committee members were involved in the process because of an administrative mandate not out of a desire to develop curriculum or a need to solve a practical problem. This Committee remained under the influence of the source of initiation and failed to reach the stage of problem formation in which their present practice was viewed as being problematic.

The Geography Committee began their project with a similar perspective. During the development process of the Geography Committee, it was evident that the contextual factors described above were affected by and affected the dynamics of the interactions of the individual members and the need to complete a task. This need was first influenced by the 'source of initiation' contextual factor. However, a further need to clearly delineate the problem eventually eclipsed the negative aspects of the external motivation.

Problem formation was not an easy process for the Geography Committee and they struggled with conceptualizing alternatives to their past practices. Contrary to some of the traditional curriculum models, the Committee did not rationally define the problem and then find ways of addressing the issues through the curriculum document. Rather, the Committee gradually formed the problem as they made curricular decisions. Often a decision advocating a new approach created a state of cognitive dissonance with status quo. The 'curriculum orientation' contextual factor greatly influenced the cognitive dissonance experienced by committee members. Committee members had to deal with their personal orientations in light of the issues arising from their curriculum deliberations and the new Ministry of Education guideline. For example, the decision made in meeting 2 to use concepts and skills instead of factual content as the curriculum base eventually led to a discomfort with their existing teaching strategies. This, in turn, led to an examination of more interactive methods of teaching. It was through such an on-going, back and forth process that the Committee gradually made their practice problematic.

The problem formation phase took the Geography Committee five out of their total eight days. They did not spend this time in a theoretical discussion but made design decisions and produced material throughout the process. However, as they added a new dimension to their problem, Committee members returned to earlier decisions to ensure congruency with the added dimension. The process can be represented as a deepening spiral with each return to a previous decision or previous work having more depth and new insight.

A premature forcing of the problem formation might have been detrimental to the process. These teachers added a dimension to their criteria for making curriculum decisions as they became uncomfortable with past practice or needed to solve an issue as it arose from their practical discussions. Gradually, the source of initiation changed from an external force to an internal need because the Committee members were addressing issues they perceived as useful and practical. The problem dimensions emerged from, and became grounded in, their daily practice. If the Committee had been forced into developing their criteria at the outset of the process, it might have been perceived as a theoretical task with little practical application. Also, without the benefit of the reflective dialogue, the problem might have been defined in terms of their past practice and the richness that was developed through the process would have been lost.

The contextual factors of 'leadership' and 'resources' were especially crucial in facilitating the problem formation and subsequent completion of the development project. Time was one of the key resources. The Geography Committee had eight meetings which were held approximately once a month for a school year. Not only were the number of in-school days devoted to the process important but the time between sessions was crucial to allow for reflection and assimilation of new ideas.

Facilitative leadership was also very important to the success of the geography project. The process leader had a firm understanding of the nature of deliberative curriculum development and encouraged a back and forth dialogue that allowed individuals to express their ideas or concerns. She also stressed the importance of reflective dialogue over the need to quickly produce a written document. The leader modeled an acceptance of alternative views and gently guided the Committee members to question their past practice. She frequently guided the process through asking questions in tentative terms rather than stating a direction or viewpoint. By addressing the questions posed, the Committee members explored alternatives to their past practices of teaching geography. Gradually, the Committee established a group climate where it was acceptable to take risks and to disagree with other perspectives. The Committee became very supportive of each other and operated in a collaborative manner. This climate allowed the participants to reflect upon and to question their beliefs. The facilitative leadership had assisted the Geography Committee in gradually forming a problem and in developing criteria from which to make their curriculum decisions.

Evaluative Comments on Successes and Failures

The History Committee and Geography Committee had very different experiences with their efforts at school-based curriculum development although they began with similar attitudes. Three of the four contextual factors were the same for both committees as they entered into the process because of an external source of initiation, faced a change of curriculum orientations in their new provincial guidelines, and had access to the same resources. Yet one Committee failed to complete their project and the other Committee developed a curriculum they felt was useful for their practice.

The Geography Committee was able to adapt and overcome the initially negative contextual factors influencing their project. Committee members gradually perceived an internal need to be involved thus overcoming the initially negative influence of the external 'source of initiation'. The Committee members modified their curriculum orientations through their involvement in the process and used every resource at their disposal. The key difference between the two committees was leadership. The History Department Head did not perceive curriculum development as a useful task and failed to take advantage of the opportunity to promote change. He never encouraged his Department to reflect on their past practice of teaching history and, consequently, the Department staff members never conceptualized the process in problematic terms. The curriculum development process remained a task that must be completed to meet an administrative mandate, and was not considered a useful process to enhance their teaching.

The geography process leader, conversely, viewed the process as a growth opportunity for the teachers involved. She actively encouraged teachers to reflect on past, present and future practice. She viewed the purpose of school-based curriculum development not only as document production but also as a means of professionally empowering teachers. The leader was able to use her facilitative skills to help the Committee overcome the initially negative contextual factors and to produce a sound and useful document.

Facilitative leadership skills seem essential if we are to help teachers develop their own curriculum. The leader of the Geography Committee had a great deal of experience acting as a change agent and had extensive academic training in curriculum as a field of study. Very few teachers who are asked to chair a development committee have similar training. Leading a school-based curriculum group is difficult and we must consider means of training teachers to perform this role.

Before entering into a school-based curriculum development project, a careful analysis should be made of the characteristics of the contextual factors evident at the site. By determining the potential negative factors, facilitators can decrease the detrimental impact of these factors on the project.

Conclusion

As the two case studies have illuminated, school-based curriculum development can be a difficult process for practising teachers for several reasons. The contextual factors interweave throughout the development process and can enhance or impede the project. The necessity of, and the difficulty in, defining the task in problematic terms has also been emphasized. The process is time consuming as participants need time to reflect critically, consider alternatives, deal with the cognitive dissonance, and assimilate new ideas into their personal knowledge. Yet schools often demand that curriculum be developed in a very short time period. If curriculum development is to go beyond a cut and paste of past practice to become a reasoned process facilitative of participant growth, then sufficient time must be allocated to encourage reflection on, and the assimilation of, new ideas. If that time is not available then the curriculum development process might become a rush for the solution without the existence of a well-defined problem.

When curriculum development is conceptualized to include a dimension of school improvement, the process can become very complex and difficult. This is especially true for school-based curriculum development projects as the participants might perceive the task in product terms rather than as a reasoned, reflective process. If the innovation includes a change in curriculum orientations either for the individuals directly involved or the school, then the difficulties are further heightened.

School-based curriculum development involving a substantial change in teaching style or beliefs requires that teachers work collectively, reflect critically on past practice, and accept the philosophical basis of the innovation. Such requirements can be contrary to the subjective world of the teacher as described by Fullan (1982) and must overcome with the state of isolation most teachers experience as described by Lortie (1975). Failure to address these issues can mean the school-based curriculum development process becomes a 'cut and paste' effort that results in a reissuing of past practice.

School-based curriculum development, consequently, must be conceptualized as a professional growth experience for teachers. The individuals facilitating the process must allow sufficient time for teachers to reflect and assimilate the changes included in the innovation. They must conceive of the process not just as a product driven endeavour but must incorporate professional development into the process. Only then will the participants gain the full advantage of their involvement and empower themselves professionally.

Notes

1 Funded by the Social Sciences and Humanities Research Council of Canada, Grant µ410-85-0531, 1987.
2 Pseudonyms are used for the participating teachers and the school.

Chapter 5

United States of America: School Based Curriculum Development in Chester: Revising a Curriculum for the Gifted and Talented

Background Details

The Setting[1]

At one time Chester sat in the midst of cornfields outside a large city in the midwestern United States of America. As has happened elsewhere, the city has recently been expanding and all but engulfs Chester and several other once-separate towns north of the city. These towns are affluent and seem eager to preserve their own identities instead of being seen merely as suburbs of the metropolis. Chester is a fast growing community and school system in Ohio. By 1992, kindergarten through grade 8 enrolment is projected to be 7000 students, with 4000 in high school. Chester can neither be thought of as a blue collar nor white collar community. Perhaps it is best considered a 'silver collar' community in that its residents are typically health professionals and business executives. Homes are large in Chester and sit on spacious, well-groomed grounds, costing $120,000, on the average. Only 0.26 per cent of Chester's residents rent. For people who live in Chester, the American system has worked well, and they want it to work well for their children. People in Chester are proud of their community. Clearly it seems difficult for Chester's teachers (whose average salary is $26,590) to live here unless their spouses also work, but many of Chester's teachers actually do reside here due to double income families.

The Chester Public Schools serve an area of forty-seven square miles in three counties.

National and State Curriculum Policies Affecting Chester

It is important to remember that the United States of America has no formal, national curriculum. Educational matters are the province of state control because matters not considered to be federal are reserved to the states, as stated in Article X of the Constitution of the United States of America:

> The powers not delegated to the United States by the Constitution, nor prohibited by it to the States, are reserved to States respectively, or to the people.

It could be argued that several large textbook companies and companies that develop nationally-normed achievement tests informally constitute a national curriculum, because of their widespread use. For instance, the California Test of Basic Skills and Ginn 720 Reading are currently popularly used achievement tests and reading series throughout the nation, so in a way they constitute a national curriculum. This is not the result of a national policy, however, but the result of school system committees' deciding to adopt them. Since such materials profoundly affect what is taught and learned in schools, these two are currently major shapers of the curriculum.

Each state has curriculum policies. While some of these policies suggest or mandate the content of schooling, others suggest or mandate a process for developing curriculum guides or graded courses of study. Currently, the State where Chester is located does the latter.

To be sure, national initiatives that fund particular areas of the curriculum affect curriculum materials, what teachers teach and therefore what students have an opportunity to learn. However, for the most part, in the United States of America, state policies appear to affect the curriculum more directly and profoundly. This state's policy adopted in 1983, rather than mandating specific content, is primarily a process mandate in that each school district is to develop graded courses of study to prescribe what is to be taught in a given subject or program in its schools. Since 1953, Ohio's Revised Code 3313.60 has served as the legal basis for these courses of study in the state. According to the *Process Model for Courses of Study* of the state (Department of Education [1983:9–11]), the Revised Code, Section 3313.60, specifies subjects which must be taught and establishes specific requirements for some subjects. The following is the text of the statute, effective June, 1980.

> Section 3313.60, Boards of education of county, exempted village, and city school districts shall prescribe a graded course of study

for all schools under their control subject to the approval of the state board of education. In such graded courses of study there shall be included the study of the following subjects:

(A) The language arts, including reading, writing, spelling, oral and written English, and literature.

(B) Geography, the history of the United States and of the state, and national, state and local government in the United States, including a balanced presentation of the relevant contributions to society of men and women of African, Mexican, Puerto Rican, and American Indian descent as well as other ethnic and racial groups in the state and the United States.

(C) Mathematics.

(D) Natural science, including instruction in the conservation of natural resources.

(E) Health education which shall include instruction in the nutritive value of foods, including natural and organically produced foods, the relation of nutrition to health, the use and effects of food additives, and the harmful effects of and legal restrictions against the use of drugs of abuse, alcoholic beverages and tobacco, and venereal disease education, except that upon written request of his parent or guardian, a student shall be excused from taking instruction in venereal disease education.

Minimum Standards

Minimum Standards for Elementary and Secondary Schools, effective September 1, 1983 include requirements regarding course of study. Standards related to courses of study are presented below:

Standards

3301-35-02 Educational Programs

The kindergarten through twelfth grade educational program shall be implemented in accordance with adopted policies which cover paragraphs (A) to (E) of this rule. Board policies shall be available to parents, pupils, and school personnel.

(A) A written philosophy of education and educational goals shall give direction to the educational program and shall provide a basis for daily operations.

   (1) The educational program shall be provided without discrimination on the basis of color, national origin, race, or sex.

   (2) The philosophy of education and educational goals shall

reflect pupil interests and needs identified by broad representation of community, pupils, and staff.

(B) Curriculum and instruction shall be characterized by systematic planning, articulation, implementation, and evaluation.

(1) A course of study shall be adopted for each subject taught. Each course of study shall:

    (i)   comply with the provisions of 3313.60 of the Revised Code;

    (ii) be based on the philosophy of education and educational goals;

    (iii) prescribe what is to be taught;

    (iv) specify subject matter objectives;

    (v) establish a scope and sequence;

    (vi) provide a basis for pupil evaluation.

    (b) Courses of study shall provide for the following topics to be a part of the curriculum: career education, citizenship, human relations education, multicultural education, energy and resource conservation education and instruction in study skills.

    (c) Courses of study shall be reviewed and updated at least once every five years.

(2) Locally developed competency based education programs shall be implemented for English composition, mathematics, and reading.

    (a) Pupil performance objectives shall be established for English composition, mathematics, and reading.

    (b) Provisions shall be made for periodic assessment of pupil performance, including testing at least once in grades one through four, grades five through eight, and grades nine through eleven.

    (c) Guidelines shall be established for the use of assessment results for instruction, evaluation, intervention, guidance and promotion decisions.

    (d) Intervention shall be provided according to pupil needs.

(3) Daily lesson plans shall give direction for instruction and implementation of courses of study.

Such a policy virtually mandates school-based curriculm development, and similar policies exist in several other states as well.

Chronology of Events and Persons Involved

The people involved in this development for the summer of 1988 project included:

B.J. — an elementary school teacher of the gifted
Wilma — an elementary school teacher of the gifted
Rachel — administrator of the gifted program
Leonard[2] — district level coordinator of curriculum and staff development responsible for orchestrating this effort
Mary — a middle school teacher of the gifted
Rhonda — an elementary school teacher of the gifted
Michelle — an elementary school teacher
Terence — an elementary school teacher

As these people spoke about the project, their faces lit up and they gestured. They seem to be 'true believers' in gifted education and their roles in it and seemed to be morally committed to doing the 'right' thing during the summer's deliberations, although as we shall see what constituted the 'right' thing differed for each person.

A timeline of events occurring until the autumn of 1988 for developing the curriculum for the gifted in Chester's schools follows:

September–April 1987 — original curriculum developed
January 1987–May 1988 — ad hoc committee meetings among classroom teachers, teachers of the gifted, a member of the Board of Education and several administrators to discuss common problems. Because of these meetings, the ensuing curriculum revision was needed.
Summer 1988 — curriculum revision

So this case exemplifies school-based curriculum development at the district level brought about by teachers, administrators and parents.

History of the Curriculum Project

While gifted education is not prescribed as a course to be developed in the aforementioned state code, Chester, like many other school systems in the United States of America, developed such a curriculum. The first such venture in Chester occurred in 1987, resulting in a matrix of skills to be taught as well as a set of mandated units about economics, architecture, space, mysteries, law, Disney, ecosystems and old England. The matrix was partly compiled and adapted from a list of State Department of Education recommendations and objectives contained in the district's other graded courses of study, specifically language arts, social studies and science.

Almost immediately, several curricular issues ensued. One was teachers' differential knowledge of these units. For example, Wilma teaches in the elementary gifted program. In her view:

> You have to know economics before you can teach it. I had a list of goals and objectives for the unit and boxes of materials to pull from, but no meat because I didn't know economics. As a course of survival, I began to meet with Rachel, who knew economics. I had a feeling of incompetence, though. Here I am in my *ninth* year of teaching, *six* in gifted education in a variety of schools, socioeconomically! But there were certain expectations here and I had to work hard to get to them. I had nothing to fall back on merely because I didn't know economics.

Other issues leading to the revision concerned the schedule for gifted education, community relations, a lack of materials, space for teaching, articulation of the program among elementary, middle and senior high schools (for example, whether isolated grammar lessons should be taught), and relations with regular classroom programs. About the schedule, B.J. (an elementary school teacher of the gifted) said, 'Before we revised the curriculum, we'd teach at one school, and at the end of five weeks we had to move to our other school.'

At this point, an ad hoc committee began meeting and continued to meet for five months, ultimately requiring that the program be initiated in fourth grade (rather than second), which led to the curriculum revision that occurred for eleven days during the summer of 1988.

It is not surprising that the beginning of the curriculum development meetings witnesses these problems boiling out in deliberations even though the ad hoc committee had aired issues during the 1987/88 school year. The early deliberations are characterized by a clarification of some of the problems being faced:

June 7 1988: Gifted GCOS Committee Meeting

Leonard: Michelle's concern is a concern I share. She's saying if we are mandated (Mary, we're talking about the grammar issue. Here's a copy of the minutes.) the issues here are that we have received a mandate from the Board of Education to give students a comprehensive grammar proficiency test at the middle school level. Because of this order, it's relatively counter productive and contradictory to what we're trying to do in language arts education district-wide and that is writing process. Although the Language Arts Graded Course of Study does prescribe the teaching of grammar, it does so as a tool for editing.

Michelle: Right! It's not isolated.

Leonard: This mandate is to be that kind of thing.

Leonard: It came out of a board member's request for a Board Curriculum Committee meeting.

Michelle: You mean at the last Board meeting or something?

Leonard: No. Not exactly. All year long representatives for the Board have been attending these curriculum meetings have been expressing concerns about the secondary gifted program. So finally we asked, 'What are these concerns?' And the two Board of Education representatives on the sub-committee, who speak on behalf of the community, and then fellow Board members, . . .

Mary: It's interesting. One thing that came out that they wished. I would pretest grammar. It's in our plans.

Leonard: Right! And you said that at the last meeting too — you said the same thing . . .

I think the Board wants to make teachers more aware of the concern that students need more formal instruction in grammar. So, you at the middle school need to articulate better to your students and parents that we are giving them grammar proficiency tests to determine where they are in grammar and that I, as a teacher, will provide independent work or group activities if need be in the areas that are deficient.

Wilma: Right, in the case of group work, it's the gifted kind of syndrome coming out. The kids told me we don't want grammar; we don't need it. Being new to the district, I read the graded course of study as grammar being in there and that I need to teach it — whether it was misinterpreted or not. I thought this was part of my job. So, I went ahead with it and I may have 6 students out of 100 who did not do well in the proficiency tests. I didn't think that was not something I wanted to send home — such a weakness — and I would take care of it — get them up to par — and continue onward . . .

Michelle: This is part of a much larger philosophical problem and I think it needs to be put on hold and let language arts graded course of study people handle it. I think it's a part of the problem.

Michelle: And I know of those two members. I know how each one feels about grammar. But there lies the challenge through the year. We have to . . .

Leonard: Yes. It's a matter, too, of educating people about what the writing process is all about.

Michelle: Something that's never done . . .

Mary: Yes, it's more of a middle school type problem and you are all here.

Michelle: Leonard, my point is that I don't want something to go down here and have what we do be in violation of some other graded course of study. Nor do I want us to be locked into something . . .

Mary: I want to be aware of what you want from me.

Leonard: What we could do is just — to satisfy this request — and since you basically do it anyway — we'll look at what you do and illustrate it to the Board — and say this is our response to what you want us to do. But Michelle is bringing up an important philosophical question — this is what curriculum-building is all about — we have prescribed curriculum — but how it's interpreted and how it's taught — is up to various forces — sometimes those are not in our power to control. Students determine the curriculum — obviously in gifted ed. this is essential — but you can see here community expectations influencing the written curriculum. This type of thing happens in every curricular area. What we need to do — I tried to set the stage for this at our preliminary meeting — is to respond to outside forces that we are listening to them. It would be in our best interest to say to the Board members who are interested in what we are doing — you might not think it appropriate — but the research clearly indicates that grammar studied in isolation has little to do with composition. But getting people to understand this takes a while — not even the entire teaching staff accepts this — let alone the community-at-large. What's happening, you see, you at the middle school are held accountable for what some of the high school English teachers expect . . .

Mary: And this is what I've gone by this year. I've heard feedback from the high school.

These problems and frustrations set the tone and formed a subtext for much of the work of the group, although another subtext concerned the strong personalities of members of the curriculum development team. Of them, B.J. says:

During the summer, human dynamics were involved — a lot of personalities, *strong* reasons why people cling to an idea: difficulty with change, it's the only thing they know . . . I came to the point of wondering what's crucial. I fought for those things.

Rhonda reflects, 'We had strong personalities there . . . *opinionated*, strong philosophies'.

Mary echoes a theme of conflict among dedicated professionals when she reflects:

The stress level and flexibility of different people really came into play. There was a lot of tugging and pulling, but tension — tension can be positive sometimes, you know? — but we met our goal of curriculum development. I wanted certain skills taught in elementary school. I'm not a hard pusher, but firm. I wanted a bibliography form to be taught in research skills in elementary. But me — I'm a quiet deliberator.

Quite possibly, this situation has been overly emphasized as teachers reflected on the curriculum development process. It may be a human phenomenon to recall our lives' stories in terms of points of conflict. A novel is not a good story without some conflict; one about fields of clover or peaches and cream would not be seen as a serious novel. Similarly, when we tell the stories of our lives, we might organize them around points of conflict. However, in the deliberations themselves we can see these conflicts when they converse about what (and whether) to mandate particular skills:

Rhonda: You know what's going to happen? We, at either the 4th or 5th grade, are going to have to emphasize an objective. And I don't agree with that.

Rachel: How about if elementary look at all the objectives — everything under Program Objective I and star for 4th or 5th grade those that they think should be starred — where you use it the most.

Mary: On the other hand, Rachel, there are some of these areas where I feel an objective is emphasized at 6th, 7th and 8th grade level.

Leonard: Maybe we are attempting to do the impossible. Maybe we should forget a matrix and just list the skills — and through the unit planning blueprint indicate where you're going to teach those objectives. For example, in the state model all they do is prescribe objectives. These are objectives for critical thinking or whatever — your job as a gifted teacher is to take the objectives and then plug them in to what you are doing.

Michelle: . . . it puts it on a continuum.

Rachel: And it gives us a scope and sequence.

Leonard: Another concern is how are you going to know which Matrix skills will be emphasized if you don't know what units you will be teaching.

Rhonda: Because these are — this is a scope and sequence — they are generic things for gifted education — creative problem solving that is going to exist in the 4th and 5th grades.

Mary: . . . and the maturity of the child at a given level.

Rhonda: Right, however, you've brought up a really good point — with everyone of those there is a very specific thing when we get into research — how do we know when we are going to put our trust on research?

Jean: Look at Objective H. Students will differentiate. C'mon guys, you can tell them all you want in elementary school — but seriously.

Wilma: Why don't we plan to emphasize all of those at the 4th

> grade or at the 5th grade? And somewhere in the middle school and somewhere at the high school. So we have to get together and decide what we want to emphasize where.

Leonard: What do you want to do? How should we go about this? Ultimately, we all have to do this together. Are you making a motion to reconvene the sub-committees?

Jean: Ok here's the other option. Take down the information that Mary and I have and let them look over it again tonight and come back in and hash it out again — that's the only other option we have.

So, we can envision this symphony of curriculum development here with violins playing a constant percussive undertone (the violins of practical problems these teachers faced), and individual arias or solos being performed (about the facet of the curriculum for which they argued) that were sometimes discordant with each other's solos. Nonetheless, all of these teachers were pleased with the curriculum they developed, although each believed that others (presumable of a different philosophy) were probably unhappy with it. Perhaps, this is because each soloist listened more to her or his own soloes than to anyone else's. Perhaps this is also why the curriculum now emphasizes the skills to be taught rather than specific content of individual units, so when visited, Wilma was teaching about archaeology and Rachel about inventions. Yet, the curriculum does not look like an ungainly unbelievable creature designed by a committee, nor does the product of deliberations resemble the discordant symphony of the process used to develop this curriculum.

In the absence of an ongoing community of enquiring professionals, when they do meet infrequently, perhaps we can expect strong opinions and difficulties in working together for any group. Added to the frustration with the practical problems with the curriculum being revised, it is no wonder that strong positions were held by individuals. Perhaps such dogmatism can occur as the result of not having other adults with whom to discuss practice on an ongoing process, so goals and practices weren't publicly questioned, compared or deliberated about. In isolation, teachers reflect about their own practice and may not do so as critically as would occur within a community of dedicated professionals. In isolation teachers can come to believe they're right because what they do appears to be working, so it's difficult to see why everyone shouldn't do the same thing. Moreover, they knew this curriculum was going to control their actions to a certain extent, so decisions appearing in the written document were important, for they knew from personal experience that uncomfortable and unworkable constraints on their practice could result (such as an unworkable involved schedule or having to teach a unit whose content they did not know); they had a vested interest in improving the curriculum.

Emerging Patterns and Issues

The problem preoccupying the Chester team was the scope and sequence they were revising. The content focus and emphasis of objective across different grades lay at the heart of their deliberations. We can look at these deliberations as consisting of several phases: conversation, confrontation and consolidation. Let's examine each in greater detail.

Conversation

At this stage, the Chester teachers deliberated about what was currently taught and learned in gifted education, and what learning expectations seemed to be appropriate or inappropriate. When the gifted education specialists in Chester had the opportunity to meet with the regular education teachers many discoveries and revelations ensued. During this process, the most basic questions about the scope and sequence in use for gifted education in the district arose. (At what grade do you introduce research writing? Do you do much with oral speaking in Grade 6? Where in the curriculum do you introduce self-awareness skills?) In so doing, the focus of the curriculum team's work was on the formal, written curriculum. Consequently, the group invariably attempted to anchor the formal curriculum to an understanding of what actually was in the hearts and minds of the teachers and therefore transpired in the district.

It made sense for teachers to share with each other and clarify current practice in their field in this manner. For one thing, the Chester teachers had a definite need to exchange perceptions, beliefs, and feelings about the curriculum they were presently teaching. If the team members did not have the opportunity to make explicit their assumptions about the scope and sequence they were currently using, it would not have been impossible for them to interpret and 'size up' proposals for innovation — either from scholarly literature or from reform-minded colleagues.

If this preliminary phase of conversation and clarification were skipped, the team members might have responded to new ideas by saying, 'Yes, we already do that.' It is easy to think our actual practice conforms to the 'ideal' when our understanding of our own practices is implicit and vague. One reason for spending time in making current practice explicit is to provide a firm basis for assessing the extent of change called for in proposals for curriculum improvement.

Confrontation

Although perhaps overly dramatic, the term 'confrontation' is used here to refer to the process of facing head-on recommendations for curriculum change. For the Chester group, a series of such recommendations had been suggested by a special ad hoc committee convened to review the gifted education curriculum. It was the team's task, then, to sift through the recommendations in an effort to determine how they might be manifested in the revised curriculum. Teaching writing as a process, for example, has become the *leitmotiv* of the district's instructional improvement projects in language arts. This meant that learning objectives in the Gifted Education Graded Course of Study placed considerable emphasis on such aspects as prewriting, planning, drafting, peer editing, rewriting, etc. At the same time, it was suggested that the gifted education program should place some attention on grammar instruction. The Chester team thus had the difficult task of integrating instructional objectives in sentence structure and grammar with the more fundamental aspects of thinking and communicating. Another aspect of 'confrontation' that the Chester group encountered involved the issue of grade-level sequencing in their curriculum. Curriculum scholars and subject matter specialists generally are hesitant to suggest what should be taught at particular grade levels, because given the large variation in individual growth and development that can be readily observed in all areas of learning, talk about a formal, grade-related sequence of learning seems artificial and constraining. However, while nobody wants to be bound to a fully prescribed lock-step sequence, members of the Chester curriculum team were at times disappointed that theory and research contained few firm guidelines for defining growth in a particular gifted skill from one year to the next.

Consolidation

Once the Chester team members had the opportunity to converse about and clarify current curriculum patterns in the district, they needed time to consolidate what they had discussed, and reach agreements about specific aspects of the curriculum. This process entailed bringing together the old and the new, and establishing areas of particular emphasis and priority in the curriculum. One principle that guided the group during this consolidation phase was the idea that 'more is not necessarily better'. Ultimately the team decided that a curriculum that prescribed in depth a reasonable small number of essential skills and concepts was preferred over one that covered in a superficial way a wide range of content. Thus, the Chester team devoted much time determining the essential core of their curriculum, and discarded objectives they considered to be of secondary or peripheral importance.

Because the people who developed the curriculum were also the teachers who taught it, they knew the curriculum very well by the time they finished the revision. Through this process of deliberating about the content, the teachers most closely involved with teaching the gifted students in Chester learned the curriculum intimately. As a result, the skills to be taught are not merely words on 168 pages of paper, but rather have life and meaning. Each person seems to have a sense of ownership of the document, for each can see his or her 'item worth fighting for' in the document. Further, the regular classroom teachers who engaged in the process understand the document and as a result can communicate clearly with their constituents, which had previously been concerns.

Page 19 further clarifies the program:

> Chester's Gifted and Talented Program is designed to provide differentiated educational and high school mentorship experiences for identified, academically able students. It is qualitatively different from other curricular offerings. This program provides both a solid cognitive foundation for learning as well as opportunities for creativity and independent study.

The remainder of the document describes how gifted students are identified and details the scope and sequence in a matrix indicating grade levels where the skills are to be given special emphasis.

It is clear from this case that curriculum development is messier than many describe because people were involved who bring with them their strong commitments. The people involved here were polite, but firmly committed to particular ideas. As these commitments were deliberated about, people came to understand their own and others' commitments more clearly and a group position resulted.

Page 6 of the curriculum development they wrote describes the nature of gifted education in Chester:

> The content of the graded course of study scope and sequence is organized according to the major areas of emphasis determined by enrichment teachers, namely, the acquisition of thinking, skills and processes, research skills, interpersonal/intrapersonal relationship skills, and communication skills and concepts.

Page 13 goes on to state:

> The program provides necessary experiences and options for identified, academically able students. In all cases, these experiences will provide opportunities for higher level thought processes. The program helps students to develop and refine their ability to think at the higher levels of the cognitive domain (i.e., analysis, synthesis, evaluation), as well as develop creative and problem solving skills.

On page 17 of the same document, the program is further overviewed:

> At the primary elementary level (2–3), the Program provides direct service to identified students, which establishes cognitive experiences for extension of regular curriculum as well as opportunities for creativity and problem solving.

> At the intermediate level (4–5), the program provides a differentiated program for identified students through topic seminars in social studies and science, taught in five-week cycles.

> At the secondary level (6–8), identified and academically able students are provided with a differentiated program. This program offers opportunities for the identified students to pursue curriculum experiences to meet the unique intellectual, social and personal needs of each student.

> At the HS level (9–12), identified students are offered topic seminars as a flexible class designed around selected topics. In addition, the students are offered a variety of shadowing experiences within the private sector to be followed by qualified mentorship opportunities.

When administrators begin to organize a local curriculum development project, one of the more important decisions concerns personnel.

One way to designate the developers would be to appoint like-minded people who presumably could efficiently and quickly list goals, write a philosophy and iron out details. Another way, is to appoint the most prominent actors and recognize that they may have trouble reaching agreement, but that in the process of deliberating many important ideas will be brought to light, examined and argued over. Each position then can have its warts rubbed off as people strive for resolution of problems despite the personal strife involved. This second process may not seem as efficient as people consume much time in the deliberations and may not follow a rational sequence in their work as they deliberate about a matter, seem to drop it and turn to another one only to return to the previous one. The result may be a rich curriculum with great depth, and the deliberations may serve to educate all about their own positions and the positions of others involved. In this case, the deliberators say they now know their colleagues very well as about the curriculum itself. Mary said:

> I've been here a short time. I knew Rachel [the coordinator] and knew she and I agreed about some things. But it was interesting to see where everyone else was coming from. I needed to get to know the gifted educators I work with as well as the eight team leaders. Here in the middle school I needed to know what they all expected of me so I could mold somewhat to fit into the focus here in Chester. The deliberations were healthy.

In Chester, these learnings may be particularly helpful because these educators seem likely to remain with the Chester schools for quite some time. Stability of a program seems to be threatened when widespread, rapid turnover occurs, but it seems unlikely to occur in Chester. So, between that and the development of what appears to be a workable curriculum, things seem auspicious for gifted education in Chester.

One way of interpreting practical problems is to note the absence of an overall conceptual design of the curriculum. When each graded course of study is developed separately by discipline (as mandated by the state), the separate pieces may not fit together well; like tektonic plates they may grind and bump into each other yielding earthquakes in the geologic world and the sorts of practical problems experienced here in the schooling world. Developing individual programs — noteworthy though they may be — in the absence of a plan for the grand scheme of the curriculum may cause some of those programs that are noteworthy to run into problems. The state's curriculum policy mandates the development of a graded course of study for each discipline; this mandate may lead Chester and other school systems not to design an overall scheme for the curriculum but rather to focus on each part. We can envision someone cooking dinner who makes each dish superbly but lacking an overall conception for the dinner failing to serve an excellent meal because neither carrots in butter and thyme nor the salad-based with curry mayonnaise goes well with cheese enchiladas. This is further true in selecting clothes in an outfit, or furnishings for a room, which must be harmonious to create the effect one desires.

For self-contained elementary school classrooms this may not be as problematic as in cases where students are pulled out of class to attend other classes and where students exchange classes. In self-contained classrooms, a teacher filters all of the separate courses of study and has the opportunity to weave common threads through them and to encourage students to do so, but in the other cases the weaving may not occur and made more difficult for students to do because of large differences among the separate courses.

This has usually been done by administrators writing a policy about the design of the curriculum, but this could also be treated through staff meetings where teachers and administrators deliberated to discuss and come to develop and thereby understand the common mission of their school. Teachers could further examine the extent to which various levels of schools in the system fit together so the elementary and secondary schools curricula are not at odds with one another. In this manner, teachers' personal understandings would become an aspect of how each filtered the graded course of study for her or his field, and some of these understandings would be held in common because of the group's deliberations, and curriculum coherence would be a likely result. However, in the absence of either a curriculum design conceiving of the nature of content of schooling and the absence of the practice of faculty deliberation about it, the pieces of the curriculum may well remain separate and glitches such as the ones witnessed here continue to occur.

The absence of such an overall conceptualization permits courses such as gifted education, in this case, and special education to be seen as peripheral, and hence not an integral part of what is to occur in Chester schools. As a result, problems arise such as a lack of space, lack of appropriate materials and so forth. If teachers and administrators saw it as an important aspect of the mission of Chester's schools, the problems would be treated as part of a whole.

These teachers say they are happy or comfortable with the curriculum they developed, although they do not believe everyone is. Margaret reported that in her view, 'most of the classroom teachers are pleased because we have something we can put our hands on about what's happening'.

Notes

1 The city's name and all others have been changed to preserve anonymity. In addition, incidental details about people such as approximate age and appearance have been changed for this purpose.
2 'Leonard' also helped gather data for this case and critiqued facts presented and interpretations offered.

Chapter 6

United Kingdom: Managing Curriculum Development at Branston School and Community College

The SBCD activity described in this chapter was TRIST (Technical Related In-Service Training) funded, though not all the projects within it were concerned with technical and vocational education. Indeed this school-based curriculum development scheme is typical of many which have been funded under TRIST and provides an example of the ways in which local education authorities and schools still are able to exercise their own judgments to support what they consider educationally valuable activities within imposed funding frameworks — particularly those which promote more active, student-centred curriculum development. Although the work described in the chapter is particular to one secondary school in Lincolnshire, England, it is typical of many throughout England now that financial devolution of INSET funds is occurring under the Local Authorities Training Grants Scheme (LEATGS) described in chapter 1. This, and the changes in teachers' conditions of service, has caused a shift in the locus and focus of professional development work towards on-site, school-centred development work. The chapter raises issues of learning and change, and the management of school-based curriculum and professional development which are fundamental to all who are engaged in this work.

The chapter is divided into four sections. The first provides the social setting for the scheme, its historical context and purpose within the school development plans. The second section provides a summary of the planning, processes and outcomes of the three school-based curriculum development projects, principally from the participants' viewpoints. The third section provides a formative evaluation of the scheme itself; and the fourth section focusses particularly on the management of school-based curriculum and professional development which embodies principles and practices of action research.

Background Details

The study covers the period September 1986 to December 1987. During this time five separate projects were undertaken by different groups of teachers on a voluntary basis. Three of these are reported in this chapter. The numbers of teachers involved constituted almost half of the total school teaching staff of seventy-three. Each group had a leader who was allocated two periods each week off timetable, and the groups themselves were allocated between ten and twenty days of supply cover to enable members to conduct their investigations. The key feature which underpinned the scheme was that:

> teachers themselves can be active in promoting changes of style or content which will lead to significant developments across the curriculum. (Branston, 1986)

This view of teachers as experts represents an assertion by the Principal of the school and those who supported his initiative — taken only months after arriving at the school — of 'the creative power inherent in the group of teacher colleagues' in his school (Schmuck and Schmuck, 1974). The involvement of teachers in a 'generative' role is both a valuing of their capacities to (actively) evaluate and design as well as to deliver the curriculum and of their resistance to (passively) implement other people's ideas. This valuing has practical implications for all those in positions of management who have line responsibility for curriculum development and reform.

Significantly, monitoring and evaluation processes were built into the scheme from its inception. Traditionally, most of the resources and effort to promote curriculum and teacher development have been concentrated on the initiation and developmental stages themselves, and little, if any, have been devoted to monitoring (i.e., the systematic collect of information) and evaluation (i.e., making judgments, whether formative or summative, based upon information collected). The scheme avoided this temptation in two ways.

(i) *Internal monitoring* — First, although the principal transferred ownership in the ways described above, he continued an involvement in the work through the scheme overall coordinator who had the explicit responsibility of reporting back to him, 'so that I can account to the MSC and the LEA' (Branston, 1986b) and through 'adcom' (the Academic Development Committee) members of whom played a role in the projects as individuals, and who were also to be available 'when plans for possible implementation are thrown up for discussion' (*ibid*).

(ii) *External evaluation* — In addition to internal monitoring, one condition of LEA support was that 'full documentation and evaluation' (Branston, 1986a) would be ensured. The 'launch pack' had already expressed the Principal's perceived need for, 'a major evaluation by a significant credible outsider . . . It is extremely important that when we succeed we have "proof" . . . We also need sympathetic outsiders to tell us what is happening as we go along . . . People who will *really* listen to us as we try to manage our own INSET and school development, and later be able to report our feelings as people, our perceptions as professionals, our achievements as educators . . .' (*ibid*). The Staff Bulletin (Branston, 1986b) reported further that an external evaluation would provide the Branston scheme with the necessary status and support for the 'teachers-as-experts' approach to curriculum development.

> Fundamentally, the most important evaluations of professional services are those conducted (or commissioned) by the professionals themselves . . . (Stufflebeam and Shinkfield, 1985)

It is important at this point to define more precisely the role of the external evaluator in this school-based curriculum development work. Clearly, he/she cannot be 'the' authority, since every member of every project group is an authority within the teacher-as-expert model. His/her role is to 'objectify' the conditions, purposes, processes and outcomes of the projects by documenting the perceptions, over time, of those who are involved directly and indirectly. In order to achieve an evaluation which is derived from the cultural perspective of the participants, the evaluator has to seek inside information and respect indigenous definitions and values. This kind of evaluation, 'tries to define how people see things from within' (House, 1981). It is thus qualitative, placing 'literacy above numeracy' (Stufflebeam and Shinkfield, 1985). Its purpose is to provide feedback to participants in the particular projects, other staff in the school, management and others responsible for the management of school-based professional and curriculum development. It is collaborative rather than hierarchical, relying upon the collection, interpretation and validation (by the participants) of information through documents, observation, and face-to-face interviews. The evaluator must thus establish credibility by encouraging the creation of a climate of openness and trust with each of the individuals with whom he/she works. Essentially, he/she also has an investment in, and commitment to, the professional growth of teachers, the improvement of schools in general, and teaching and learning in particular. The assumption here is that outside experts who 'know best' cannot easily improve schools and teaching. Indeed:

This trend in thinking that there surely is someone somewhere who knows best and can decide for one is a form of self-domination that is profoundly ironic (and is) destined to promote infantilisation of teachers rather than secure their growth. (Bell, 1985)

Two major themes will be addressed in the chapter. The first concerns the extent to which the projects 'succeeded' in terms of the criteria established at the outset; and the second concerns the management of school-based curriculum and professional development — which is of increasing concern in relation to the developing support within national and local government structures for work which is school-based.

The School

Branston School and Community College is situated in the village of Branston some four miles from the centre of Lincoln. The school catchment is widespread and includes several villages, many of which have experienced considerable growth in recent years as the dormitory function of the area has grown. The student intake is, therefore, of a broad social mix, but predominantly rural. Most students are 'bused' in and out of school. Branston is an 11–18-year-old mixed comprehensive school of some 1200 students which include a sixth-form of 125 and an integrated county unit for students with moderate learning difficulties. Staffing totals seventy-three teachers (including the Principal, two Deputies and two senior teachers). The school is largely purpose built and includes a sports complex with sports hall, swimming pool and youth wing, and specialist provision for the sixth form, the special unit and areas of curriculum provision including business studies, computer studies, drama, art, science, craft design and technology, music, languages and home economics. The published aims of the school are

> to provide for every student an equal opportunity to attain his or her fullest personal development; to provide students with the confidence and maturity to handle whatever life may have in store; to provide, through the resources of our College, a welcoming setting for a varied programme of community activities; to encourage good home–school relationships; and to foster the fullest professional development of staff.

In *year 1* students with the possible exception of those identified as having special educational needs enjoy a common curriculum experience. In *year 2* an opportunity is given to students to add media studies or a second foreign language to their programme and *year 3* continues the same pattern. In *years 4 and 5* students follow a core curriculum of physical education, personal and social education, English, mathematics, a science and a technical/creative subject. French or German form part of the core for the great majority and the study programme for all students is completed by four option choices at examination or non-examination level.

The sixth-form curriculum offers a general education 'core', opportunities for work and community experience and examination subjects at General Certificate of Secondary Education (GCSE), Certificate of Extended Education (CEE) and 'A' level, and a Certificate in Prevocational Education (CPVE) with business studies and caring for people clusters. With the exception of a very small group of students who have identified special educational needs, first year students (11-year-olds) are placed in mixed ability teaching groups. Second year students are divided into two similar populations; within each of these there is the facility for arrangement of teaching groups according to department wishes. In the third year the second year pattern is continued. Fourth and fifth year students are divided into half-year blocks for core subjects and are organized for options according to the demands of individual subject areas. The sixth-form is open to all students of the school. Students with moderate learning difficulties usually join the integrated unit at 11. They integrate socially within the house organization and, where appropriate, within teaching groups in the spirit of the Warnock Report (DES, 1987b) and the 1981 Act. These students come from a wider than the normal catchment area.

When the project began pupils in years 1–5 were organized pastorally in six houses, each led by a Head of House. Nine house tutors in each house were responsible for the social and educational welfare of a 'family group' of approximately twenty pupils in all-age tutor groups. The range of social, cultural and sporting activities within the school was predominantly house based. This system was changed in 1987 to a horizontal year pattern principally to facilitate the introduction of a more coherent scheme of tutoral activity throughout the school.

The senior management team of the School and Community College comprises the Principal, two Deputy Heads and currently three senior teachers. Branston enjoys the support of a 'Friends' organization which embraces all strands of the College structure.

In the spring term of 1986, the Principal of the School, as a result of meetings which he had initiated with the Director of Education, the Chief Inspector of Schools and the local TRIST Director, and following a paper which he had written in support of school-based curriculum development, called a full staff meeting in school time. At this meeting support was sought and given for a written submission to TRIST and the LEA of a scheme for curriculum development which indicated both 'the Principal's perception of major areas for future development and his belief in Branston teachers as their own experts' (Branston, 1986a). The Principal wrote the detailed submission which was approved both by the Academic Board, Heads of House and the Governing Body of the School. The submission gained support as 'a special pilot scheme to assess the effectiveness of timetabled INSET as a model for replication in the future . . .' (*ibid.*). At this stage (May 1986) the Principal issued a 'Launch Pack' informing all staff that the scheme had gained financial support, outlining the rationale and methodology of the scheme, and seeking responses from individuals to their involvement in five project areas; three of which are reported below.

Project Areas

1 The Curriculum (to become known as Curriculum Descriptions).
2 Teacher Research into Classroom Phenomena (to become known as Learning about Learning).
3 The Role of the Tutor/Tutorial Structures, styles activities.

Teachers were asked to indicate their desired involvement in one or more of the project areas at one of six levels:

LEVEL OF INVOLVEMENT (tick the box nearest to your present wishes)

1 *No* involvement — on reflection the scheme is unsound.

2 No involvement in 1986/7. Too many priorities this year, but count me a sympathetic non-participant.

3 *Some* involvement — (am interested in hearing speakers, whether colleagues or outsiders, and in reading reports etc., but not in group membership, discussing, writing or visiting other institutions).

4 *Significant* involvement (interested in hearing speakers, considering reports and issues, exploring issues as a member of a group, possibly helping write brief reports, possibly suggesting INSET activities, possibly visiting other institutions. Prepared to set work for supply teacher on one or more occasions next year if

the group requests me to undertake a task for them, so I can take time out.

5 *Major* involvement (interested in co-ordinating the work or findings of a group, and playing a leading role in the tasks listed in 4 above, possibly organizing outside visits, speakers in, ensuring colleagues' work is coordinated, written up and disseminated to group bodies such as Adcom, Academic Board, Heads of House, staff meetings. etc.). Willing to accept one–two periods reduction in class-contact (if timetabler can manage) in order to undertake research or team-leadership role.

6 *Ultimate* involvement (willing to eat, drink and sleep research and development, freely to give up the hours between 4–10 p.m. each night, if necessary, marking books before breakfast in order to keep up. Able to vow, as the Good Lord is my witness, that I will earn the professional staff at Branston a national reputation for pioneering work in school-based INSET, willing to sacrifice . . . (*ibid.*)

A staff bulletin posted at the end of June recorded that fifty-three staff (80 per cent of the full-time teaching staff) had responded and that, of these, 20 per cent had sought 'major' involvement (5 above), 60 per cent for 'significant' involvement (4 above) and 20 per cent for 'some' involvement (3 above). The response had been so great that the Principal was moved to report that, 'the resources we have will be stretched' (Branston, 1986b). The areas for investigation were selected by the Principal and agreed by the Academic Board prior to being 'offered' to the staff of the school; and the following criteria were established:

(a) projects should centre on an important school issue (of curriculum or learning styles, and related organizational/structural implications);

(b) projects should be collaborative. Participation in them, the process, should be regarded as an important outcome in itself, as a way of supporting the view that school self-analyses and self-renewal are key aspects of a teacher's professionality;

(c) projects should lead to, or clearly prepare for, an actual change, or the central aim of TRIST proposal will not be achieved;

(d) project teams should be deliberately and clearly linked to the normal, on-going processes and bodies which in theory 'manage' curriculum maintenance and review (eg. Academic Board or Heads of House or staff conferences) so that the danger of TRIST isolation is avoided, and so that the proposal has maximum status and impact. Every effort should be made to relate TRIST projects to other aspects of school development, including other school INSET, secondments, departmental curriculum development etc;

(e) projects should clearly relate, immediately or less directly, but always, to classroom interactions. The stimulation of direct consideration of, or research into, what happens at the point of learning should be an aim. Teachers should be encouraged to become their own researchers into classroom phenomena. (Branston, 1986)

Those who had expressed interest in team membership/coordinator roles (and whose chosen topics fell within the TRIST range) were approached and the staff common room bulletin indicated which individuals had been selected. This was a significant moment in the history of the development of the scheme, since it not only marked its practical launch — only six months after its inception — but also emphasized management support for principles of ownership and collaborative participation through the ways in which the process was organized. First, there was a deliberate move by the Principal to distance himself from his initial 'ownership' of the scheme by placing control of its development in the hands of the individual project leaders (almost all of whom had 'middle management' positions in the school) and by appointing an overall coordinator whose role was 'to liaise with the teams and leaders, facilitate whatever they plan to do, promote the feedback from each project to everybody else, and keep an eye on the submission criteria . . .' (Branston, 1986b). Second, within this organizational structure, his intention that all participants should feel ownership was clearly indicated:

Needless to say, the title 'team-leader' implies nothing about where the ideas, plans for development come from. He/she is simply the focus/coordinator of the team effort . . . Lists of interested colleagues can go to co-ordinators, so expect to be approached by them this term or early next, or approach them first . . . (*ibid.*)

The projects, it seemed, were to be pursued by communities of equals and success would therefore be the result of collaboration. Third, support was to be provided for all participants:

> It would be good to think that every team member could have at
> least one day off timetable on behalf of the group during 1986–87.
> Probably the best way to organize resources is to allow each group
> its own supply day budget, and let people concerned decide as
> they go along how to spend it . . . (*ibid.*)

Thus was the Branston scheme launched, and already the achievements were notable, for the broader educational and political contexts
pertaining were not conducive to the kind of curriculum development
which has teachers centrally and actively involved. At its inception, for
example, teachers' professional associations were in dispute with the
government policy and were 'working to rule' (This dispute was resolved
in time for the start of the project proper in September 1986.) The
teaching profession as a whole had perceived itself to be under attack
since 1975 with the launch of Prime Minister Callaghan's 'Ruskin'
Speech (Day, 1986), and new initiatives concerning teachers' conditions
of service and the 'National Curriculum' were being launched.

Against this wider social context, however, was the view of the
overall project coordinator that:

> The climate in the school is good for this kind of action research.
> It's right for this school at this stage in its development . . . it's
> got a tradition for progressiveness and forward thinking. Here is
> a project which is central in that it is going to look at curriculum
> and curriculum delivery, and this is what many staff think their
> schools should be addressing themselves to now . . . in the light
> of all the initiatives and comments that have been made about
> school in recent years.

The school had a recent history of school-based curriculum development. Three years previously three voluntary study groups had been
formed through the initiatives of the previous (newly-appointed) Principal and Vice Principal to engage in cross-curriculum review. They had
met after school over the course of a year, and then submitted their
reports. However, the national industrial action by teachers had, in
effect, hindered implementation of the recommendations contained in
the reports, so that, for some members of staff, the exercise had been
unproductive. The risks of embarking upon this new enterprise were all
too clear, and during an interview conducted a year later, the Principal
recollected his feelings:

> I did it because I believed in it, but it felt to me at times very very
> high risk . . . it was in the middle of industrial action . . . it felt
> like leaving myself very vulnerable indeed . . .

The Branston Scheme in Action — Teachers as Experts: Teachers as Researchers

This section contains brief descriptions of, and comments upon, each of three projects. These are based upon attendance at, and documentation of, meetings, and data gathered through tape recorded interviews with project participants and non-participants during the autumn, spring and summer terms of the projects themselves, and during the following autumn term when preparation for the dissemination of the findings occurred. All the work was innovatory.

Following the summary descriptions of the projects the extent to which the specific criteria described previously were met will be discussed within a general consideration of teacher learning and change, and the management of school based curriculum development.

Curriculum Descriptions Group

All teachers are concerned with the curriculum. It's fundamental to what we do . . . What we all do is to close our classroom door and shut the school out . . .

The group of six teachers from across the disciplines led by the then Head of the English Department, aimed to produce a 'summary of the curriculum offered to Branston pupils, such that all staff could gain some insight into the experiences children were receiving in areas other than personal specialisms' (Williams, 1987).

The project was divided into two areas:

(a) discovering what the curriculum is, and how it is delivered;
(b) investigating a means of presenting a description of the whole curriculum in a comparatively immediate and accessible form.

The group had a total of twenty days of supply cover for its researches and meetings. During term 1 of the project members devised a questionnaire, based upon elements of learning identified in *Curriculum Matters 2* (DES, 1985). This was approved by Heads of Department and then administered to all staff who taught first year (11-year-old) pupils. The questionnaire format was adopted as being 'the most expedient means of soliciting information from a comparatively large number of subject areas' (Williams, 1987). The intention was to discover and describe the framework of the curriculum, what overlap of subject areas and interests, and what complementary material and approaches were present.

A further intention (not realized) was that the questionnaire be used as the basic model for analyses of other year curricula (TRIST Team Leaders Meeting Notes, 10 December 1986). Despite doubts as to its adequacy the questionnaire results did provide the desired base for analyses and description.

Term 2 was spent in pupil pursuits in order to 'gather a flavour of the curriculum on offer'. In this exercise five members of the group observed the same class of first year pupils on each day of the same week in order to gain an overview of curriculum in action. Five viewpoints were felt to be of value — despite the recognition that there would not be a single conformity of view. Because the group had decided to describe, rather than interpret, only the overt curriculum was recorded. It was recognized also that there would 'probably be distortions in any single week'. Teaching purposes were taken into account, activities in lessons were recorded sequentially and timings were taken. In addition, pupils were interviewed. The results were analyzed and discussed and provided the information for a display which was to form the centre piece of a presentation designed to disseminate the group's findings. The group worked on the displays during term 3 and presented the results in terms 1 and 2 of the following year at two separate meetings.

The group reported on issues concerning the curriculum (balance of age and experience of staff; possibilities of gender stereotyping) and the relationships between the ways in which different subject departments 'delivered' the curriculum. Some of the findings are illustrated in this excerpt from the final report:

> Far more listening takes place than might normally be supposed — In many subjects far less was anticipated. Less discussion takes place than might be expected. Similarly, far less exercising and developing of reading and writing skills takes place than might have been supposed. . . . The project raised many pertinent questions, the answers to which cannot but help shape future curriculum planning, and indeed it suggested further areas where INSET research would be rewarding to both researchers and researched. For example, such an area could be an attempt to effect a comparison between (1) how children learn (best) with (2) how children are expected to learn. The percentage of time children (should) spend working individually, in pairs, in groups, in classes etc. needs to be researched. This work would need to be in careful conjunction with an analysis of what is taught (or learned) (1) by example, (2) by telling, (3) by investigation etc. A weighing of physical skills, what children learn to *do*, with mental skills, how

children learn to *think* needs to be made, and a measure taken on the amount of curriculum time devoted to each. Finally, the more staff can observe other staff teaching, and students learning, the more will be the general awareness of what the curriculum really is, and less the need for a description. (Williams, 1987)

> *Learning About Learning Group* (originally entitled 'Classroom Phenomena')

The support for this kind of project was fundamental to the Principal's belief in teacher-as-expert; and the purposes were described as being:

(i) to stimulate the teacher–as–researcher/analyst model;

(ii) to emphasize classroom experience as worthy of primary, personal analysis by teachers themselves, as the obvious and in fact only possible 'experts' in promoting learning. (Branston, 1986)

There was an overlap between both the work and membership of this group and that which has been described. All but two of the group of ten were English and mathematics teachers and the eight included the team leader from 'Curriculum Descriptions'. The team leader of the 'Learning about Learning' group was also a member of that group. 'It's important because he's describing curriculum, what I'm doing is almost a mirror image. . . .'

The most important intended outcome was described as 'an increase in confidence among teachers that they can discuss, theorise about and be active in the management of learning (or the environment it happens in) and that they are the natural experts at analysis of its features'. This coincided with the group's aspirations for a heightened awareness of what they were doing which would 'rub off in conversation with other people'. None of the group had any previous experience of classroom research.

Members agreed to focus upon classroom interaction initially and they began by observing their own classrooms, focussing upon areas which were of particular personal interest. The main aim of this was, 'to enable us to clarify our ideas about possible fruitful areas of research'. These observations were then shared in the group. Impressions recorded at the end of the first term were described as 'striking, particularly the "blinkerdness" and isolation of much pupil experience in the classroom'. As a result of discussion, the main areas of interest which emerged were: teacher questioning as an aspect of teacher/student exchanges; and how best to motivate students and encourage them to take greater initiative in their learning. A decision was made to focus first upon the volume and types of teacher questioning through the observation of colleagues' classrooms from within and outside the immediate project group. This was to fulfil the group's agreed secondary aim, 'to acquire experience of methods of research, especially of observing each other teaching'. An aim which was of equal importance, however, was, 'to achieve a greater sense of team identity, greater ease of coordinating the group's work and . . . being able to meet to discuss common ground'.

To help in the systematic observation of teacher questioning, the group used its own, modified version of one devised some years previously by Douglas Barnes (Barnes, Britton and Rosen, 1971). They wanted to discover how many times in a school day students were invited by teachers to reflect upon their own experience. The major difficulty in using the system was in achieving a consistency of interpretation of different categories. Members were aware of this and other difficulties but decided to, 'trust our instincts'. This pragmatic and apparently naive approach to research processes was mirrored by the group's decision to look at classrooms on the basis of 'whether the observer got on with the teacher' rather than any other. The result was that no two people looked at the same subject. Below is an extract from the team leaders' report on this part of the group's research.

Teacher Questions

Six members of the group each observed at least seventy minutes worth of lessons, recording the types of questions used by teachers on an analysis sheet adapted largely from the one described by Douglas Barnes . . . The strongest impression formed by the group was of the sheer number of questions generated by teachers. This surprised both the observers and the observed. The most startling case involved a teacher who had been happy to have a lesson of hers observed though rather apologetic that the lesson would not involve many questions; in fact 110 were recorded in thirty-five minutes . . .

Observers were left with the impression that rather too often questions were just a method teachers had of controlling or dominating a discussion; rather than provoking thought they could in fact dull the student's receptiveness to the occasional really valuable question. (Laycock, 1988)

Whilst seasoned researchers from outside schools will find little to surprise them in this information it is worthwhile emphasizing that many of the teachers were learning this for themselves for the first time and were deeply affected by their discoveries.

As a result of this, the group decided to try to view the experienced curriculum from the pupils' viewpoint, and five members engaged in student pursuits each following a different student from the same mixed ability first year class (11–12-year-olds) through a day's lessons on different days of the week. The report cited above observed that:

> We had come a long way since the group's first tentative exercises in observing fellow group members. Two factors may have been particularly important in ensuring the success of the exercise: we were seen to be a reasonable cross section of . . . teachers directing our own research; and, furthermore, our emphasis was now on observing students and learning rather than teachers and teaching.

Clearly this was a group which grew in confidence through the year. The final report reflects this and the learning which occurred from the student pursuits:

> One of the strongest impressions to emerge from this section of our research was of how isolated many of the students seemed to be — from their teachers and from their peers. A well motivated and academically able girl whom we observed even managed to remain unaware of the excitement caused in a science lesson by a minor fire in another part of the laboratory. Perhaps more interesting, however, was that her periods of deep concentration would be broken regularly — typically about every twelve minutes — by a pause for taking stock or simply relaxing. During the science lesson already mentioned, for example, she left her table ostensibly to fetch some apparatus but in fact simply to be able to wander round and look out of the window. In a remarkably sophisticated way her learning was already largely self-directed.
>
> This girl was in many ways exceptional but for different reasons the activities of their peers and their teachers seemed to have very little impact on at least two of the other students to be observed, boys of average and weak academic ability. One member of staff commented on the latter that school was a phenomena in his universe that wouldn't hurt him if he didn't hurt it. In this context it seemed significant that observers commented on the very small amounts of time when students were expected to produce or discuss work in groups. This was corroborated by the findings of the Curriculum Descriptions TRIST

> Group which suggested that the first year spent more time
> engaged in listening than in any other activity and very little time
> learning through structured discussion. (*ibid.*)

This part of the work naturally led on to investigating group work as
a means of countering the sense of isolation noted in the student pursuits. Six members of the group volunteered to act as observers of group
work in different departments. They found that, 'While there was some
debate about whether group work could provide an appropriate teaching technique in all subjects and for all abilities most members of the
group had their belief in its potential confirmed'. It was the project
group leader's belief that of all the questions raised by his group's
observations, 'the ones about how group work can be implemented,
structured and evaluated are probably the ones most worth pursuing.
Certainly, they seemed to get as close as any others to the central,
underlying question: what happens when students learn?'

The Role of the Tutor Group

> We've got a different job in that we've *got* to have done something
> by next September . . .

This statement illustrates the urgency of this group's task. Initially, the
project had been described as having 'the potential for initiating major,
whole-school review' of the pastoral curriculum, with the aim of providing 'examples of practice and some real lines of development for
future teams of tutors'. By the time it was launched, there had been a
'statement of intent . . . on an eventual move to horizontal groups'; and
by the end of the first term an 'imminent change from a vertical to a
horizontal pastoral system' was reported. Ten staff were involved
actively in the project, five of whom were Heads of House under the
current pastoral system, and not all were committed to changing this.
This project was unique within the context of the other TRIST funded
projects in that it became clear during the first term that its role was
not to conduct research in order to describe or make recommendations
for change but rather to plan for the implementation of a policy decision
taken by the Principal which did not have the unanimous support of
staff:

> We felt that there was a need . . . to justify this change. There
> was no staff consultation on a major scale at all . . .

Although the Principal responded to this feedback by producing a paper

154

and holding a meeting as far as the progress of this group's work was concerned, 'a term had been lost'.

The first term was spent by the whole group meeting together at two-weekly intervals at lunchtimes to discuss the advantages and disadvantages of change, to assimilate literature about horizontal pastoral systems and to define the role of the tutor:

> But it's very difficult, because with a change like this, depending upon somebody's age and what job they have in the school and how settled in a rut they are, talk about change to them, especially people in middle management positions, if these people are facing change and reject that change they're in the working group . . . then it is a very very difficult working position . . . so we're working under constraints of all sorts . . .

Additionally, the whole team attended a part-time externally-directed in-service course. At the end of the first term there was still a certain amount of ambiguity and uncertainty perceived concerning the role of the project group. The parameters of its work had not yet been clearly defined:

> If you've not got a firm foundation to start with, all your preparation and hard work will be no good. We still don't think that the senior staff have taken on board the many day-to-day things — geographical, location of first year groups, reporting systems, sport and competition. Who's going to think about that? . . . We're still worried because we think a lot of things that need doing will not have been done, and that might affect how effectively the tutor can operate from the start . . . We're actively conscious that we need to have time to be together as teams as often as possible before next September . . . At the start of the summer term we've got to be there ready to kick off our in-service training . . . the half-term before Easter we've got to start packaging the course, ready for September . . .

During the second term members of the team visited schools already operating a horizontal pastoral system, but the bulk of the spring and summer terms were spent working in five pairs in devising tutor materials for each of the five school years. Although, there had been reasonably effective liaison, it was reported that meetings of the whole project group, 'petered out like a car running out of petrol'. Nevertheless, despite, 'conflicting views, attitudes, opinions within the team . . . I think we are working towards a common approach . . .'; and in terms of implementing as distinct from recommending or initiating change it

was clear that some success was achieved. Speaking in the term following the formal ending of the project, one group member stated that:

> I would certainly think that the . . . team now has benefited from
> it . . . there were one or two who were very dubious about tutor
> work, a little frightened of being involved in it, the methods . . .
> but through talking about it, looking at methods, the role of a
> tutor in tutorial work, they've overcome it . . .

Emerging Patterns and Issues

During the interviews, the participants and non-participants talked
about their reasons for involvement or non-involvement in the projects,
their hopes and fears, their achievements and the constraints that hindered these. Although interviews were conducted individually, there
was a remarkable degree of consensus within each project group both
in the early interviews, those conducted during the course and after the
formal ending of the projects. Six issues in particular were raised which
are pertinent for further consideration by those involved in the management of school-based curriculum and professional development.

1 The climate — Contextual constraints.
2 Ownership and control — Participation in need identification and
  policy-making.
3 Self reflection and collaboration — Individual and group gains.
4 The fatigue factor — Time, energy and support.
5 Peer support — Group leadership.
6 Institutionalization of innovation — Expectations and outcomes.

The Climate

It is important in evaluating school-based work of all kinds to remember
that it occurs within at least three major contexts — national, local
(school) and individual (social-psychological) — and that these will
affect attitudes of participants and non-participants to learning and
change. One group leader had referred at the beginning of the project
to the previous, 'two years of discontent' during which teachers associations had been in dispute with central government over pay and
conditions of service; and a member of another group had seen the
projects as coming, 'at the end of a bad year as far as morale goes'.
One year later, another pointed out the continuing burdens of coping

with off-site initiatives promoted by central and local governments, so that, 'nowadays morale is so low that people would be reluctant to give up their time to do something like that again . . .'

Evidence has also been presented concerning curriculum development activities which had been initiated under a previous Principal and in which individuals had placed considerable time and energy but which had not been translated into action. A report on the views of thirty non-project staff conducted independently referred to *The Branston Factor*:

> Almost universally staff experience in this area had been bad. Most regarded them as ineffective talking shops that produced little of merit. Others had reacted with considerable hostility to findings critical of their departments, calling into question the validity of methodology and findings. At the end of the day nothing was done with the findings of these groups . . . Hence many dedicated and experienced members of the Branston staff, from management to Scale 1 teachers, had no intention of repeating such an experience . . . (Hall, 1987)

Thus it was perceived as vital that the Principal, '. . . persuade the staff that what's going on is actually going to be acted upon, that any initiative which he takes . . . has got to be clearly focussed . . .'.

This view was reinforced in interviews which were conducted with the majority of staff who were not project group members. Referring to the 'Learning to Learn' project, one had, 'doubts about what's going to happen to it . . . I can see the result being a lot of files and reports . . .'; another was not against changes in the pastoral system, but, 'There's too many changes . . . and we're going to have to do most of it in our own time . . .'; and another was in favour of a modular curriculum, 'providing that teachers are well trained for it'. The following statement is typical of those expressed by many non-participant staff about the speed and nature of the changes:

> Sometimes you feel as a member of staff that he's going along too fast . . . There is a feeling generally in the school that he's going along too fast . . . we teachers are a bit jealous of things that we've already established, and are very wary of change . . . he's going uphill in a way because unfortunately the previous head did not always have the backing of the staff . . . People need the human touch . . . Someone to . . . be prepared to listen to people's criticisms . . . fears . . . you can sometimes forget that you need to talk to people . . .'

Attitudes to involvement in changes (the conscious act) and changing (the ensuing processes) will inevitably be affected by these and other more personal factors. While most were positive about the ideas themselves, one had been, 'seriously put off because it would have been tinkering with my time'; another had, 'too much on my plate'; and a third had 'lost my missionary zeal'. However, it was reported that, 'without doubt the biggest single factor in deciding people that they would not get involved with TRIST was time' (Hall, 1987).

Ownership and Control

The Principal's underlying intention was to engage colleagues in collaborative activities for the 'common good' of the school (Lewin, 1946) so that there was a moral imperative implicit in his selection of the projects. The assumption (untested until the projects got underway though implied by the operative principle of voluntarism) was that this would be shared by the project members. A related assumption was the expectation that the results of the investigations — whether descriptive or in the form of recommendations — would be disseminated to colleagues in the school and an aspiration that change could result.

This raises an important issue for those who seek or are offered resource support for professional and curriculum development for inevitably there will be an 'institutional needs' dimension which will have to be taken into account and may conflict with the personal or group needs dimension. In any need identification procedures and staff and curriculum development programmes, this matching between felt individual and institutional need is bound to be potentially problematic. The Branston Scheme implicitly recognized this, but did not fully account for it, although the Principal did see the scheme as being the first of three one-year phases which would account for differently perceived needs. Nevertheless, as this chapter has indicated, some problems arose in the course of particular projects in 1986/87 in which changes in school policy, which were perceived as necessary by the Principal and senior management colleagues, conflicted with the views of some of the staff members involved. Much attention, particularly in England (Elliott, 1980; Simons, 1979 and 1987; Day, 1981) and also Australia (Kemmis *et al.* 1981; Smyth, 1987) has been given to establishing a particular ethical framework for the control of teacher research, so that, for example, 'involvement should be voluntary and teachers should retain a high degree of control over the direction of the teacher research and the confidentiality surrounding their contributions' (Wallace, 1987). In this conception the primary focus is upon groups of teachers using action research frameworks (practical and ethical) to support the improvement of their own practice. Kemmis (1981) has distinguished between 'practical' and 'emancipatory' action research:

> Action research . . . can be practical (i.e. deliberate groups decide the best ways to act within existing constraints) or emancipatory (the process of reflection leads to action based upon a critique of the social milieu). Just as the patient is emancipated from the oppression of his psyche through the process of self-reflection, so also in social theory, the act of self-reflection within critical communities is emancipatory . . . The emancipation of partici-pants in the action . . . from the dictates or compulsions of tra-dition, precedent, habit, coercion, or self deception'.

Whilst the *process* of action research which occurred in the project groups was emancipatory in the sense that their participants were free to opt in, design and implement, and evaluate, the emancipation of the mind and spirit did not always lead to empowerment in terms of the ability to change individual and collective practices and policies. For example, in the case of one of the project groups emancipation was circumscribed by the knowledge that the Principal had taken a policy decision to change the pastoral system — an area of school life which was controversial. It was not, perhaps, surprising, that even the project group itself was characterized by occasional dissension and conflict, since it became clear during the first term of the project that a decision had been taken by senior management to change the pastoral 'House' system to a horizontal 'year group' system.

One of the group commented that: 'Its like building your house on poor foundations'. Many staff were not committed to the planned change, 'even in our own team' and there was initial and continuing resentment that 'there had been no staff consultation on a major scale'. It was 'very difficult early on to get a nice climate at meetings', because, 'there's a lot of ill feeling and a lot of dissension'. A member of the group summarized the difficulties that, ultimately, caused the project group to split into year group pairs in order to set the scene for the new system:

> Every meeting we have, somebody puts a spanner in the works about something. If we'd all been committed we'd probably have got our ideas together now . . . I think there's a feeling at the back of people's minds that, 'I'm keen, but am I wasting my time? Will the things that we have suggested be taken up . . .'

Clearly, the project members felt that they were being denied the opportunity to conduct a 'reconnaissance' of pastoral systems and to consider relative merits before reporting on these to colleagues. 'We were overtaken by events . . . so that the work of the group, in the summer term, seemed to stop, because we were so busy trying to get everything ready for the tutors to operate in September . . .'. Commitment to the process of investigation was not universal and, far from empowering, this project appeared to frustrate many of its participants. The decision on change had already been taken, and it took some time for members to adjust.

In the other two of the groups, however, it was clear that members had similar interests, motivations and prejudices, and that school and individual needs coincided.

For one member of the 'Curriculum Descriptions' group involvement in the project was a 'natural extension' of work in a particular subject area in which a curriculum had been designed and developed for years 1–3. He anticipated that this would help him to look at 'broader issues'. Another had 'always been interested in cross-curricular links' and had tried to build these up in his previous school. His 'prime motivation' was to 'try and find out what is being done elsewhere'. A third member was keen to 'learn more that will help *me* develop, help me be a better teacher' and he too wanted 'a lot more cross-curriculum activity to take place'. The fourth project member expressed similar sentiments, feeling that 'there should be a tie up between what we're doing and other departments . . .'

'I always do reflect a lot on what I do. I always have done. I'm that sort of person really' seemed to characterize the backgrounds of those ten teachers (all but two of them from the English and maths departments) involved in 'Learning about Learning'. The key activities of observing classroom action, whether from the viewpoint of the teacher or the pupil (as in the pupil pursuit tasks) suggested that this was a 'doing' group. 'It's all very well to sit and philosophize about education, but unless it's going to do something then . . . I've got 101 things I can be doing . . . *The reason that a lot of people are doing this is that they're at the heart of it . . . We're deciding what we're doing as we go along'*.

Yet, despite this, much of the group's time was spent in designing observation schedules, analyzing results and hypothesizing on the processes and outcomes of teaching and learning. Perhaps the key feature of the work of these groups is that it did not threaten the existing order in the school.

It seems then that school-based curriculum development which meets institutionally-perceived needs is likely to be more successful providing that these coincide with those of the individuals involved and that they do not and are not perceived to affect the structure of the organization or curriculum of others in the school. Expressed differently, managers of schools need to take account of principles of ownership and change when taking an initiating role in school-based curriculum development.

In a real sense, then, work undertaken which attempts to support curriculum and staff development through teacher research, runs the risk of being seen as ultimately an instrument of control rather than empowerment where the research is proscribed by curriculum needs or policies defined by an individual or group of staff who hold senior positions within the management structure of an institution. Teachers recognized this and commitment by those who did not share this value position was adversely affected.

Self Analysis and Collaboration

> It was well worth doing . . . the chance to see what's actually going on in school . . . just to see what activities were going on has helped me . . .' 'It's been an eye opener . . .', 'We've enjoyed the tasks we've set ourselves . . . the minutiae of educational research . . . looking at the data and drawing conclusions. The very process we've enjoyed, as well as the final benefits . . .

The model of teacher professionality promoted by management explicitly recognized the importance to teachers' learning of the use of their personal, practical knowledge (Elbaz, 1983) and, as a means of utilizing this, a dialectical process of reflection both 'on' and 'in' action (Schön, 1983; Connelly and Clandinin, 1985).

Participants across all groups spoke of personal gains that had been made as a result of the activities of visiting other schools, discussing values and ideas with colleagues, reading, looking at life in classrooms. The projects had provided '. . . an opportunity to look at other people's ways of looking at things . . .' and although in one group, 'a majority think that we didn't achieve as much as we ought . . . all in all I'm glad I had the experience . . .'. 'If nothing else comes of this . . . approach, it will have brought me into contact with more pieces of material, and I've been made aware of other methods . . . topic areas . . . which cannot but help . . .'.

Three gains in particular are worth highlighting in the context of professional development and change. The first concerns the recognition — perhaps the re-recognition of *the gap between intentions and practice*:

There's the inevitable problem that you have a vision of what you want to do, and what you actually accomplish is only going to be a fraction of that vision . . .

The second concerns the *changing of individuals' perspectives of their own work from a narrow departmental to a broader school context*:

I think it's helped us all to see the school as an organism, that whatever you contribute can inevitably only be a part of the whole. And it's been interesting to see how other parts of the organism work, what they contribute . . .

A third gain identified related to the *collaborative nature of the work which brought teachers from different disciplines together*. Two comments, in particular, illustrate the perceived value of this:

The biggest value is just opening communications between groups of teachers who would otherwise not necessarily talk about teaching . . . I've never done that before . . .; It's valuable not just to confirm hunches that you may have had yourself, but to share those with other people and see that they too share them.

and

I think it was important that we did spend time together as a group in school time. I think that adds a greater kudos to what we do . . . that the school thought it important enough to give it time . . .

It is sometimes assumed that schools are social and sociable places. Writing after the project had ended, one member made this comment:

I think that in a big place like this the biggest weakness is that staff don't know each other. They pass like ships in the night . . . We began to appreciate people far more, and . . . working together like that you get a greater appreciation of people. You get to know them better. And I think the better you know somebody, the better the opportunity of achieving things working together . . .

The Fatigue Factor

The provision and giving of time were identified by the project participants as being the biggest single factors affecting both motivation and energy levels. It was generally observed that, 'a lot of people have given up considerable amounts of time' to the work. This theme was repeated through all the groups, as the comments below illustrate:

> I think I put in far more time than I was actually given . . . so having an afternoon or morning session a week working on it (the project) wasn't a bonus, but it did make us feel that we were doing something which other people were going to look at . . .

> If you're given TRIST time to observe a lesson, then you're going to have to spend many times that to do anything meaningful with it afterwards . . .

> The spin off was to be given the opportunity to study in working time . . . That was one of the very positive things where you've got that time and it's a facility, and I think that in itself is a very motivating factor . . ., The question is, would we have done it without the TRIST scheme?

> You might get a couple of periods, and this is classed as time off, but in reality it isn't necessarily time off because you've taken a substantial part of that time in setting work for classes that you'd normally be teaching, and then you've got to go back and mark all the work that they've done . . . It's a relocation of resources . . . not a free gift . . .

It would appear that in terms of economics as well as professional growth those who financed and managed the scheme obtained 'value for money'. However, there are two further issues which relate to provision of time support. The first is that not every member of every group will necessarily provide the same level of commitment, and this may have adverse effects upon the dynamic and learning processes of groups. One leader spoke of the need to 'reconcile' himself to people's individual commitments — which ranged from one who, 'just stopped coming to meetings with five seconds notice each time . . .', to others who, 'after Friday night's meeting which finished at five o'clock . . . spoke for a further twenty minutes about it . . .'. The second is the issue of *fatigue*.

It was observed in two of the groups that, 'People started getting fairly tired through the year', and we have read that one group's work began to 'peter out'. Additionally, when asked whether they would wish to continue to participate in school-based curriculum development work in the following year, a significant number of participants stated that they, 'wanted a break from it'. This was not it seemed because they were no longer interested, nor, for the vast majority, because they had had negative experiences. One, for example, had been studying on his own for a number of years, and so wanted to, 'tick over on my responsibility and enjoy my teaching'. Another said that he would probably continue what his group had been doing after a year's break; and a third stated that he, 'felt it was detracting from my lessons quite a lot. . . .'

It is worth reflecting on the issue of involvement in projects which require extra time and energy in relation to the notion of 'bounded' or 'containable' time. Here the problems of research fatigue and increasing lack of confidence by individuals in their ability to focus upon the central task of teaching would be taken into account at the planning stage of school-based curriculum and professional development work. Whilst it has been noted that, 'The best way to improve practice lies not so much in trying to control people's behaviour as in helping them control their own by becoming more aware of what they're doing' (Elliott, 1977), and whilst adults undoubtedly benefit most from those situations which combine action and reflection, it is nevertheless incumbent upon those who manage school-based curriculum and professional development to ensure also that 'commitment' does not become associated with 'stress'. Perhaps teaching should not be regarded purely or even predominantly as teacher-pupil contact time:

> There should be an in-built time to discuss teachers' problems and things that happen in the classroom, because we tend to keep problems to ourselves, or discuss them with perhaps one to two close colleagues . . . I think a lot more time ought to be devoted to it . . .

Group Leadership

The roles played by group leaders are crucial to the degree of success of the various enterprises, and in view of this it is surprising that no leadership training and team building programmes were provided prior to the beginning of the projects. Team leaders' commitment and credibility were not questioned by colleagues, and while some were viewed as 'middle management' figures and others as 'very much grass roots' this did not seem to be an issue in the functioning of the groups. One member of the senior management team was 'impressed by the methods employed for getting the teams together, and the quality of the debate . . .'. Nevertheless, it is clear from the reports of the projects that leadership knowledge and skills are essential prerequisites for the management of school-based curriculum development.

Institutionalization of Innovation

In an interview after the project had ended, the Principal stated that:

At the moment what's important to me is that kind of (open) attitude and awareness and openness, especially in view of the fact that teachers do feel kicked about and treated as menial (a reference to the national context of centrally initiated change through legislation). It's more important to me that their sense of professionalism has been increased . . . than that any specific change has been achieved . . .

Evidence that individual project members had changed has been presented already. The change in the pastoral system had been serviced by rather than resulted from the work of the 'Role of the Tutor' group. So to that extent its work was disseminated and utilised (although it is too early to judge how effective this has been.) Both the 'Curriculum Descriptions' and 'Learning about Learning' groups had entered the projects with expectations that they would share their findings with their colleagues in the school. Both hoped that their work, 'will affect the work of the school . . .' and that the information would, 'enable people to understand what they are doing . . . what's happening in the school . . . then decide is this the right thing, is this the right way to do it? What changes do we need?' One member stated that, 'it is very important in a large school with so many different subjects that the left hand should know what the right hand's doing and when and how'; and another envisaged it as, 'an exercise in information sharing which then could be used department to department . . . as a means of breaking down subject barriers . . .'.

Evidence of the participants' perceptions of TRIST has already been provided, and it is clear that overall the scheme had been valued. It had, 'made people feel that there is life after their classroom-lessons'. It had been welcomed as being important in, 'making people aware of issues in education . . . because it means that we are looking at ourselves to see what we are doing with children . . . which will either confirm or help people to look again at some of the ideas . . .'. The scheme itself recognized that, 'as teachers we want to do something about our own profession, about what's going on here. We want to examine it . . . to look objectively at what we are doing . . .'.

Hall's (1987) report confirmed the data gathered during the evaluation that, 'Those significantly involved believed quite firmly that the scheme overall had benefited the school, even if they had doubts about their own particular sub-group'; and the perceived gains for the participants themselves have already been enumerated. It is worth recording, however that, 'Those who had no or little involvement felt they had not benefited at all . . .'.

In effect the hope for adoption or use of the findings was in part based on an act of faith, a belief that if they had intrinsic merit and were perceived as being 'valid', then acceptance by others could be achieved through traditional modes of dissemination (for example, a report and presentation).

In the Branston TRIST Scheme the school management ensured that the new practices which were necessary as part of the imminent change in the pastoral system were planned through the 'Role of the Tutor' project team. The findings of both the 'Curriculum Descriptions' and 'Learning about Learning' groups were not accompanied by structural and procedural changes. Whilst these groups planned for dissemination by producing, and in one case presenting, their findings, no detailed consideration was given to the very principles of participation, collaboration and ownership which had characterized their own learning throughout the projects. One is led to conclude that perhaps the expectation in the scheme that participants would act as agents for change for others' as well as their own thinking and practice was a worthwhile dream but a reality which remained out of reach.

Conclusion

A number of specific and general issues which arise from the scheme and which may be useful in furthering knowledge about the planning, processes and outcomes of school-based curriculum development have been discussed. This final section focusses particularly upon the management of SBCD.

In a recent study of 250 newly-appointed secondary heads in England and Wales, it was noted that:

> The strategies used by the heads to introduce change were similar across the (sixteen) case studies. In addition to the curricular reviews, the heads discussed the proposed changes with their senior management teams and the relevant heads of department or heads of year, and produced discussion papers. Working parties were usually set up if the changes were cross-curricular or affected many staff . . . It was clear that the new heads were the major initiators of the changes; but once the decision to adopt a change had been made, day to day responsibility was usually delegated

... The research indicates that it is how change is introduced rather than the change itself that is most likely to upset staff. (Weindling and Earley, 1986)

Essentially the scheme described in this chapter was the brainchild of the recently appointed school Principal, variously described by his colleagues as, 'an ambitious professional', who, 'sees himself as a fairly cerebral and dynamic head who would like to get his staff and probably to encourage some of his colleagues to think about the curriculum perhaps on a slightly more advanced level' ... and, 'a quiet operator, thinking and planning, calculating ... in logical and sensible ways'.

In a very real sense, then, the scheme was an embodiment of the Principal's ideals and values. It had begun, in his own words 'with the thought that effective change is people changing and is grass roots'. In an interview conducted after the scheme had ended, he recognized that those directly involved had been, 'people that one would expect to come through', who had, 'seized the opportunity ... It was a vehicle for them to express themselves'. He had been convinced that a 'top-down hierarchical' approach to curriculum and professional development would not work, and that the approach which he had taken had, 'has as good a chance as anything else of success in achieving change, which in a school is so linked to people internalizing'. He had been aware of the need to establish a 'right timescale for change', and had consciously determined to take advantage of his 'honeymoon period' in school:

One of the glories of being new is that you're already at the threshold before you start. People expect you to have your own agenda, expect changes . . .

Nevertheless, he recognized the 'tension between wanting to use your power as headteacher to empower the staff and then wanting to retain the controlling voice — which in certain respects I do'; and he did not think that power sharing was a necessary logical conclusion of staff development. A senior management colleague described the management model:

It was top down only to provide the initial impetus. Once the impetus was there then if we nurtured it then it should develop — as indeed it has developed. So to the extent that we opened doors to enable staff to progress, we opened those doors where we saw there was a need. So although the staff could claim ownership, in fact the options which were available to them to bid for had been diagnosed and offered by the management team . . .

This 'mandated ownership', while attractive, clearly results in problems of commitment for those who do not share the leader's value system; and empirical evidence in the Branston scheme provides support for this. One of the interesting factors in this scheme was, however, the long-range vision and alternative strategies which the Principal intended to employ. He described it as only the first stage of school-based work — 'the start of an ongoing INSET strand' — which, it was hoped, would eventually provide every member of staff with opportunities to participate:

> The ideal progression in my mind is: 1986/87 my agenda and framework, colleagues respond; 1987/88, my frameworks colleagues respond and fix much of their own agenda/topics as individuals; 1988/89 whole school agree on INSET agenda and possibly select framework . . .

So, even before the formal end of the TRIST scheme, an invitation had been issued for colleagues to participate in a new scheme which, 'invited bids for development time from individuals, groups, or departments on any area', though, 'whole-school research/development, or at least whole departmental ones remain likely to get preference over individual, self-contained ones'. The scheme attracted bids from two departments (the thirteen staff in these were allocated a total of twenty-one 'supply' cover days) and nineteen individuals who were allocated between two and six periods each week in order to pursue investigations into a range of curriculum issues.

Essentially, managers of schools must adopt principles of collaboration based upon assertion of teachers' ability as learners and partners (if not equal partners) within a continuing professional development programme. In doing so, they must adopt strategies which take account of a number of learning and change principles.

Figure 7 is an attempt to operationalize these. It represents a planning — action — review — planning cycle which accounts for the need of all those engaged in SBCD to engage in a process which minimizes potential problems caused by disjunction between, for example, individual and institutional need. It recognizes that 'need' may be identified by any individual or group or by collaborative need identification procedures but that the key to progress is in contract building and contract making. It is at this stage that the kinds of responsibilities and answerabilities (by management to teachers and vice versa) for the duration of the work may be clarified, established and negotiated. The model avoids making judgments upon the effectiveness of particular management stances, so that the opportunity exists for 'pro-tem' power

Figure 7: A model of management-participant roles in school-based curriculum and professional development

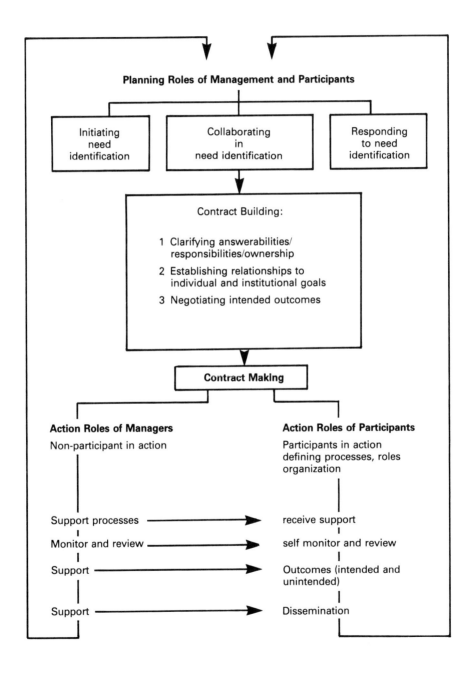

and authority relationships to be negotiated. However, it is implicit that where the culture or ethos of the institution is expressed through antagonistic management — staff relationships, then success will be difficult to achieve.

.Perhaps the final words should be those of the person who had initiated the idea, who had been passionately convinced of the necessity for professional research and development to be seen as an, 'utterly natural part of every schoolteacher's role within his own institution'; and who had undertaken considerable searching and lobbying for resources from outside the school to support the project:

> Of course, the projects were perhaps not equally successful, and certainly not in the same ways, but my own subjective view is that the process at least began to diffuse into the bloodstream, and although neither the projects nor their reports may have broken new ground, that they happened here was enormously significant for our future development. Some tied in directly to whole-school curriculum and structural changes (though the question of the relationship between teacher groups and whole-school policy, as determined by senior management, is itself worthy of a separate report) while others were far more akin to basic research, with no immediate outcome. This was a deliberate mix.
>
> I myself believe that the year paved the way for a better understanding of several major school changes, as well as acting as a spur to professional in-house activity. For example, when in the following year as stage 2 of the campaign 'Teachers as Experts' I invited bids for research development time, over twenty staff responded individually and ten more as members of departments. Two of the resulting individual projects are forming the major part of a Diploma in Professional Studies, validated by Nottingham University, and this is one more necessary step forward, for in these GRIST days off-site secondment to award-bearing courses is much reduced. Besides which, professional activity of the school-based sort just should be validated, by certification as well as in other ways.
>
> Only the future will tell whether school-based research and development will become as natural as breathing here, but I am confident, especially since Lincolnshire has made a move towards giving schools control of part of the County INSET budgets. From an LEA view school-based work certainly proves to be very cost-effective in terms of 'activity generated per pound of resource', but of course it needs *some* funding.

Overall, despite our imperfections, we have I believe, shown that there truly is an appetite for school-based, teacher-centred collaborative research. I also believe that this school is healthier and stronger because of the activity its members have participated in than it would otherwise have been. I intend to continue to pursue the 'Teachers as Experts' approach.

Issues and Prospects

Chapter 7

Re-Examination of Factors Affecting SBCD

Introduction

The task of this chapter is to re-examine some major features of SBCD which were conceptualized in chapter 2 and illustrated in the case study chapters presented in section B.

The four case studies presented in section B were selected by the authors because they felt that they exemplified some of the salient features of SBCD — the enthusiasms and energies of groups — the advances and achievements but also the inevitable impediments and shortcomings.

SBCD would appear to be alive and well from these four case studies. Yet how representative are the case studies on the total educational scene? Is it possible to make any summary statement when SBCD encompasses such a variety of approaches, scales of activity and levels of participation? It is not always easy to disentangle the numerous assertions and idealised accounts of SBCD from comprehensive evaluative accounts.

A Conceptual Map of SBCD

Some major factors relating to SBCD and depicted in figure 8. Three factors, motivations of stake holders, awareness of innovative approaches and ownership are given a central focus. It was argued previously in chapter 2 that these are major factors. Yet there are also many other interrelated factors as depicted in figure 8.

It is important therefore, to consider each factor in some detail, namely:

Motivations of stakeholders
Interest in innovative approaches
Control, responsibility and ownership
Type/scale of activity
School climate
Leadership
Time
Resources
External initiatives and support

Motivations of Stake Holders

If a school Principal and his/her teachers are relatively satisfied with what is happening at their respective school there is little likelihood that serious SBCD activities will be initiated unless there is an externally generated initiative. As noted in chapter 2, most teachers strive for stability, routines and practices that work — it is a source of sanity for

Figure 8: A Conceptual Map of SBCD

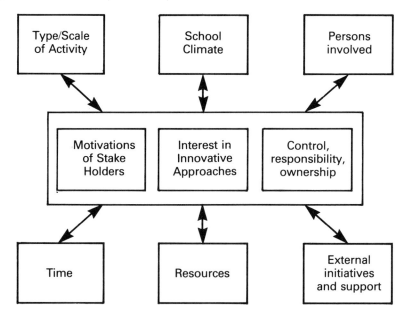

the myriad of conflicting activities and turmoil that can occur during the course of a school day — although there are always those 'hero innovators' (Georgiades and Phillimore, 1975) who thrive on the management of uncertainty and the experimentation with new practices.

It is often the school Principal who jolts staff out of these accepted routines. The motivations may be diverse. They can involve personal ambitions and goals or they might be part of a long-term goal of development for school staff as a whole.

Some fascinating examples were included in the case study chapters. In chapter 3, the Australian Principal was depicted as being very ambitious, outgoing, outspoken and tending to be almost aggressive. He had established a reputation for being an innovator, although at times this was perceived by others as a desire to be the first to try out an innovative practice regardless of its appropriateness or consequences. Notwithstanding, it was his initiatives that attracted other staff to be involved and eventually led to the whole school activity.

The school Principal at Branston, as described in chapter 4 was also highly motivated to initiate SBCD projects. Although he had only been at the school for a matter of six months he seemed to want to demonstrate his 'innovative spirit' to others. He obviously had a sound knowledge of how to obtain external funding for SBCD projects and used this to good effect to galvanize the staff into action. Perhaps he was also motivated to strike early with the intention of destabilising staff work patterns established under his predecessor.

The Canadian Principal, as described in chapter 5, had staff professional development as his major motivation for commencing an SBCD activity. He was able to use the Ministry requirements as a reason for embarking upon an extensive five-year plan in all subject-area departments.

These examples refer only to school Principals but of course other stakeholders can also be very influential in motivating their colleagues. An interesting example in the Australian case study was the senior science teacher who took on the task of change agent at the school. His computing expertise and problem-solving skills enabled him to convince other staff to make greater use of microcomputers in planning their teaching and in the recording of assessment results. The group leaders in the UK school also had a major role in motivating and maintaining their groups as the school head had deliberately delegated major decisions to them. Some leaders emerged during the ensuing meetings and discussions, such as the physical geography teacher in the Canadian case study example. In the American case study the coordinator of curriculum and in-service (Leonard) was highly involved in motivating colleagues.

Recent research studies provide some interesting insights and caveats about the motivations of stake holders. For example, Huberman and Miles (1986) noted as a result of their involvement in the study of Dissemination Efforts Supporting School Improvement (DESSI study, 1984) that persons who are highly motivated to initiate SBCD activities can enthuse but they can also destabilize staff because of their subsequent career shifts. During their period of time at a school these leaders can establish enthusiastic work groups only to leave them abruptly and leaderless at short notice. The UK case study commented upon those in the school who were sceptical of the newly-appointed Principal's initiative because a previous Principal had done just this. The high visibility that these leaders develop can often cause them to be upwardly mobile and to be given rapid advancement to other educational positions. Kirk (1988) also refers to the biographies of school personnel and how their past and anticipated future career positions can affect the intensity of their efforts.

An SBCD project can provide the opportunity for teachers and principals to undergo extensive self-criticism (Reid, 1987). This process can become most enlightening and motivating to the individuals concerned, even though the extent of this development might not be anticipated prior to their involvement. Various writers have outlined the emancipatory qualities of school-based activities. Carr and Kemmis (1986) refer to the opportunities for teachers to 'organise themselves as communities of enquirers, organising their own enlightenment' (p.221). Day (1987) emphasizes the need for stakeholders to have opportunities for private and public reflection. Teachers may have already developed their private solutions to classroom problems but once the issues are discussed in public forums they may be willing to reconsider their initial solutions. The reports of two group leaders in the UK case study demonstrate the extent to which teachers involved had reconsidered their classroom practices.

The development of appropriate policies and practices as a result of private and public reflections are termed 'practical theories' by Sanders and McCutcheon (1986). It is evident that SBCD projects can provide powerful opportunities for teachers to inquire deliberately and systematically about their practical theories.

Interest in Innovative Approaches

This factor is interrelated closely with the motivation of stakeholders in that the former can be a vehicle for the latter. For example, if teachers or principals are dissatisfied with their present effectiveness they may decide to use a specific innovatory process or product to alleviate the problem. Taking an altruistic stance, they may opt to use an educational innovation because they anticipate benefits for their students. But there may also be some self-interest motives involved to the extent that an innovation is used to give individuals higher levels of visibility and to increase their prospects of promotion. In real-life situations it is difficult, if not impossible, to separate out the genuine altruistic motives from those of self-interest as most individuals are probably affected by both considerations.

Be that as it may, the educational scene is inundated with persons and organizations plying innovative processes and products. As explained in chapter 2, teachers and principals are very susceptible to innovations because there is still no unequivocal evidence about the superiority of specific methods of teaching. The pressures of account-ability from various organizations, especially the government and the media, all have the effect of persuading school principals (and teachers to a lesser extent) to demonstrate that they are willing to consider innovative approaches.

There were examples of these influences at work in the case study chapters. For example, the Principal in the Australian secondary school had a reputation as an innovator. Rogers's (1983) ideal characteristics of an innovator seem to apply very closely to this Australian Principal, namely:

> Venturesomeness is almost an obsession with them. They are very eager to try new ideas. This interest leads them out of a local circle of peer networks and into more cosmopolite social relation-ships. . . . He or she desires the hazardous, the rash, the daring and the risky. (p.248)

This school Principal certainly took risks. He implemented new policies and later advised Ministry officials about his actions. He was very outspoken at meetings with senior education officials. Local papers and education newsletters and journals often included feature articles and 'letters to the editor' which were authored by this person.

We are told in the UK case study that the Principal of Branston School initiated and negotiated the SBCD activity with external agenc-ies such as the Director of Education, the Chief Inspector of Schools and the local TRIST Director. It was evident that he was perceived by his staff as an innovator and that he regarded his innovations as 'high risk' activities for him. The Principal, in turn, encouraged the leaders of each study group to take over ownership of their project and to embark upon innovative approaches and solutions.

We are informed in chapter 4 that the Canadian Principal wanted his staff to be involved in reflective curriculum development processes. This in itself is a relatively innovatory goal. He was certainly keen to support this goal by allowing teacher release time and sponsoring district in-service sessions.

It is interesting to note that in each case the innovations were expressions of the Principals' philosophies of 'teachers as experts', as practitioners who, with support could take responsibility for their own professional and curriculum development.

It is likely that principals have more opportunities to initiate innovatory practices not only because they are expected to perform a leadership role, but because they have greater access to the latest information about innovatory products and processes. However, as Kirst and Meister (1985) remind us, well established practices are not easily jettisoned in favour of new ideas and products. Further, some innovations which are asserted at the time to be a major advance, never get beyond a very short period of adoption. Examples of innovations that have been ephemeral, include 8mm projectors, voucher systems, programmed learning and cuisennaire rods in mathematics. Innovations which are selected by a central office for all schools run the risk of being used by only a small number of teachers. The contents of many storerooms provide evidence of items which were deemed to be an innovatory advance by a head office but which were not accepted by classroom teachers and were subsequently relegated to a dusty shelf.

Control, Responsibility and Ownership

There will be a number of stages in the developing commitment of participants in SBCD to the project/tasks/activities. Motivation and interest in innovations are only the first albeit important steps on the path towards commitment to learning and change. Initial motivation may well become soured or decline if, for example, there is little support, time, energy and resources, if the task is too large or if the school climate is not right (figure 8).

However, a central feature of the case studies presented is that of felt ownership and control. Whether the project is initiated by the

Principal or an individual or group of teachers where others who were not the originators become involved, it is important to ensure that they feel able to exercise control and ownership of the processes of the tasks and responsibility for these and the outcomes. The UK case study provides examples of what may occur where this exists and, in one project, the negative responses which occurred when external policy makers intervened to destabilise ownership, responsibility and control. The need at the outset to establish ethical frameworks which ensure that teachers retain a high degree of control over the direction of work of this kind which is essentially voluntary has been highlighted by Kemmis (1981), Elliott (1980), Smyth (1987), Wallace (1987) and Sabar *et al.* (1987) among others. If this is not established, work which purports to support teachers in a central role as curriculum developers runs the risk of being seen ultimately as a means of control rather than empowerment.

Type/Scale of Activity

SBCD activities can be classified into many types/forms and as explained in chapter 2, this will depend in turn upon such factors as time availability, funds, and purpose.

One way of categorising SBCD activities is in terms of whether the focus is upon creating new curriculum products or selecting or adopting existing ones. Clearly, the creating of new products is a far more time-consuming and complicated project than merely adapting them. The Canadian case study chapter refers to Miller and Sellers' (1985) three orientations of 'transformation', 'transaction' and 'transmission'. The first of these terms, 'transformation', can be related to SBCD activities which involve creating new products, structures or processes for a school. The emphasis is upon personal and social change. The other two terms of 'transaction' and 'transmission' can be linked to SBCD activities which emphasize more effective ways of teaching with given content, skills or values. There is little interest in any problematics of 'why'. Rather, the emphasis is on the 'how'.

However, SBCD activities can also be concerned with processes rather than the creation or adaptation of products. Various writers, such as Schiffer (1979) argue that SBCD activities are often undertaken to 'improve aspects of organizational health: communication adequacy, the ability of the staff to solve problems collaboratively, cohesiveness and morale' (p.10).

Because SBCD activities are concerned with advancements for the total school staff, or at least departments or sections, it is most important to consider processes that will facilitate this, rather than merely advantaging individuals.

In undertaking these SBCD activities, whether they are product or process-oriented, there will be some sequences of events, or procedures. For example, Loucks-Horsely and Hergert (1985) suggest that typical procedures include:

establishing the project
assessment and goal-setting
identifying a solution
preparing for implementation
implementing the project
reviewing progress and problems
maintenance and institutionalization

Lieberman and Miller (1986) remind us that these procedures are neither linear nor prescriptive. Enormous variations can occur. Some school staffs might spend inordinate amounts of time on needs analysis (assessment and goal-setting). Others might undergo rigorous evaluation exercises using internal as well as external personnel. Huberman and Miles (1986) note that the contextual factors affect the extent to which procedures will be followed in any SBCD activity.

The case studies exemplify the diversity of SBCD activities ranging from a study of whole school changes to establish a new curriculum structure, to concurrent studies on three relatively independent curriculum issues, to a study of problem-solving and how it might be incorporated into several subject areas.

The Australian case study illustrates how a major organizational change was planned and implemented. All staff were affected by the changes and had to develop new skills in lesson planning, in different forms of assessment, and in the use of microcomputer packages for analyzing test results. The school Principal used a set of well-defined planning principles to bring about the change. He was careful to enlist the support of key individuals whom he could rely upon to develop collegiality and to foster a supportive environment. Although negotiations were very open and egalitarian between administrators and teachers, it should be noted that parents and students were only marginally involved in the planning process, even though they were fully informed at a later stage.

The UK case study provides a fascinating account of three concurrent projects although some staff were involved in more than one. Each project team was formed to focus upon a particular school need but some were more tightly organized than others. For example, 'the role of the tutor group' had a very tight schedule. It was discovered at a later stage that participants in this project were not required to research a problem but 'rather to plan for the implementation of a policy decision taken by the Principal which did not have the unanimous support of staff' (p.20).

Although the topics for each of these three projects varied considerably, similar procedures were followed for each. Researching the problem, followed by collecting classroom data and the identifying of solutions, were practices followed in each project. There seemed to be a considerable emphasis upon monitoring of the group activities and the decision-making points.

The Canadian case study was a different type of SBCD activity again in that the major emphasis seemed to be upon subject department staff being involved in redesigning their teaching subjects. It was not monitored very closely although substantial resources were made available to groups if they needed it. One group did not reflect very critically on their curriculum planning, and not surprisingly, quickly came to the decision that there was no need to take any action. The second group was able to obtain the assistance of an external facilitator to help them appreciate some of the issues. Once a perceived need for action was realized by members, this group followed through with a series of activities which involved reflection, exploring alternatives and establishing some viable solutions.

The American case study was also quite different in that the scale was system-wide but the curriculum development activities were undertaken by class teachers. The interpersonal conflicts that occurred between participants created a positive tension in the long-run. The conflicts highlighted the complexities of curriculum planning when system level targets have to be reconciled.

School Climate

The concept of school climate/organizational climate has been recognized by many writers as a major factor in school change. Croft (1963) introduced his Organizational Climate Description Questionnaire (OCDQ) in the early 1960s. Many studies have been completed since then using the OCDQ and modifications of this instrument (for example, Thomas and Slater, 1972). The studies have highlighted such dimensions as principal supportiveness, motivating teachers by example, social cohesiveness among teachers. Brady (1988) examined the relationship between organisational climate and aspects of SBCD and concluded that 'principal supportiveness' was the most consistent predictor of successful SBCD activities.

Other writers have used an ecology metaphor to explain the importance of school climate. For example, Goodlad (1987) refers to the school as an ecosystem. He extends this analysis to consider how a school can become healthy and renewing. School communities need to be constantly self-examining the functions they perform. A healthy school is one which realizes that it is an incomplete culture and that it is necessary to articulate and confront problem areas.

Lieberman and Miller (1986) examine the school culture in terms of the 'routinization and regularities of school life and the strong informal norms that grow up among teachers and which govern their working life' (p.98). They argue that SBCD activities have to build upon the school norms that operate. Initiators of SBCD projects should not underestimate the complexity of these relationships, and the tensions that often occur in schools that are either structurally loose or tight (Hoyle, 1986).

Huberman and Miles (1986) provide some rather different, if not provocative, arguments about certain aspects of school climate. They suggest that a positive school climate for SBCD is one in which there is

administrative decisiveness bordering on coercion, but intelligently and supportively exercised . . . because powerful people tend to be able to exert directional control over the environment — to shape the surround, to reduce the uncertainties, to reduce the degree of freedom of actors having countervailing plans — and to offer assistance resources. (pp. 70–1).

In the Australian case study an interactive system of decision-making had been carefully nurtured by the school Principal. Teachers were encouraged to take on leadership roles as leaders of the four houses (a vertical system of grouping students for academic and sporting activities); as heads of subject departments; and as elected members of the school board and finance committee. There was also a Staff Social Officer and a Curriculum Coordinator. A spirit of informality and collegiality seemed to span across all groups including students, clerical staff, administrators, teaching staff, cleaners and community members.

In the Branston case study it appeared that the staff had been involved in SBCD activities under the previous Principal and Vice Principal. There was a great deal of interest expressed by staff in the new projects as revealed by their responses to the 'Launch Pak'. A number of staff volunteered to be involved in more than one project and the overall level of collegiality seemed to be very high. Notwithstanding, there were pockets of discontent. Reference has already been made above to the 'Role of the tutor' project group who considered that their task had been pre-empted by an earlier decision made by the Principal. In addition, the industrial actions which were occurring nationally during this period would have been unsettling and not conducive to any SBCD endeavours.

The Canadian case study highlights very dramatically the importance of school climate in terms of group cohesiveness and collaboration. The History committee did not want to share their individual expertise with each other. The group members were apparently hostile toward the project and preferred to work in isolation from each other. The group leader did little to establish a congenial group climate. By contrast, the leader of the Geography Committee was experienced in deliberative decision-making and strove hard to get members to conceptualize their problems and to work toward possible solutions. Gradually an open, supportive, group climate was established and this allowed the project to reach a successful conclusion. The American case study also highlighted the need for school climate but it was even wider than that and could perhaps be termed 'system climate'.

Leadership

The number of persons involved and their type of involvement are important aspects of any SBCD activity. Numerous studies on school principals over recent years attest to their role as a key agent in SBCD at both primary and secondary school levels and to the important skills they need to use (see table 6). Rutherford (1984) emphasizes the 'vision' that a school principal can bring to SBCD activities. Glatthorn (1987) refers to the support and resources that a principal can bring to a SBCD project. Leithwood and Montgomery (1982) maintain that the principal has the responsibility and the opportunities to develop interpersonal and organizational skills among his/her staff. School principals are also able to monitor the degree to which SBCD projects are succeeding. Various principal styles have been advanced in the literature, especially by Hall and Rutherford (1983) and Leithwood and Montgomery (1986). The former suggests that there are three typical styles of 'responder', 'manager' and 'initiator'. The latter suggest that there are four discernible levels that principals progress through over a period of years, namely 'administrator', 'humanitarian', 'program manager' and 'problem solver'. To facilitate SBCD activities it would appear that 'initiator' and 'problem-solver' principals would be particularly successful.

However, it is too simplistic to place all the leadership burden for SBCD upon school principals. Other key figures can also undertake leadership roles in a school. Some of these figures may have achieved respect from others because of their past accomplishments, or special personal qualities. Others might undertake leadership roles because they occupy formal staffing positions or because special authority has been delegated to them.

Marsh and Bowman (1988) report that many key players in the Californian School Improvement Plan (SIP) program have been class teachers. Hall *et al.* (1984) and Hord (1986) refer to Second Change Facilitators (Second CF) as being key actors also in SBCD activities. They can be assistant principals, an appointed teacher from within the school, curriculum coordinators or external, district-level advisers. The Second CF tends to take a complementary leadership role to the principal. Hord (1986) maintains that 'principals provide planning, guidance, reinforcement, and supervision directed to the individual teachers and teacher groups, while the Second CF does more training and problem solving work with individual teachers' (p.18).

Caldwell and Spinks (1988) have demonstrated how organizational structures can be developed (Collaborative School Management Approach (CSM)) which enable class teachers to become leaders in SBCD activities. They advocate a policy group of administrators, teachers and parents, and various program teams whose task it is to review current programs and to produce viable plans and budgets for school improvement. As a result of their involvement in such project teams, class teachers can develop important leadership and interpersonal skills. It is these kinds of experience that enable teachers to become valuable key actors in SBCD activities (see table 6).

The four case study chapters illustrate very clearly the pivotal role of the school principal/administrator. Various examples were provided in these chapters of their vision, and their ability to provide resources and encouragement for SBCD activities. For example, the Principal of Branston School used the SBCD projects as the first stage of an ongoing school-based in-service strand. Even before these projects were completed he had issued invitations for colleagues to become involved in a new scheme. To use another example, the Principal of River Valley School seemed to be ahead of his time. He was experimenting with new approaches to individualized instruction, via a vertical timetable, several years before the Ministry of Education announced it as a new

186

policy. This Principal was always keen to take on new ideas and he had the flair and the conviction to persuade others to be involved. 'Leonard', the administrator in the American case study, was a very experienced facilitator and was highly regarded by the teacher-participants.

Yet there was also ample evidence of other key figures, akin to the 2 CF role advanced by Hall and Hord (1987). At River Valley High School the Deputy Principal was a driving force in solving the problem of creating viable vertical timetables for the school. He used various workshop situations to demonstrate to senior staff how they could rearrange and sequence their teaching units. The external consultant who undertook the role of leader of the Geography Committee at the Canadian school was able to turn around a district-generated activity which produced little initial support from the geography staff into a rewarding SBCD project which became a significant professional growth experience for all participants; and the leaders of the individual projects at Branston clearly played vital roles in the management and maintenance of their teams and tasks.

1 *Curriculum skills*
  (a) Subject knowledge
    (i)   updating subject knowledge
    (ii)   identifying conceptual structure of subject(s)
    (iii) identifying skills in subject(s)
  (b) Professional skills
    (i)   reviewing existing practice
    (ii)   constructing scheme/programme
    (iii) implementing scheme/programme
    (iv)   assessing scheme/programme
  (c) Professional judgment
    (i)   deciding between available resources
    (ii)   deciding about methods
    (iii) identifying links between subjects
    (iv)   ordering, maintaining resources
    (v)   relating subject to its form in other schools

2 *Interpersonal skills*
  (a) Working with colleagues
    (i)   leading workshops/discussions
    (ii)   translating material into comprehensible form
    (iii)   liaising with head and/or senior staff
    (iv)   advising colleagues informally
    (v)   teaching alongside colleagues
    (vi)   visiting colleagues' classes to see work in progress
    (vii)   maintaining colleagues' morale, reducing anxiety, etc.
    (viii) dealing with professional disagreement
  (b) External representation
    (i)   consulting advisers, university staff, etc.
    (ii)   consulting teachers in other schools.

(after Campbell, 1985, p.57)

Table 6: Skills needed for the management of school-based curriculum development

Time

Having sufficient time is a major factor for all SBCD endeavours. It can be considered from several different perspectives, namely 'project' time in terms of schedules and target dates and 'personal' time in terms of commitment required by participants.

Most schools are governed by tight schedules such as term dates, daily timetables, monthly tests, and many more requirements. Typically, SBCD activities need to be undertaken within one school year as staff mobility and other changes make it extremely difficult to extend a project for longer periods. Sometimes the project has to be of a much shorter duration such as a term or a number of weeks. Caldwell and Spinks (1988) suggest procedures for keeping SBCD activities within reasonable time limits. For example they advocate that project teams should consist of only six to eight persons; that no school should become involved in more than three to five projects per year; and that policy recommendations from a project team should be kept to a maximum of two pages per team. These authors have a very task-oriented focus for SBCD activities and this may be appropriate on many occasions, but there may be other situations where such efficiency-oriented priorities don't allow sufficient time for self-reflection and discussion sessions for participants.

For individual teachers, time spent on non-teaching activities can be a very real cost. There are, of course, the attractions of involvement in a group project with all the bonhomie, excitement, and camaraderie that can develop, and a welcome relief from isolation, but this is only the positive side. On the negative side there is the very real danger that a person will over-extend himself/herself and become fatigued. It is also possible that earlier convivial meetings can be transformed into sessions of friction and conflict. Fullan (1982) refers to personal time costs of doing SBCD in terms of actual time lost, energy expended and perceived threats to a person's sense of adequacy. Teacher stress and burnout is frequently featured in the media and it may be related to unrealistic expectations about how much SBCD activity can be undertaken by teachers in addition to their normal teaching loads. Professional development programs which provide teacher release time is an obvious solution but it is becoming increasingly difficult to provide in a period of restricted education budgets.

The case study chapters provide some interesting insights into how time was a significant factor in SBCD activities. The staff at River Valley High School had time on their side in that senior staff were experimenting with vertical timetables and pastoral care approaches for almost two years before a decision was made to implement a new school-wide curriculum structure. This considerable amount of 'lead time' enabled the new curriculum to be implemented relatively painlessly. Nevertheless there was evidence at this school that some teachers were suffering stress due to over-work. The majority of teachers were highly committed and accepted the teaching of large classes, they worked on various committee loads and they had leadership responsibilities for a school house or subject area. This level of commitment could not be maintained and it was unrealistic to presume that it could. Fortunately, teachers union pressures on the Ministry of Education brought about new regulations about maximum sizes of classes under the new Unit Curriculum and this brought about some relief.

The Principal of Branston School opted for some SBCD projects which could be completed within one school year. He was also mindful of time commitments by allocating a number of teacher relief days to those teachers involved in the projects. It is apparent from chapter 4 that project participants embarked upon self-analysis, undertook observation sessions in colleague's classes, and reflected upon substantial issues with other team members. Some staff members received personal gains and feelings of professional growth from undertaking these experiences, despite the onerous loads. Others were less sure and complained of fatigue.

The Canadian case study example also revealed concerns about the effective use of time. The Principal provided teacher-relief time so that the two project groups could work during regular school hours. It is interesting to note that members of the History Committee opted not to use their allotted teacher relief days. They resisted any efforts to reflect upon their current teaching practices and were not willing to produce a common course of study. By contrast, the Geography Committee needed all of their eight teacher-relief days to accomplish their SBCD activity. Their needs only emerged after protracted discussions. It is argued in this chapter that if periods of reflective dialogue had not occurred in the Geography Committee, the group process would have been lost.

The American case study example was also constrained by time limits. Although the team was able to work full-time on the project during their summer vacation and were paid for eleven days of this, they had to make decisions on the run, and were always mindful of the product they had to complete by the conclusion of the time period.

Resources

The provision of appropriate resources is of course a major concern in any SBCD project. As indicated in table 7, resources can take various forms. Grants of money paid direct to a project team might be perceived by recipients to be the most ideal solution but it is becoming far less prevalent in the current period of budget downturns and concerns about accountability. Grants of money tied to the purchase of materials can be of considerable assistance to a project team. Then again, consultants with subject matter expertise or process skills can be hired to work with a project team. These experts can give demonstrations and workshops or be used in the role of group leader or project evaluator.

Money grants
Materials
   examples   teacher readings
                                   activity sheets
                                   curriculum kits
                                   class sets
                                   equipment

Expert advice/modeling
   examples   arranges for presentation by external experts
                                   arranges for demonstrations
                                   arranges for visits to attend workshops

Timetabling assistance
   examples   reduces number of teaching periods
                                   rearranges classes
                                   provides teacher relief

Information retrieval/circulation
   examples   answers requests for information
                                   circulates information to others
                                   exchanges tips/solutions

                                       (after Huberman and Miles, 1984, pp.94–5)

Table 7: Resources for SBCD

There are also many other avenues by which a Principal or Deputy Principal can provide human resources. For example, project members can be given reduced teaching loads if the Principal has access to a fund for teacher-relief days. Even without such funds, the administrator responsible for the school timetable can reallocate duties so as to optimise the block times or free periods available to SBCD project members.

The school Principal and other experienced teachers can be a resource to a project team by providing moral support — offering advice, assisting with the location of sources, or simply being willing to react to proposals and to discuss their reactions in some detail.

However, there can be problems with the provision of resources to project teams. Too often funds are depleted before a project is completed and so team members are not able to get the resources they need for the lifetime of the project. Sometimes the resource providers lose interest in the project or they become committed to other more immediate problems.

An equally serious problem is that resource provisions are often tied to specific conditions. Pressures may be applied to ensure that resources are used for special purposes, whether that is congruent with the intentions of the SBCD project team or not. In these circumstances it is likely that the provision of resources could lead to resentment by project team members with resultant negative outcomes for all concerned.

With reference to the case study chapters, it was evident that River Valley High School was fortunate in receiving considerable resources from the Ministry of Education because it had agreed to become a pilot school for the Unit Curriculum. The salaries of three additional teachers were made available to the school. This money could be used to provide teacher-relief days, to hire consultants or to purchase additional equipment. Specialist personnel from the Ministry were also made available to assist with the development of appropriate computer programs to generate vertical timetables and to provide computer-bank remarks for student reports. Officers from the examination authority (Secondary Education Authority) provided assistance on the planning of the new units and the development of viable forms of assessment. There was considerable moral support from many of these external personnel as well as considerable funds from the Ministry of Education.

Substantial resources were also made available to Branston School as a result of TRIST funding. The school principal had sufficient funds to provide a number of teacher-relief days to project members. He was also able to hire an external consultant to document the SBCD activities and to provide valuable feedback to the participants. This external evaluator was able to provide considerable moral support and expertise to the project teams. However, it is interesting to note that the principal had already made decisions about one of the three SBCD research topics. In this case there was little opportunity for project members' actions to lead to improvement of practices and policies. Rather, this project group considered that they were being used as an instrument of control and they resented this imposition by the principal.

At the Canadian school there was also ample resources to undertake the SBCD activities. This was largely in the form of teacher-relief days although in addition, the Principal hired an external consultant to chair one of the committees and to take on the role of process consultant. This appears to have been a major factor which led to the success of the Geography Committee. Once the Geography Committee members had developed an openness toward each other and a group purpose, they used each other as resources. Those with special expertise in certain areas of geography, such as physical geography, shared their knowledge with others. Community personnel were also used as resources for particular materials needed.

In the American case study considerable financial resources were made available for the team of ten teachers and administrators to be employed full-time for eleven days over their summer vacation. Leonard, the district level coordinator, was able to allocate considerable periods of time to the project during the winter and spring terms.

Although the six developmental stages of SBCD, as described in chapter 2, were only intended to be illustrative, it is interesting to note that examples were highlighted in some of the case study chapters, especially at the Australian school and the Canadian school. There does appear to be some merit in considering stage theory development for teachers as a means of explaining their commitment and their leadership capacities for SBCD activities.

External Initiatives and Support

External agencies such as state/province/local education authority systems have the resources to initiate various changes in schools. Farrar (1987) adds to the list by including state legislatures, a most important force on educational matters over recent years. Various British authors, such as Lawton and Chitty (1988), Reid *et al.* (1988), Campbell (1985) and Simons (1987) refer to the powers of the Secretary of State for Education and Science and the Department of Education and Science. These external agencies are increasingly applying pressure to schools by establishing policy priorities and linking funds to each. They also have the capacity to redistribute staff and to provide consultants to facilitate the implementation of these policies.

The literature is replete with assertions and counter-assertions about the benefits and/or problems of top-down and bottom-up curriculum initiatives (for example, Berman and McLaughlin, 1977; Datta, 1980; Crandall *et al*, 1983; Marsh and Huberman, 1984; Marsh and Bowman, 1988; Sabar *et al*, 1987).

Berman and McLaughlin (1977) argue that a grass-roots approach is the most successful. In an ideal, closed system most would agree that a school community should initiate their own SBCD efforts. In actual practice it is virtually impossible to avoid political interventions by external agencies. Some top-down initiatives will invariably occur and are occurring in most countries during the latter years of the 1980s, whether they are from general policies or specific programs.

Participants in SBCD activities may not be overly concerned about the source of the initiative so long as the funding is not closely tied to specific priorities and that it is sufficient for them to undertake their respective projects. There is some recent evidence in the literature to support this stance. For example Huberman and Crandall (1982) concluded that 'locally adaptive, democratic enterprise is a caricature. The source of innovations is quickly blurred once local implementation begins' (p.80).

Each of the case study chapters involved initiatives by external agencies. In the Australian example, the Ministry of Education had developed a new curriculum structure termed the 'Unit Curriculum' and sought out seven individual schools to adopt the structure and then to develop and implement their particular versions of it. Although staff at River Valley High School were given relative freedom in planning and implementing this major curriculum change, the Ministry did monitor their progress and made available various consultants. In the British example, a central agency, the Manpower Services Commission (MSC) (now the Training Commission) provided funds through its Technical Related In-Service Training program (TRIST) to Branston School. It is interesting to note that the SBCD projects initiated at Branston School were not directly concerned with technical education as might have been anticipated by the funding source. It appears that the focus on school-centred development work was sufficient to attract the grant. One can assume therefore that either MSC and TRIST did not closely monitor the SBCD projects in operation, or that they had a broad definition of the term 'technical'.

The Canadian example exemplifies a typical top-down approach with Ministry of Education policies and provincial guidelines. Both committees were initially hostile to the mandate from the Ministry and in fact the History Committee never progressed beyond one meeting. By contrast, members of the Geography Committee soon lost their hostility to head office when they discovered that the curriculum development process was intrinsically satisfying, due in no small measure to the leadership qualities of the external consultant. As noted above by Huberman and Crandall (1982) the source of this SBCD activity was soon forgotten by the Geography Committee as they became engrossed in reflective dialogue and action.

Conclusion

In this chapter some of the major SBCD factors whicch were conceptualized in chapter 2 were revisited in the light of the case study chapters (chapters 3–6).

The case studies, despite different age levels of school students and the very different contexts selected from Australia, Canada, USA and the UK, revealed some fascinating patterns. There do appear to be some common factors that are important in promoting SBCD. Although many of these factors are interlinked and interrelated, the motivations of stakeholders, interest in innovative approaches and ownership do seem to be factors of paramount importance. Of the six other factors which were also discussed in this chapter, those of considerable significance include time, type of activity and external initiatives.

Chapter 8

Current and Future Issues

The overwhelming feature of schooling over recent decades has been its politicization. Political activity occurs at all levels from politicians and bureaucrats to community and parent groups, to teachers and students. Each interest group endeavours to use its power to achieve certain ends.

In this chapter general political issues with regard to education are examined in Australia, Canada, the UK and the USA followed by a more detailed analysis of specific, current issues such as the role of parents and students in decision-making, initiatives for teacher appraisal and school evaluation and professional development needs.

Introduction

Politicians have taken an active interest in schooling, especially over the last decade. Various writers have indicated that schooling has been deteriorating and so interventions by politicians are not unexpected. For example, Hewlett (1987) states that:

If the politicians came to the conclusion that education was too important to be left to the educators, bear in mind the massive input of public resources, education's failure to demonstrate significant improvement of standards, poor marketing; uncertain professional leadership, and the fact that every year youngsters leave school ignorant of much they might reasonably be expected to know and lacking skills that could have been acquired in 11 years of schooling. (p.31)

Boyd and Smart (1987) emphasize that schooling has become increasingly under the scrutiny of politicians and state that

> it can be characterized by turbulence and change. Everything about our education systems — their organizational structures, their leadership, their political and judicial environments, their teacher organizations and their financial underpinnings — is unquestionably in a state of flux and ferment. (p.12)

A great deal has been written about the politicization of education in the United Kingdom. Various events have been charted — from the Prime Minister's Ruskin speech in 1976, which led to the so-called Great Debate on education, through to increasing decisions being made by Department of Education and Science (DES) officials, to major policy changes made by successive Secretaries of State for Education and Science, especially Sir Keith Joseph and Kenneth Baker, under the watchful guidance of the Prime Minister, Mrs Maggie Thatcher (Glatter *et al.*, 1975; Becher and Maclure, 1978; Lawton, 1980 and 1986; Day *et al.*, 1985; Day and Moore, 1986; Simons, 1987).

The coalitions of power-brokers seem to be constantly changing. In a recent publication Maw (1988) suggests that there has been

> an eclipse of DES civil servants and of Her Majesty Inspectors (HMI), and we are witnessing the domination of the politicians. Mrs Thatcher's deep suspicion of DES officials has been reported on a number of occasions, as has her determination to oversee the passage of the Education Reform Bill . . . (p.58)

The Great Education Reform Bill (GERBIL) was passed by Parliament in July 1988 and has brought about massive changes in terms of:

*   A National Curriculum for all 5–16-year-olds in maintained (government) schools in England and Wales.
    (a) it includes foundation subjects and of these English, maths and science will form the core (secondary schools 30–40 per cent of total time; primary schools — majority of their time);
    (b) attainment targets will be set for the three core subjects for 7, 11, 14 and 16-year-olds;
    (c) themes, such as health education and information technology, are to be taught through foundation subjects;
    (d) programmes of study for each subject will set out the content, knowledge, skills and processes pupils must be taught (but not how they will be taught);

    (e) national tests will measure pupils' progress against the attainment targets;

    (f) records of achievement are to be introduced nationally by 1990.

* Control over school budgets to be given to governing bodies of schools.

* Maintained (government) schools can opt out of local education authority (LEA) control, with grants from the DES being made directly to the school.

In Australia similar patterns have been occurring at the federal level, especially since the creation of the combined Department of Employment, Education and Training in 1987. There has been an increased emphasis upon skills and training needs of students, both in terms of quality and quantity. An economics orientation to education is evident in policies which are demanding that state systems identify tangible educational outcomes and which can justify the costly inputs of funds. As a forerunner to possible National Curriculum initiatives, task forces have been established to review curriculum development activities in all states, to examine ways of reducing duplication of effort and resources, and to 'map' content in specific subjects (for example mathematics) across all state systems.

But the picture is complicated by what is also occurring at state levels, which traditionally has been the locus of power for educational decision-making. In some states, elaborate plans, carefully nurtured and orchestrated by state Ministers of Education, have brought about considerable devolution of decision-making to regions and individual schools. Frazer *et al.* (1985), Marsh (1988) and Caldwell and Spinks (1988) have documented the series of events in Victoria which led to parent and community participation on school councils by an Act of Parliament, a devolution of decision-making powers to schools, and various school-initiated school improvement activities. Similar developments are currently occurring in Western Australia. By contrast, some other states, such as New South Wales, have maintained a strong centralist stance with recent developments including state testing for all students in English and mathematics.

The US has also been involved in establishing national priorities in education by commissioning various reports and studies. These reports have focussed especially on deficiencies in the quality of education and they have made recommendations about how the dilemma of a 'nation at risk' might be resolved (Peters and Waterman, 1982; Deal, 1985; Ginsberg and Wimpelberg, 1987).

Yet it has been individual states which have taken the difficult political decisions of producing legislation and mandates for schools and teachers relating to:

- strengthening graduation requirements and course requirements in the 'New Basics';
- requiring more rigorous, measurable standards;
- requiring more instructional time for learning the New Basics by increasing the length of the school day and lengthening the school year;
- requiring improved teacher preparation. (Harvey *et al.*, 1984)

Some states, especially California and Florida, have been extremely active in implementing major reforms, particularly at the secondary school level. Marsh and Bowman (1987) refer to the top-down and content-oriented developments by the state department of education in California in implementing its School Improvement Program (SIP) and which was based on state legislation passed in 1983.

Features of this legislation include:

- over eighty educational policies and programs ranging from curriculum and instruction reform to revised financial structures.
- increased high school graduation requirements.
- development of model standards for all foundation subject areas.
- development of new criteria for textbook selection.
- strengthening of the alignment between local curriculum and the state testing program. (*ibid.*, pp.5–6)

The accession of George Bush to the Presidency has undoubtedly brought about some reshuffling of policies at the federal level, but the continuance of the Republican line of minimal intervention is likely to be maintained.

The Canadian education system is based upon centralized control at the provincial level, with school boards charged with the responsibility of implementing these policies. Most provinces, but especially Alberta and Ontario, have also been heavily involved in the drive for higher achievement standards, especially at the secondary school level.

Specific SBCD Issues

The key actors involved in political decisions about schooling in their respective countries tend to use several terms to describe or promote their efforts. Such terms include 'quality of schooling', 'school improvement', 'school-focussed improvement', 'self-managing schools' and many others. The term school-based curriculum development (SBCD) is still used in some quarters but more vogue slogans appear to have superceded it, even though they are used synonymously.

Be that as it may, there are a number of interesting issues about SBCD (and its synonyms) which are currently of considerable interest and are likely to remain so in the immediate future. They include:

(a) the role of parents and students in decision-making;
(b) financial management by schools;
(c) professional development for teachers;
(d) professional development for principals;
(e) teacher appraisal;
(f) school evaluation;
(g) pressures of tightening central control.

The Role of Parents and Students in Decision-making

There seems to be a growing realization that the practices of schooling should not be confined to the initiatives and care of the teacher professionals. It is argued that parent participation increases the richness and variety of the school learning environment because of the wide range of skills that can be provided by parents (Beattie, 1985). Many would advocate that parents and other citizens have the democratic right to participate in school decision-making.

Yet, there are enormous difficulties in achieving this end. Although school councils may be created by law (such as in the Australian state of Victoria) there can still be considerable problems in achieving active parent participation because of their work commitments and their perceived or actual lack of skills in group situations. It is interesting to note that parents did not figure prominently in the four case study chapters included in Part II. In the UK the enactment of GERBIL has brought about new powers for school governors but numerous problems are already occurring with regard to the provision of appropriate training skills needed to cope with staff appointments, financial management, running meetings, discipline and related matters.

Similar arguments and problems can be applied to student participation in SBCD activities. Vallance (1981) argues that students have the 'lived-in' experiences of schooling. Their experiences are extremely valuable in providing information to those involved in planning subsequent learning activities. Andrews (1985) asserts that students have legal rights which cover various aspects of schooling including curriculum decision-making. Some of these legal rights have in fact been tested in the courts, especially in the USA since the 1960s.

Students are becoming active participants in some secondary schools, especially where there is support from other agencies to provide skills-training. Darling and Carrigan (1986) suggest that some major problems for student participation include prejudice and negative attitudes by adult school councillors; lack of student skills in communicating ideas, meeting procedures and organizing tasks; and resource and accreditation issues.

The issue of increased participation by parents and students in SBCD activities is likely to remain a problem in the next decade and beyond. Limited resources in already stretched education budgets will make this a very difficult area in which to achieve results.

Financial Management by Schools

In many countries there have been moves to shift the responsibility for financial management to individual schools. The motivations for this could be partly educational in that it can be argued that personnel at each school are in the best position to make decisions about the structures and curricula and deployment of staff to create the best possible learning conditions. It might also be construed as an economic measure by head offices, thereby forcing local schools to demonstrate moderation and economies in handling very limited resources. A number of writers, such as Caldwell and Spinks (1988), applaud the opportunities for self-management of finances so long as this is linked to educational plans. These authors have developed a model for linking goal-setting, need identification, policy-making, planning, budgeting, learning and teaching and evaluating. Their approach is widely used in several Australian states and has the advantage of involving school staff in collaborative planning activities. Staff acquire various financial management skills by on-the-job training.

Although the Caldwell and Spinks (1988) model (and others found in the literature) provide useful procedures for personnel to develop on-the-job skills, there is still an urgent need for school principals and senior teachers to receive training in basic skills of financial management. They need to develop an awareness of programme budgeting and the skills needed to initiate and maintain financial records, balance sheets, short and long-term policy planning, long-term contracts, inventory planning and control and cash management and related matters.

This problem is far from resolved. Pre-service/initial training programs do not deal with topics of financial management. Their respective programmes are already overloaded with what are considered to be basic survival topics needed for the neophyte classroom teacher. Funds for professional development of practising teachers have not been plentiful over recent years due to budgetary restrictions upon education. The ideal is to provide training for senior school personnel via intensive workshops and by periods of secondment to industry. The limited degree to which this is actively occurring must be a continuing dilemma for senior education officials.

Professional Development for Teachers

Successful SBCD activities are dependent upon the collaborative efforts of skilled professionals. Simons (1988) echoes this point when she states that:

> The professionals I have in mind evaluate what they do against self-generated critical standards, they research shortfalls in provision and performance, they respond to changes of context or clientele, they experiment, they reflect, they develop new programmes to solve identified problems, they collaborate, they engage in persuasive negotiation with the constituencies whose support and approval they need. (p.78)

As indicated in earlier chapters, more teachers (and other stakeholders such as parents and students) have to develop skills such as those identified above over time. Leadership skills are acquired by taking on new roles in different circumstances and learning from the experiences. Confidence and commitment among participants takes time to develop and requires opportunities for group-sharing and reflection.

Despite all the evidence from the mid 1970s and early 1980s about successful professional development practices (for example, Crandall *et al.*, 1983; Huberman and Miles, 1984; Little, 1981; Louis and Dentler, 1982; Marsh and Berman, 1984; Showers, 1982; and McLaughlin and Pfeifer, 1988), it is most disappointing to note that education authorities do not appear to be willing to commit the same level of resources into professional development in the late 1980s.

To achieve budgetary economies in Australia, for example, major professional development programmes have been terminated and personnel associated with them (for example, process consultants) greatly reduced in number. The new focus is upon a relatively narrow set of management skills. In the UK a new set of in-service provisions under the LEA Training Grants Scheme (LEATGS) have produced a reduction in the extended, intensive in-service programmes and a far greater emphasis upon mass model professional development days (school-focussed training days for total school staff) placed adjacent to school holidays so as to cause minimal administrative disruption (Bamber and Nash, 1988), and other short intensive programmes which do not allow for the kinds of support, reflection and deliberative enquiry essential for learning and change.

It would appear that the lessons of the 1960s and 70s have not been learnt by senior education officials:

> where education reform efforts fell short primarily because planners seriously underestimated teacher-training needs. . . . An important lesson of the so-called 'Decade of Reform' (1965–1975) is that even the 'best' educational practice is unlikely to fulfil its promise in the hands of an inadequately trained or unmotivated teacher. (McLaughlin and Marsh, 1979, p.69)

Furthermore, Simons (1988, p.85) notes that the language for professional development has now changed with terms like 'task force' 'objectives' 'delivery' and 'managers' but there is no evidence that these power-coercive strategies will be any more effective in the years ahead. Insufficient attention to the professional development needs of stakeholders as we move toward the 1990s might well be a problem of monumental proportions.

Professional Development for Principals

As indicated in chapter 7, school principals can play a major role in SBCD activities. They are often instrumental in initiating an SBCD activity or on occasions they may act to hinder it. There are various changes to the principal role which have been developing over the last decade and these are likely to continue on into the 1990s. Hopes (1986) refers to the pressures coming from various groups including parents, teachers and the community. These groups are demanding, and in some countries obtaining, greater degrees of participation by Acts of Parliament.

School principals exert their leadership role (along with other senior staff) in different ways. They develop techniques for communication and consultation based upon past experiences and/or special training they have received. They have to persuade indifferent staff to

202

become involved in SBCD projects; and to be able to tolerate hostile reactions, cynicism and apathy.

In chapter 7 reference was made to particular leadership styles such as 'responders', 'managers' and 'initiation' (Hall and Rutherford, 1983). These and other typologies point to some leadership styles which seem more effective than others in fostering successful SBCD ventures but the research evidence is equivocal. What is clear from recent studies (for example, Bailey, 1985; Bolam, 1987) is that the impact of current short (ten–twenty days) and long (one term or more) training courses for school principals are only effective if sufficient preparation and follow-up is included. Education authorities at present seem to make little provision for school principals (and aspiring principals) to have time to reflect upon their role prior to attending these in-service courses. Even more important, there is little encouragement for principals to follow through with post-course activities such as discussion groups, management tasks, and review sessions.

Some recent developments, such as those programs operating in Canada by Leithwood *et al.* (1984) are of special interest as they make the assumption that principal effectiveness is a continuous process which can be enhanced through training rather than a personality character-istic which some have and some have not. They consider that the ultimate purpose of such a training programme is to train principals to become systematic problem-solvers.

> The training program consists of diagnosing the entry behaviours of each principal by the use of interviews and questionnaires and then providing a particular package of activities that will assist each person to get to the stage of systematic problem-solver. To achieve a truly individualised approach it is clear that the training program must have follow-up activities between trainer and prin-cipal extending over many months. The communication between each must be kept strictly confidential to avoid invidious compari-sons between principals. Above all, the employing authority must be committed to the training program in terms of providing the necessary resources for trainers and relief-time for school principals.

In the United Kingdom, the National Development Centre for School Management Training, which was established at the University of Bri-stol in 1983, is another interesting approach to the training of school principals (and other school leaders). They prefer to use the term 'school manager' and have developed a number of successful programs using techniques derived from industry.

Lack of resources to support these necessarily expensive and time consuming programs for school principals is likely to be a major concern in the ensuing years. The rapidity and intensity of changes to schools make such training programs for principals a necessity. System officials cannot expect new and major policy decisions to be implemented without providing the necessary support and training to their school leaders/managers.

Teacher Appraisal

Teacher appraisal is currently an important issue and it is likely to remain so into the 1990s. The enduring preoccupations of government with accountability and efficiency are such that teacher appraisal is not likely to fade away. As noted by Bunnell (1987)

> Schools are no longer and never again will be private places. The community and parents want increasingly to know what is happening and want better evidence for claims made. (pp.9–10)

In any case, there are some very real advantages if teacher appraisal is considered from a formative, developmental perspective. Various writers such as Reid *et al.* (1988), Bunnell (1987), Day *et al.* (1987) and Wragg (1987) suggest that teacher appraisal can be justified because:

(a) it enables teachers to know themselves;
(b) it provides feedback for curriculum planning and general school planning;
(c) it provides the basis for professional development;
(d) it provides accountability data.

However, these justifications can only be substantiated if teacher appraisal schemes are widely discussed, if teachers are represented at all planning stages, and if certain safeguards are included. This is especially important for schools which are heavily involved in SBCD activities. The collaborative, trusting climate developed through SBCD team efforts could be severely strained if teacher appraisal schemes were initiated unilaterally and without sufficient negotiation among all staff. Evans (1988) reminds us that too often bureaucratic schemes are hastily introduced and inadequately funded.

> They include crude carrot-and-stick mechanisms which ensure that teachers gloss over, or avoid altogether, any major difficulties or constraints. They do nothing to promote teachers' professional

development; they do not encourage teachers to participate actively in the appraisal process, nor to suggest changes or make criticisms of the management of their schools and colleagues; they do not set realistic targets for teachers to work towards.

Above all, such schemes fail because their central aim is not to improve teaching and learning, but to provide some superficial form of accountability, either to bureaucrats or to the public at large. (p.4)

The experiments with teacher appraisal are many and varied in the four countries considered in this book and go under different titles such as 'teacher evaluation', 'performance management' as well as 'teacher appraisal'. Most would agree that teacher appraisal is worth developing so long as certain caveats can be upheld such as:

(a) teachers are widely consulted over all aspects;
(b) it is non-threatening and is kept separate from disciplinary and dismissal procedures;
(c) the information collected is strictly limited to the appraisee, the appraiser and to the school principal;
(d) appraisal is used as an integral part of the process of professional development;
(e) appraisal is undertaken of all teachers and administrators at a school;
(f) the appraisal exercise must be properly resourced.

Some of these caveats are difficult to achieve. For example, Reid *et al.* (1988) maintains that the resource implications are daunting and would involve each appraisee in at least twelve hours per annum. Add to this the training time needed for appraisers (ten to forty hours per annum) and time required to undertake appraisals (ten to twenty hours per teacher) and the total annual costs for a school could easily exceed $6–10,000 (Australian dollars) per annum.

There is an important link between teacher appraisals and professional development. Teacher appraisals provide the information required to identify training and professional needs of individual teachers. The credibility of teacher appraisals revolves around this premise.

There have been examples, especially in the USA, of teacher appraisal schemes which have been inappropriately biased toward easily measurable outcomes such as teacher qualifications and teacher effectiveness based on student achievements on standardized tests. Teacher appraisal is a very complex task and easy solutions will need to be resisted as new and exploratory approaches are developed over the coming years.

School Evaluation

'School evaluation' or 'school self-evaluation' has been given prominence in many countries during the 1980s and it is likely to become even more widespread. It is, of course, a vital process for any SBCD activity. Many writers such as Van Velzen (1982) and Bollen (1987) consider that the diagnosis achieved by a school evaluation is a vital first step, an inevitable phase in any SBCD process.

However, there are often other purposes. Evaluations can be carried out in different ways, some of which may be more desirable than others. For example Simons (1986) and Clift *et al.* (1987) both concede that school evaluations may be initiated to provide the catalyst for SBCD activities but pressures may also be brought to bear to use the information for accountability purposes. There has certainly been evidence of this in the UK where LEAs have supposedly assisted schools with their self-evaluation schemes but the hidden message has been to acquire accountability data for the LEA's (Simons, 1986). In some state systems in Australia, funds for SBCD activities have been tied to schools undertaking school evaluations and making this data available to regional or central offices.

It seems inevitable that school evaluations will be used for both purposes. Local communities, as well as school systems/departments, do want to know how their school is faring. Independent (public) schools which rely upon full-fee paying students have to maintain an image of excellence and they often embark upon comprehensive school evaluations so that they can use the results in their publicity literature. For example many independent schools in Australia have used the New England model of school evaluation (New England Association of Schools and Colleges, 1972) which uses an external panel of eight to ten people, comprising experts, citizens and teachers or principals from other schools, to review a school's activities and to uncover dysfunctions between reported and actual practices. These schools may use their evaluation reports as the basis for ongoing SBCD activities, especially where deficiencies in the school curriculum have been uncovered. However, the predominant purpose is one of producing information which will be selectively used for recruitment purposes.

Be that as it may, there are many schools which are embarking upon school evaluations because they perceive it as an essential aspect of the SBCD process. The scale of the evaluation can vary from school to school. For some it might be an evaluation of a subject department, or an age level grouping such as the junior primary grades, or the total school. Various authors such as Elliott (1979), McMahon *et al.* (1984), Brennan and Hoadley (1984), Simons (1987), Caldwell and Spinks (1986) cite important criteria for school evaluations. They consider that school-focussed evaluation should be:

- holistic in nature;
- owned by the school;
- an integral part of the school's function;
- process- rather than product-oriented;
- continuous and incremental;
- inclusive rather than exclusive;
- cooperative and collaborative;
- purposeful and judgmental.

Of these authors, McMahon *et al.* (1984) produced the Guidelines for the Review and Internal Development of Schools (GRIDS) which has been widely used by UK schools. Day *et al.* (1985, pp.160–1) highlight a number of positive aspects about the GRIDS approach, such as the detailed advice it provides to heads and senior staff on how to conduct a school review and development exercise, and the emphasis upon staff to take a broad look at their school to select priority areas which are manageable within typical time constraints. In Australia, the Collaborative School Management Model (CSM) developed by Caldwell and Spinks (1986) is being used very widely in several states. Although writers have been critical about certain aspects of the GRIDS and CSM models (for example Simons, 1987; Marsh, 1988), the models do provide useful frameworks for school staffs intent on seeking out information about their school needs/deficiencies as a preliminary to initiating SBCD projects.

It would appear that school evaluations will continue to have a high priority for school staffs in the foreseeable future. Although it is desirable that these school self-evaluations are broad-based and use inputs from parents and students, it is likely that this will continue to be the exception rather than the rule. Teacher skills in undertaking evaluation tasks will be dependent upon them attaining the necessary training, and for this purpose, professional development resources will be of considerable importance (Clift *et al.*, 1987).

There may be increasing pressures for school self-evaluations to include data on student outcomes in addition to their usual categories. More elaborate data-collecting methods are now available and computer programs make the task of processing data far easier. Pressures from education authorities and the media may force school evaluations to look far more closely at school performance indicators. As noted by Harrison (1988, p.23) in a feature article in the *Times Educational Supplement*, it is up to school staffs to develop indicators which embody educational integrity and which are fair. If these are not developed within schools there is a grave danger that unfair ones will be imposed by external agencies.

Pressures of Tightening Central Controls

In the four countries studied it is disquietening to note the tightening central controls which have occurred over education policies and practices and which appear to show no signs of abating in the near future. If these central controls also apply to curriculum decision-making then the opportunities for SBCD in the future are very limited indeed. However, in most countries, the type of controls being applied display some variable attributes, some of which provide opportunities for the support and expansion of SBCD while others are clearly restricting SBCD.

Possibly the prime example is in the United Kingdom where the Thatcher government since 1979 has accelerated central control (Simons, 1987). As noted in the beginning of this chapter, GERBIL plans are now underway to introduce a National Curriculum for 5–16-year-olds in government schools and to be linked to national testing at ages 7, 11, 14 and 16. This will have a massive limiting effect upon what is taught in schools as few teachers will dare ignore the importance of the national tests. The scope for SBCD in this situation would seem to be extremely bleak. Yet, it should be noted that GERBIL also expands the role of school governors and community control of local schools. Further, the National Curriculum applies only to maintained (government) schools. It is still possible, therefore, for schools to embark upon SBCD projects especially in schools where enlightened governors perceive the need for local curriculum endeavours.

The Australian scene is complicated by somewhat different emphases at federal and state levels. At the federal level a new super ministry, the Department of Employment, Education and Training (DEET) appears intent on establishing new national policies including a National Curriculum. However, it does not have the powers to dictate policy direct to schools because this is a state preserve. Some states are moving toward state testing (for example the state of New South Wales is producing state tests for mathematics and English for years 3, 6 and

10) but others are taking a very strong stance against any form of state-wide testing.

Some Australian states have brought about structural change, such as school boards and decentralized regions to encourage SBCD activities. This has occurred especially in three states, the Australian Capital Territory, Victoria and Western Australia. In these states, funds have been provided to individual schools to embark upon school self-evaluations and to develop their own school improvement plans. Yet, over recent months, increasing accountability pressures are being applied as management priorities, programme budgeting and curriculum frameworks are being developed centrally and applied to all schools.

The American picture is also complicated by the different state priorities to education. Some states, such as California, have produced far more centralized directives to schools over recent years in an attempt to improve the quality of schooling, especially at the secondary school level. The Californian School Improvement Program provides strict guidelines for aligning curriculum content with appropriate textbooks and with state testing programs. Yet there is still considerable opportunity and funds available for school staff to become involved in SBCD projects. A similar situation seems to be occurring in many provinces in Canada.

Conclusion

Although the term SBCD is not used as frequently in the literature in the late 1980s as in the 1970s, the practices embodied in the term still seem to be occurring, and in some situations, even flourishing. It is unlikely that schools will ever retreat back to an isolated, private existence where the superordinate position of the school principal was sacrosanct, where teachers had strict procedures to follow and where parents and the community were virtually excluded from all decision-making.

The spirit of schooling in the 1980s is one of collaboration and sharing. In some countries the opportunities for SBCD are greater than in others and more advances are likely as we move into the 1990s. Parents are demanding a greater share in the decision-making and in most countries the provision of new or improved structures is facilitating this process. Teachers are developing more skills in group decision-making as a result of initial training/pre-service and in-service programmes.

Against this backdrop of commitment and collaboration are of course the political initiatives. Some of the recent political announcements may prove to be ephemeral as political parties go in or out of government. Notwithstanding, it is certain that the politicization of education will continue to be a major force in the 1990s. Whether political parties perceive centralized or decentralized priorities to be important will have a marked impact on the continuance of SBCD activities.

Bibliography

ADAMS, M. (1984) 'A school coping with change: St John's Girls High School', *Curriculum Exchange*, **2**, 1.

ALEXANDER, K. (1985) 'Political intervention and curricula accountability', paper presented at the annual conference of the South Pacific Association of Teacher Educators, Hobart.

ANDERSON, B.L. and COX, P.L. (1988) *Configuring the Education System for a Shared Future: Collaborative Vision, Action, Reflection*, Andover, MA, Regional Laboratory for Educational Improvement.

ANDREWS, G. (1985) *The Parent Action Manual*, Melbourne, Schools Community Interaction Trust.

ANGUS, M.J. (1974) 'Traditionalism and openness in Australian primary schools', *Education*, **23**, 2.

ARMSTRONG, M. (1980) *Closely Observed Children*, London, Writer & Readers.

BAILEY, A. (1985) *Support for School Management*, Falmer, University of Sussex.

BAKER, K. (1980) 'Planning school policies for INSET: "The SITE Project"' in HOYLE, E. and MEGARRY, J. (Eds) *World Yearbook of Education 1980 Professional Development of Teachers*, London, Kogan Page.

BAKER, K. (1982) '"The SITE Project"', in BOLAM, R. (Ed) *School-focussed In-service Training*, London, Heinemann Educational Books.

BAMBER, P. and NASH, J. (1988) 'Inset or ensa?', *Times Educational Supplement*, 22 July, p.16.

BARNES, D., BRITTON, J. and ROSEN, H. (1971) *Language, the Learner and the School*, London, Penguin.

BARROW, R. (1984) 'Teacher judgement and teacher effectiveness', *Journal of Educational Thought*, **18**, 2, pp.76–83.

BATTEN, M. (1987) 'Students' views of the year 12 courses', *Curriculum Perspectives*, **7**, 2.

BEATTIE, N. (1985) *Professional Parents*, Lewes, Falmer Press.

BEAZLEY, K.E. (Chairman) (1984) Report of the Committee of Inquiry into Education Western Australia, Perth, Government Printer.

BECHER, T. and MACLURE, S. (1978) *Politics of Curriculum Change*, London, Hutchinson.

BELL, G.H. (1985) 'INSET: Five types of collaboration and consultancy', *School Organisation*, **5**, 3.

BERMAN, P. and McLAUGHLIN, M.W. (1977) *Federal Programs Supporting Educational Change*, prepared for the U.S. Office of Education Department of Health, Education and Welfare, Santa Monica, CA, Rand Corporation.

BOLAM, R. (1982a) *Strategies for School Improvement*, Paris, OECD.

BOLAM, R. (Ed) (1982b) *School-focussed In-service Training*, London, Heinemann Educational Books.

BOLAM, R. (1987) 'Management development: A response from the UK perspective', in HOPKINS, D. (Ed) *Improving the Quality of Schooling*, Lewes, Falmer Press.

BOLAM, R. (1988) 'The management and development of staff', keynote paper for the BEMAS Conference on Research in Educational Management, Cardiff, 12–14 April.

BOLLEN, R. (1987) 'School-based review in the context of educational policy', in HOPKINS, D. (Ed) *Improving the Quality of Schooling*, Lewes, Falmer Press.

BOYD, W.L. and SMART, D. (Eds) (1987) *Educational Policy in Australia and America*, Lewes, Falmer Press.

BOYER, E.L. (1983) *High School: A Report on Secondary Education in America*, New York, Harper & Row.

BRADY, L. (1987) *Curriculum Development* (2nd edn), Sydney, Prentice Hall.

BRADY, L. (1988) 'The principal as a climate factor in Australian schools: Overview of studies', *Journal of Educational Administration*, **26**, 1.

BRANSTON (1986a) 'TRIST The Branston Proposal', draft for discussion at Academic Board, 14 April.

BRANSTON (1986b) *Branston TRIST (Teachers as Experts)*, Launch Pack, May.

BRANSTON (1986c) *Staff Bulletin. Trist Update*, 23 June.

BRENNAN, M. and HOADLEY, R. (1984) *School Self-Evaluation*, Melbourne, Education Department of Victoria.

BUNNELL, S. (1987) *Teacher Appraisal and Practice*, London, Heinemann.

BUTT, R. (1981) 'Classroom change and scientific literacy: A case study', in LEITHWOOD, K. and HUGHES, A. (Eds) *Curriculum Canada III*.

CALDWELL, B.J. and SPINKS, J.M. (1986) *Policy-Making and Training for School Effectiveness*, Hobart, Education Department of Tasmania.

CALDWELL, B.J. and SPINKS, J.M. (1988) *The Self-Managing School*, Lewes, Falmer Press.

CAMPBELL, R.J. (1985) *Developing the Primary School Curriculum*, London, Holt, Rinehart & Winston.

CARR, W. and KEMMIS, S. (1986a) *Becoming Critical: Education, Knowledge and Action Research*, Lewes, Falmer Press.

CARR, W. and KEMMIS, S. (1986b) *Becoming Critical: Knowing Through Action Research*, Geelong, Deakin University Press.

CENTRAL ADVISORY COUNCIL FOR EDUCATION (1963) *Half Our Future* (The Newsom Report), London, HMSO.

CENTRAL ADVISORY COUNCIL FOR EDUCATION (1967) *Children and Their Primary Schools* (The Plowden Report), London, HMSO.

CLIFT, P.S., NUTTALL, D.L., and McCORMICK, R. (1987) *Studies in School Self-Evaluation*, Lewes, Falmer Press.

COHEN, D. and HARRISON, M. (1982) *Curriculum Action Project*, Sydney, Macquarie University.

COMMON, D.L. (1986) 'Who are the reformers: Teachers or policymaker?', *Comment on Education*, **16**, 4, pp.5–7.

CONNELLY, F.M. (1972) 'The functions of curriculum development', *Interchange*, **2**, pp.161–77.

CONNELLY, F.M. and BEN-PERETZ, M. (1980) 'Teachers' roles in the using and doing of research and curriculum development', *Journal of Curriculum Studies*, **12**, 2.

CONNELLY, M.F. and CLANDININ, J.D. (1985) 'On narrative method, personal philosophy and narrative unities in the study of teaching', paper presented at the annual meeting of NARST, Indiana.

COREY, S.M. (1953) *Action Research to Improve School Practice*, New York, Columbia University.

CRANDALL, D. *et al.* (1983) *The Study of Dissemination Efforts Supporting School Improvement (DESSI)*, Andover, MA, The Network.

DARLING, T. and CARRIGAN, T. (1986) *Taking Apart: A Student Action Resource Handbook*, Melbourne, West Education Centre.

DATTA, L.E. (1980) 'Changing times: The study of federal programs supporting educational change in the case of local problem solving', *Teachers College Record*, **82**, 1.

DAY, C. (1981) 'Classroom-based in-service teacher education: The development and evaluation of a client-centred model', Occasional Paper No. 9, University of Sussex.

DAY, C. (1984) 'External consultancy: Supporting school-based curriculum development, in HOLLY, P. and WHITEHEAD, D. *Action Research in Schools: Getting it into Perspective*, Cambridge, CARN, Cambridge Institute of Education.

DAY, C. (1986) 'Sharing practice through consultancy: Individual and whole school staff development in a primary school', in HOLLY, P. and WHITEHEAD, D. (Eds) *Collaborative Action Research*, CARN Bulletin No.7, Cambridge Institute of Education.

DAY, C. (1987) 'Professional learning through collaborative in-service activity', in SMYTH, J. (Ed) *Educating Teachers: Changing the Nature of Pedagogical Knowledge*, Lewes, Falmer Press.

DAY, C., JOHNSTON, D. and WHITAKER, P. (1985) *Managing Primary Schools: A Professional Development Approach*, London, Harper & Row.

DAY, C. and MOORE, R. (Eds) (1986) *Staff Development in the Secondary School: Management Perspectives*, London, Croom Helm.

DAY, C., WHITAKER, P., and WREN, D. (1987) *Appraisal and Professional Development in the Primary School*, Milton Keynes, Open University Press.

DEAL, T.E. (1985) 'National commissions: Blueprints for remodelling or ceremonies for revitalising public schools, *Education and Open Society*, **17**, 2.

DEPARTMENT OF EDUCATION AND SCIENCE (1975) *A Language for Life*, (The Bullock Report) London, HMSO.

DEPARTMENT OF EDUCATION AND SCIENCE (1978a) *A Survey of Primary Education*, London, HMSO.

DEPARTMENT OF EDUCATION AND SCIENCE (1979) *Aspects of Secondary Education in England (The Secondary School Survey)*, London, HMSO.

DEPARTMENT OF EDUCATION AND SCIENCE (1979b) *Special Education Needs* (The Warnock Report), London, HMSO.

DEPARTMENT OF EDUCATION AND SCIENCE (1982) *Mathematics Counts: Report of the Committee of Enquiry into the Teaching of Mathematics* (the Cockcroft Report), London, HMSO.

DEPARTMENT OF EDUCATION AND SCIENCE (1986) *Local Education Authority Training Grants Scheme: Financial Year 1987–88*, Circular No. 6/86, London, DES.

DEPARTMENT OF EDUCATION AND SCIENCE (1987a) *School Teachers' Pay and Conditions of Employment: The Government's Proposals*, London, DES.

DEPARTMENT OF EDUCATION AND SCIENCE (1987b) *The National Curriculum 5–16: A Consultation Document*, London, Department of Education and Science and the Welsh Office.

DOW, G. (1985) 'Curricular reforms "Caught not Taught" in Australia', *Journal of Curriculum Studies*, **17**, 2.

EGAN, K. (1986) *Teaching as Story Telling*, London, Ontario, Althouse Press.

ELBAZ, F.L. (1983) *Teacher Thinking: A Study of Practical Knowledge*, London, Croom Helm.

ELLIOTT, J. (1977) 'Conceptualising relationships between research/evaluation procedures and in-service teacher education', *British Journal of In-Service Education*, **4**, 1 & 2.

ELLIOTT, J. (1979) 'The case for school self-evaluation', *Forum for the Discussion of New Trends in Education*, **22**.

ELLIOTT, J. (Ed) (1980) *The Theory and Practice of Educational Action Research*, CARN Bulletin 4, Cambridge Institute of Education.

ELLIOTT, J. (1981a) *Action Research: A Framework for Self-Evaluation in Schools*, Teacher–Pupil Interaction and the Quality of Learning Project, Cambridge Institute of Education (mimeo).

ELLIOT, J. (1981b) 'Action-research: A framework for self-evaluation in school, Schools Council Programme 2, Teacher/pupil interaction and equality of learning project', Cambridge Institute of Education Working Paper No. 1.

ELLIOTT, J. (1983) 'School-focussed INSET and research into teacher education', *Cambridge Journal of Education*, **13**, 2, pp.19–31.

ELLIOTT, J. (1984) 'Implementing school-based action research: Some hypotheses', in BELL, J. *et al.* (Eds) *Conducting Small-Scale Investigations in Educational Management*, London, Harper & Row.

ELLIOTT, J. (1985) 'Facilitating action research in schools: Some dilemmas', in BURGESS, R. (Ed) *Field Methods in the Study of Education*, Lewes, Falmer Press.

ELLIOTT, J. and ADELMAN, C. (1973a) 'Reflecting where the action is: The design of the Ford Teaching Project', *Education for Teaching*, **92**, pp.8–20.

ELLIOTT, J. and ADELMAN, C. (1973b) 'Supporting teachers' research in the classroom', *New Era*, **54**, pp.210–13 and 215.

EVANS, A. (1988) 'The messages spelled out in the pilots' slipstream', *Times Educational Supplement*, 20 May, p.4.

FARRAR, E. (1987) 'Improving the urban high school: The role of leadership in the school, district and state', paper presented at the annual meeting of the American Educational Research Association, Washington D.C.

FISHER, R. and BROWN, S. (1988) *Getting Together*, Boston, MA, Houghton Mifflin.

FITZGERALD, R.T. (1973) 'Analaysis of context, structure and process in relation to reformist demands in education', *Australian Journal of Education*, **17**, 1.

FORDHAM, R. (1983) Ministerial Papers 1–4, Melbourne, Government Printer.

FORDHAM, R. (1984) *Curriculum Development and Planning in Victoria*, Ministerial Paper No. 6, Melbourne, Government Printer.

FRASER, D.J. and NASH, R. (1981) *Evaluation of Educational Innovations*, Sydney, Macquarie University.

FRAZER, M., DUNSTAN, J., and CREED, P. (1985) *Perspectives and Organisational Change*, Melbourne, Longman Cheshire.

FULLAN, M. (1982) *The Meaning of Educational Change*, New York, Teachers College Press.

GATHERER, W. (1984) 'School decision-making and accountability', *Education*, **33**, 1.

GEORGIADES, N.J. and PHILLIMORE, L. (1975) 'The myth of the hero-innovator and alternative strategies for organisational change', in KEIRNAN, C.C. and WOODFORD, F.P. (Eds) *Behaviour Modification with the Severely Retarded*, North Holland, Elsevier Excerpta Medica.

GINSBERG, R. and WIMPELBERG, R.K. (1987) 'Educational change by commission: Attempting "Trickle down" reform', *Educational Evaluation and Policy Analysis*, **9**, 4.

GLATTER, R. *et al.* (Eds) (1975) *Understanding School Management*, Milton Keynes, Open University Press.

GLATTHORN, A.A. (1987) *Curriculum Leadership*, Glenview, IL, Scott, Foresman & Co.

GOODLAD, J.I. (1984) *A Place Called School: Prospects for the Future*, New York, McGraw-Hill.

GOODLAD, J.I. (Ed) (1987) *The Ecology of School Renewal*, Chicago, IL, University of Chicago Press.

HALL, G.E. *et al.* (1984) 'Effects of three principals' styles on school improvement', *Journal of Educational Leadership*, **41**, 5.

HALL, G.E. and HORD, S.M. (1987) *Change in Schools: Facilitating the Process*, Albany, NY, State University of New York Press.

HALL, G.E. and LOUCKS, S.F. (1977) 'A developmental model for determining whether the treatment is actually implemented', *American Educational Research Journal*, **14**, 3.

HALL, G.E., LOUCKS, S.F., RUTHERFORD, W.L. and NEWLOVE, B.W. (1975) 'Levels of use of the innovation: A framework for analysing innovation adoption', *Journal of Teacher Education*, **26**, 1.

HALL, G.E. and RUTHERFORD, W.L. (1983) *Three Change Facilitator Styles: How Principals Affect Improvement Efforts*, Austin, TX, Research and Development Center for Teacher Education, University of Texas, also presented at the annual meeting of the American Educational Research Association, Montreal.

HALL, G.E., RUTHERFORD, W.L. and GRIFFIN, T.H. (1982) 'Three change facilitator styles, some indicators and a proposed framework', paper presented at the annual meeting of the American Educational Research Association, New York.

HALL, R. (1987) 'An alternative assessment of the Branston School and Community College TRIST Scheme 1986/7', unpublished MEd assignment, School of Education, University of Nottingham.

HALPIN, A.W. and CROFT, D.B. (1963) *Organisational Climate of Schools*, Chicago, IL, University of Chicago Press.

HANNAY, L. and SELLER, W. (1987) *Decision Making in Curriculum Development*, Ottawa, Social Science and Humanities Research Council of Canada.

HANNAY, L. and SELLER, W. (1988) 'The influence of teachers' thinking on curriculum development decisions', paper presented at the Fourth Conference of the International Study Association on Teacher Thinking, England.

HARLEN, W., MARTIN, M. and SYMINGTON, D. (1977) 'School-based curriculum evaluation', unpublished paper, State College of Victoria, Toorak.

HARRISON, M. (1981) 'School-based curriculum decision making: A personal viewpoint', *Curriculum Perspectives*, **2**, 1.

HARRISON, P. (1988) 'Winning points', *Times Educational Supplement*, 27 May, p.23.

HARVEY, G. *et al.* (1984) 'Recent reports concerning education', paper presented at the annual meeting of the American Educational Research Association, New Orleans.

HENDERSON, E.S. (1979) 'School-focussed INSET evaluation', *Cambridge Journal of Education*, **9**, 2 and 3, pp.165–74.

HEWLETT, M. (1987) 'Can we complain?' *Times Educational Supplement*, 18 September, p.31.

HOPES, C. (Ed) (1986) *The School Leader in School Improvement*, Leuven, ACCO Press.

HOPKINS, D. (1984) 'What is school improvement? Staking out the territory', in HOPKINS, D. and WIDEEN, M. *Alternative Perspectives on School Improvement*, Lewes, Falmer Press.

HORD, S.M. (1986) 'Implementing excellence in schools: Rhetoric and reality', paper presented at the annual conference of the South Pacific Association for Teacher Education, Perth.

HOYLE, E. (1986) *The Politics of School Management*, London, Hodder & Stoughton.

HUBERMAN, M. (1980) 'Finding and using recipes for busy kitchens: A situational analysis of knowledge using schools', paper prepared for the Programme on Research In Education Practice, National Institute of Education, Washington D.C.

HUBERMAN, A.M. and CRANDALL, D.P. (1982) 'A study of dissemination efforts supporting school improvement' (DESSI) Vol. IX, *People, Policies and Practices: Examining the Chain of School Improvement*, Andover, MA, The Network.

HUBERMAN, M. and MILES, M. (1982) *How School Improvement Works: A Field Study of 12 Sites*, Andover, MA, The Network.

HUBERMAN, A.M. and MILES, M. (1984) *Innovation Up Close: How School Improvement Works*, New York, Plenum Press.

HUBERMAN, A.M. and MILES, M.B. (1986) 'Rethinking the quest for school improvement: Some findings from the DESSI study', in LIEBERMAN, A. (Ed) *Rethinking School Improvement*, New York, Teachers College Press.

HUGHES, P. *et al.* (1978) *Teachers as Evaluators Project Policy Paper: A Rationale for Curriculum Evaluation in Australia*, Canberra, Canberra College of Advanced Education.

HUMANITIES CURRICULUM PROJECT (1970) *The Humanities Project: An Introduction*, London, Heinemann Educational Books.

HUNT, J. (1981) 'Community participation in school curriculum: Has any real change occurred?' in COLLINS, C. (Ed) *New Directions in School and Community Studies*, School and Community Project, Vol. 2, Canberra, Canberra College of Advanced Education.

HUSTLER, D., CASSIDY, A. and CUFF, E.C. (Eds) (1986) *Action Research in Classrooms and Schools*, London, Allen & Unwin.

JONES, A.W. (1977) 'Memorandum on freedom and authority', in JONES, A.W. *Ebb and Flow: Papers and Addresses by A.W. Jones*, Adelaide, Government Printer.

KARMEL, P. Chairman (1973) *Schools in Australia: Report of the Interim Committee for the Australian Schools Commission*, Canberra, Government Printer.

KEAST, D. (1982) 'School-based in-service and the providers', *British Journal of In-service Education*, **9**, 1, autumn.

KEMMIS, S. (1981a) *The Professional Development of Teachers Through Involvement in Action Research Projects*, Geelong, Deakin University Press.

KEMMIS, S. *et al.* (1981b) *The Action Research Planner*, Geelong, Deakin University Press.

KEMMIS, S. and McTAGGART, R. (1984) *The Action Research Planner* (2nd edn), Geelong, Deakin University.

KERWOOD, B. and CLEMENTS, S. (1986) 'A strategy for school-based staff development', in DAY, C. and MOORE, R. (Eds) (1986) *Staff Development in the Secondary School: Management Perspectives*, London, Croom Helm.

KIRK, D. (1988) 'Ideology and school-centred innovation: A case study and a critique', *Journal of Curriculum Studies*, **20**, 5.

KIRST, M.W. and MEISTER, G.R. (1985) 'Turbulence in American secondary schools: What reforms last?', *Curriculum Inquiry*, **15**, 2.

KNIGHT, P. (1985) 'The practice of school-based curriculum development', *Journal of Curriculum Studies*, **17**, 1.

LAWTON, D. (1980) *The Politics of the School Curriculum*, London, Routledge & Kegan Paul.

LAWTON, D. (1986) *Curriculum Studies and Educational Planning*, London, Hodder & Stoughton.

LAWTON, D. and CHITTY, C. (1988) *The National Curriculum*, Bedford Way Papers/33, London, University of London Institute of Education.

LAYCOCK, P. (1988) *Branston Trist: Learning about Learning*, report, March.

LEITHWOOD, K.A. (1986) *Planned Educational Change*. Toronto, OISE Press.

LEITHWOOD, K.A. and MONTGOMERY, D.J. (1982) 'A framework for planned educational change: Application to the assessment of program implementation', *Education Evaluation and Policy Analysis*, **4**, 2.

LEITHWOOD, K.A. and MONTGOMERY, D.J. (1986) *Improving Principal Effectiveness: The Principal Profile*, Toronto, OISE Press.

LEITHWOOD, K.A., STANLEY, K. and MONTGOMERY, D.J. (1984) 'Training principals for school improvement', *Education and Urban Society*, **17**, 1.

LEWIN, K. (1948) *Resolving Social Conflicts*, London, Condor Press.

LIEBERMAN, A. (Ed) (1984) *Rethinking School Improvement*, New York, Teachers College Press.

LIEBERMAN, A. and MILLER, L. (1984) *Teachers, Their World and Their Work*, Alexandria, ASCD.

LIEBERMAN, A. and MILLER, L. (1986) 'School improvement: Themes and variations', in LIEBERMAN, A. (Ed) *Rethinking School Improvement*, New York, Teachers College Press.

LIEBERMAN, A., SAXL, E.R. and MILES, M.B. (1986) 'Teacher leadership: Ideological practice', unpublished paper, University of Washington, Seattle.

LITTLE, J.W. (1981) *School Success and Staff Development: The Role of Staff Development in Urban Desegregated Schools*, Boulder, CO, Centre for Action Research.

LORTIE, D. (1975) *Schoolteacher: A Sociological Study*, Chicago, IL, University of Chicago Press.

LOUCKS-HORSLEY, S. and HERGERT, L.F. (1985) *An Action Guide to School Improvement*, Alexandria, ASCD.

LOUIS, K. and DENTLER, R. (1982) *Putting Knowledge to Work: An Examination of an Approach to Improvement in Education*, Cambridge, MA, ABT Associates.

McCLURE, R.M. (1988) 'Stages and phases of school-based school renewal', paper presented at the annual meeting of the American Educational Research Association, New Orleans.

McKENZIE, P. (1986) 'School evaluation in Australia', paper presented at the UNESCO Development Workshop on Evaluation of Educational Programs and Institutions, Seoul, Korea.

McLAUGHLIN, M.W. (1978) 'Implementation as mutual adaptation: Change in classroom organization', in MANN, D. (Ed) *Making Change Happen*, New York, Teachers College Press.

McLAUGHLIN, M.W. (1986) 'Teachers evaluation and school improvement', in LIEBERMAN, A. (Ed) *Rethinking School Improvement*, New York, Teachers College Press.

McLAUGHLIN, M.W. and MARSH, D.D. (1979) 'Staff development and school change', in LIEBERMAN, A. and MILLER, L. (Eds) *Staff Development: New Demands, New Realities, New Perspectives*, New York, Teachers College Press.

McLAUGHLIN, M.W. and PFEIFER, R.S. (1988) *Teacher Evaluation*, New York, Teachers College Press.

McMAHON, A. *et al.* (1984) *Guidelines for the Review and Internal Development of Schools: Primary School Handbook*, London, Schools Council, Longman.

McTAGGART, R. (1984) 'Action research and parent participation: Contradictions, concerns and consequences', *Curriculum Perspectives*, **4**, 2.

MANNING, J. (1982) 'School Boards and the curriculum: A case study', *Curriculum Perspectives*, **2**, 2.

MARSH, C.J. (1986) 'Curriculum implementation: An analysis of Australian research studies 1973–83', *Curriculum Perspectives*, **1**, 1.

MARSH, C.J. (1988) *Spotlight on School Improvement*, Sydney, Allen & Unwin.

MARSH, C.J. and HUBERMAN, A.M. (1984) 'Disseminating curricula: A look from the top down', *Journal of Curriculum Studies*, **16**, 1.

MARSH, C.J. and STAFFORD, K. (1984) *Curriculum: Practices and Issues* (1st edn), New York, McGraw-Hill.

MARSH, C.J. and STAFFORD, K. (1988) *Curriculum: Practices and Issues* (2nd edn), New York, McGraw-Hill.

MARSH, D.D. (1987) 'Curriculum change strategies in secondary schools: An extension of the California school improvement study', paper presented at the annual meeting of the American Educational Research Association, Washington DC.

MARSH, D.D. and BERMAN, P. (1984) 'Conceptualizing the problem of increasing the capacity of schools to implement reform efforts', paper presented at the annual meeting of the American Educational Research Association, New Orleans.

MARSH, D.D. and BOWMAN, G.A. (1987) 'Top-down versus bottom-up reform in secondary schools', unpublished paper, University of Southern California.

MARSH, D.D. and BOWMAN, G.A. (1988) 'Building better secondary schools: A comparison of school improvement and school reform strategies in California', paper presented at the annual meeting of the American Educational Research Association, New Orleans.

MAW, J. (1988) 'National curriculum policy: Coherence and progression?', in

LAWTON, D. and CHITTY, C. (Eds) *The National Curriculum*, Bedford Way Papers/33, London, University of London Institute of Education.

MILES, M.B. and EKHOLM, M. (1985) 'What is school improvement?' in VAN VELZEN, W.G. *et al.*, *Making School Improvement Work: A Conceptual Guide to Practice*, Paris, OECD.

MILLER, J. and SELLER, W. (1985) *Curriculum Perspectives*, New York, Longmans.

Murphy, J.T. (1980) 'School administrators besieged: A look at Australian and American education', *American Journal of Education*, **89**, 1.

NEW ENGLAND ASSOCIATION OF SCHOOLS AND COLLEGES (1972) *Manual for School Evaluation Commission on Independent Secondary Schools*, Burlington, New England Association of Schools and Colleges.

NIXON, J. (Ed) (1981) *A Teachers' Guide to Action Research*, London, Grant McIntyre.

OBERG, A. (1980) 'Implications of research on teacher decision-making', in *Curriculum Canada II*.

ODDEN, A.R. and MARSH, D.D. (1987) 'How state education reform can improve secondary schools', PACE Project, unpublished paper, University of California, Berkeley.

OHIO DEPARTMENT OF EDUCATION (1983) *Process Model for Course of Study*, Columbus, OH, Ohio Department of Education.

OLDROYD, D. and HALL, V. (1988) *Managing Professional Development and INSET: A Handbook for Schools and Colleges*, Bristol, NDCSMT, Bristol University School of Education.

OLDROYD, D., SMITH, K. and LEE, J. (1984) *School-based Staff Development Activities: A Handbook for Secondary Schools*, London, Longman for the Schools Council.

OLSON, J.K. (1982) 'Three approaches to curriculum change: Balancing the accounts', *Journal of Curriculum Theorizing*, **4**, 2.

ONTARIO DEPARTMENT OF EDUCATION (1968) *Living and Learning*, Toronto, Ontario Department of Education.

ONTARIO MINISTRY OF EDUCATION (1975) *Education in the Primary and Junior Divisions*, Toronto, Ontario Ministry of Education.

ONTARIO MINISTRY OF EDUCATION (1975) *The Formative Years*, Toronto, Ontario Ministry of Education.

ONTARIO MINISTRY OF EDUCATION (1984) *Ontario Schools: Intermediate and Senior Divisions, Grades 7–12*, Toronto, Ontario Ministry of Education.

ONTARIO MINSTRY OF EDUCATION (1988) *Science is Happening Here*, Toronto, Ontario Ministry of Education.

PARSONS, C., STEADMAN, S.D. and SALTER, B.G. (1983) 'Communication and the curriculum, the Schools' Council national projects', *Curriculum*, **42**, pp.25–30.

PELJO, K. and HOWELL, J. (1980) 'An intimate look at the methodology used in a reading programme evaluation', *Curriculum Perspectives*, **1**, 1.

PETERS, T.J. and WATERMAN, R.H. (1982) *In Search of Excellence*, New York, Harper & Row.

PIPER, K. (1976) *Evaluation and the Social Sciences: Teachers Handbook*, Canberra, Australian Government Publishing Service.

PIPER, K. (1977) *Evaluation and the Social Sciences: Data Book*, Canberra, Australian Government Publishing Service.

PLASKOW, M. (Ed) (1985) *Life and Death of the Schools Council*, Lewes, Falmer Press.

PODREBARAC, G.R. (1981) 'Establishing future educational priorities', in LEITHWOOD, K. and HUGHES, A. (Eds) *Curriculum Canada III*.

PRIDEAUX, D. (1985) 'School-based curriculum decision-making in South Australia: Change of policy or change of action', *Curriculum Perspectives*, **5**, 2.

PRIDEAUX, D. (1988) 'School-based curriculum decision making in South Australian primary schools', unpublished doctoral dissertation, Flinders University, South Australia.

RAWLINSON, R. and DONNAN, N. (1982) *SBCD: Curriculum Development Styles and Structures for Australian Needs*, Canberra, CDC.

RAWLINSON, R. and SPRING, G. (1981) *SBCD: Support Services for Teachers in Schools*, Canberra, CDC.

REID, K. *et al.* (1988) *An Introduction to Primary School Organisation*, London, Hodder & Stoughton.

REID, W. (1987) 'Where is the habit of deliberation?' in SABAR, N., RUDDUCK, J. and REID, W. (Eds) *Partnership and Autonomy in School-Based Curriculum Development*, Sheffield, University of Sheffield.

REYNOLDS, J. and SKILBECK, M. (1976) *Culture and the Classroom*, London, Open Books.

ROGERS, E.M. (1983) *Diffusion of Innovations* (3rd edn), New York, Free Press.

ROWLAND, S. (1984) *The Enquiring Classroom*, Lewes, Falmer Press.

RUDDOCK, J. and HOPKINS, D. (Eds) (1985) *Research as a Basis for Teaching*, London, Heinemann Educational Books.

RUTHERFORD, W.L. (1984) 'Styles and behaviours of elementary school Principals: The relationship to school improvement', *Education and Urban Society*, **17**, 1.

RUTHERFORD, W.L. and HULING-AUSTIN, L.Ł. (1984) 'Changing the American high school: Descriptions and prescriptions', paper presented at the annual meeting of the American Educational Research Association, New Orleans.

RYAN, A. (1986) 'Towards an activist role for reflection in implementation: Potential and pitfalls', in AOKI, T. *et al.* (Eds) *Curriculum Canada VII*.

SABAR, N. (1983) 'Towards school-based curriculum development: Training school curriculum coordinators', *Journal of Curriculum Studies*, **15**, 4.

SABAR, N., RUDDUCK, J. and REID, W. (Eds) (1987) *Partnership and Autonomy in School-Based Curriculum Development*, Sheffield, University of Sheffield.

SANDERS, D.P. and McCUTCHEON, G. (1986) 'The development of practical theories of teaching', *Journal of Curriculum and Supervision*, **1**, 1.

SCHIFFER, J. (1979) 'A framework for staff development', in LIEBERMAN, A. and MILLER, L., *Staff Development: New Demands, New Realities, New Perspectives*, New York, Teachers College Press.

SCHMUCK, R.A. and SCHMUCK, P.A. (1974) *A Humanistic Psychology of Education*, Mayfield, National Press Books.

SCHÖN, D.A. (1981) *Beyond the Stable State: Public and Private Learning in a Changing Society*, Harmondsworth, Penguin Books.

SCHÖN, D.A. (1983) *The Reflective Practitioner*, New York, Basic Books.

SCHOOLS COUNCIL (1973) *Pattern and Variation in Curriculum Development Projects*, Schools Council Research Studies, London, Macmillan.

SCHWAB, J. (1969) 'The practical: A language for curriculum', *School Review*, **78**, pp.1–23.

SHIPMAN, M. (1974) *Inside a Curriculum Project*, London, Methuen.

SHOWERS, B. (1982) *The Transfer of Training: The Contribution of Coaching*, Eugene, OR, Research and Development Center for Education Policy and Management.

SIMONS, H. (1979) 'Suggestions for a school self-evaluation based on democratic principles', in ELLIOTT, J. (Ed) *School-based Evaluation*, CARN Bulletin No 3, Cambridge Institute of Education.

SIMONS, H. (1986) 'School self-evaluation: A critique of local education authority initiatives in England', paper presented at the annual meeting of the American Educational Research Association, San Francisco.

SIMONS, H. (1987) *Getting to Know Schools in a Democracy*, Lewes, Falmer Press.

SIMONS, H. (1988) 'Teacher professionalism and the national curriculum', in LAWTON, D. and CHITTY, C., *The National Curriculum*, Bedford Way Papers/33, London, University of London Institute of Education.

SKILBECK, M. (1974), 'School-based curriculum development and teacher education policy', unpublished paper, New University of Ulster, Ireland.

SKILBECK, M. (1975a) 'School-based curriculum development in the task of in-service education', in ADAMS, E. (Ed) *In-Service Education and Teachers Centres*, London, Pergamon Press.

SKILBECK, M. (1975b) 'The school and cultural development', in GOLBY, M. *et al.* (Eds) *Curriculum Design*, London, Croom Helm and the Open University Press.

SKILBECK, M. (Ed) (1984a) *Readings in School-Based Curriculum Development*, London, Harper & Row.

SKILBECK, M. (1984b) *School-Based Curriculum Development*, London, Harper & Row.

SMITH, D. (1983) 'On the concept of perceived curriculum decision-making space', *Curriculum Perspectives*, **1**, 1, pp.21–30.

SMYTH, J. (1987) *A Rationale for Teachers' Critical Pedagogy: A Handbook*, Geelong, Deakin University Press.

SOLIMAN *et al.* (Ed) (1981) *A Model for School-Based Curriculum Planning*, Canberra, CDC.

STEADMAN, S.D. *et al.* (1978–81) *Reports on the Impact and Take-Up Project*, London, Schools Council.

STENHOUSE, L. (1975) *An Introduction to Curriculum Research and Development*, London, Heinemann.

STENHOUSE, L. (Ed) (1980) *Curriculum Research and Development in Action*, London, Heinemann Educational Books.

STENHOUSE, L. (1981) *Curriculum Research and Educational Process*, mimeo, Centre for Applied Research in Education, University of East Anglia.

TANNOCK, P. (1983) 'Interview', in BATES, R. and KYNASTON, E. (Eds), *Thinking Aloud: Interview with Australian Educators*, Geelong, Deakin University Press.

TAWNEY, D. (Ed) (1973) *Evaluation in Curriculum Development: Twelve Case Studies*, Schools Council Research Series, London, Macmillan.

TAWNEY, D. (Ed) (1976) *Curriculum Evaluation Today*, Schools Council Research Series, London, Macmillan.

THOMAS, A.R. and SLATER, R.C. (1972) 'The OCDQ: A four factor solution for Australian Schools?' *Journal of Educational Administration*, **10**, 2.

THOMSON, L. and THOMSON, A. (1984) *What Learning Looks Like: Helping Individual Teachers to Become More Effective*, Schools Council Programme 2, London, Longman.

VALLANCE, E. (1981) 'Focus on students in curriculum knowledge: A critique of curriculum criticism', paper presented at the annual meeting of the American Educational Research Association, Los Angeles.

VAN VELZEN, W. (1982) *Conceptual Mapping of School Improvement*, Paris, OECD.

WALLACE, M. (1987) 'A historical review of action research: Some implications for the education of teachers in their managerial role', *Journal of Education for Teaching*, **13**, 2.

WALTON, J. (1978) 'School-based curriculum development in Australia', in WALTON, J. and MORGAN, R. (Eds) *Some Perspectives on School-Based Curriculum Development*, Armidale, University of New England.

WALTON, J., HUNT, J. and MAXWELL, T. (1981) *SBCD: Processes and Involvement of Tertiary Institutions*, Canberra, CDC.

WALTON, J. and MORGAN, R. (Eds) (1978) *Some Perspectives on School-Based Curriculum Development*, Armidale, University of New England.

WEINDLING, R. and EARLEY, P. (1986) 'How Heads manage change', *School Organization 1986*, **6**, 3.

WHELAN, T. (1982) 'School evaluation and catholic schools: Approaches and issues', in RUSSELL, N. *et al.* (Eds) *Curriculum Evaluation: Selected Readings*, Canberra, CDC.

WILLIAMS, D. (1980) 'A hundred children bloom', *Curriculum Perspectives*, **1**, 1.

WILLIAMS, F. (1987) *Curriculum Descriptions*, Report 1987.

WRAGG, E.C. (1987) *Teacher Appraisal*, London, Macmillan Education.

YOUNG, J.H. (1985) 'Participation in curriculum development: An inquiry into the responses of teachers', *Curriculum Inquiry*, **15**, 4.

Index